C AR

Ruier Vanspeult

Rm Batama

Water placts
Ruier Veen
P E N

Vereenigde Riuier

Water placts

Ruier Nassau
TARIA
Staten Ruier

Van Diemens Riu

APRICORNE

TERRE AVSTRALE

decouuerte l'an 1644

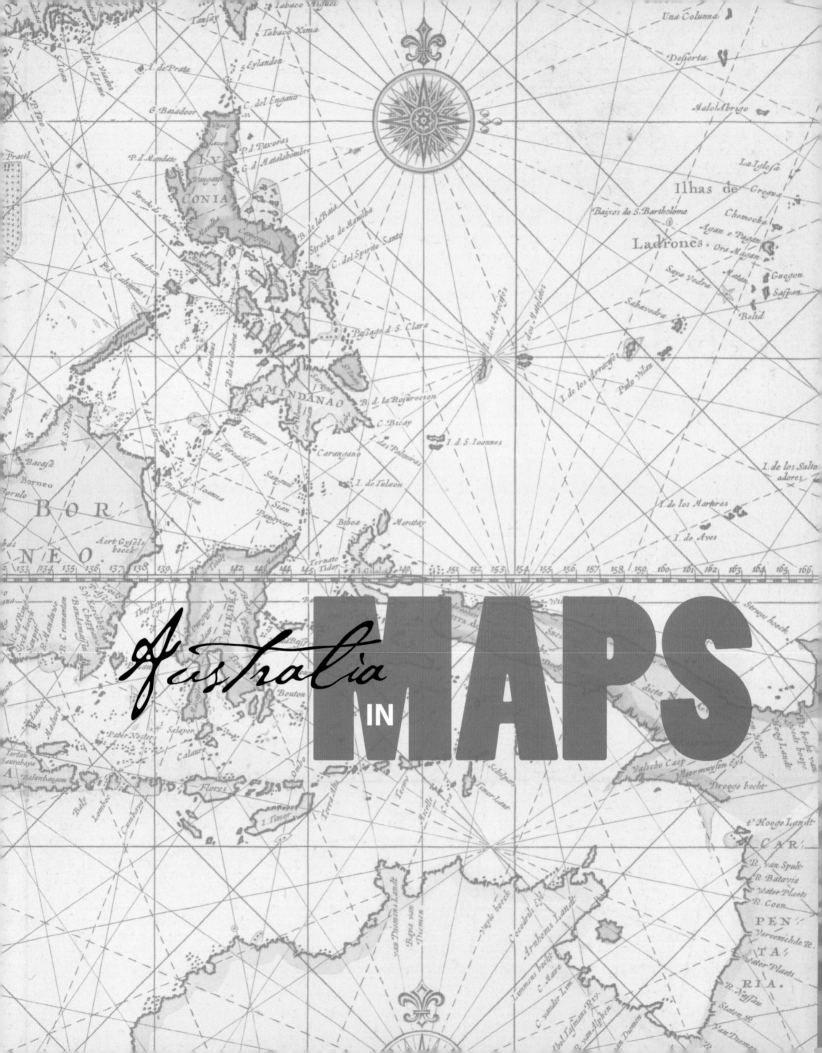

Australia IN MAPS

Australia IN **MAPS**

Great Maps
in Australia's History
from the National
Library's collection

National Library of Australia 2007

Published by
the National Library of Australia
Canberra ACT 2600 Australia

© National Library of Australia

Australia in maps : great maps in Australia's
history from the National Library's
collection.

Bibliography.
Includes index.
ISBN 9780642276353.

1. National Library of Australia -
Map collections. 2.
Maps - Catalogs. 3. Maps, Manuscript
- Catalogs. I.
National Library of Australia.

016.912

Text:	**Maura O'Connor** **Terry Birtles**
Editorial Consultant:	**Martin Woods** **Maps Curator** **National Library** **of Australia**
Editor:	**John Clark**
Publisher's Editors:	**Michaela Forster** **Stephanie Owen Reeder**
Project Management:	**Susan Hall**
Designer:	**Andrew Rankine** **Design Associates**
Printer:	**Tien Wah Press**

Acknowledgments

The National Library of Australia would like to thank the following people for their assistance
with this publication:

Peter Sutton for 'Aboriginal Australia: Mapping the landscape'.

Michael O'Connor for 'The Daisy Bates Special Map Collection'.

Col. (Ret.) Clem Sergent for his advice on 'Plane-table surveys'.

Roger Rees for his advice on all aspects of military mapping and assistance with associated
illustrations.

Allen Mawer for his assistance with 'Charles Wilkes' charts of the Antarctic continent'.

Roderick Ptak for his assistance with 'Ferdinand Verbiest'.

Jane Roberts for her assistance with 'Murray–Darling river pilot charts'.

Ian O'Donnell and Graham Baker, GeoScience Australia, for their assistance with 'Automap
and the development of Australian digital spatial data'.

Bob Pillifeant for the preparation of a number of illustrations for the book.

Front cover images
from left
Ferdinand Verbiest, **World Map c.1674** (page 29); Victor Levasseur, **Oceanie 1847** (page 1);
Ricardus de Bello, **Hanc Quam Videtis Terrarum Orbis Tabulam 1872** (page 2);
Landsat 7 Picture Mosaic of Australia 2000 (page 124)
background
Melchisédech Thévenot, **Hollandia Nova Detecta 1644** (pages 32-33)

Back cover images
top
Klaus Hueneke, **Old Currango ... in 1978** (page 96)
background
Melchisédech Thévenot, **Hollandia Nova Detecta 1644** (pages 32-33)

Title page image
Pieter Goos, **Oost Indien Wassende-graade Paskaart ... c.1690** (page 4)

Half title page image
Royal Australian Air Force, **Sydney Survey 1928** (page 123)

End paper image
Melchisédech Thévenot, **Hollandia Nova Detecta 1644** (pages 32-33)

Foreword

The National Library of Australia is the custodian of the largest and most significant map collection in Australia, with a collection of more than 600 000 maps of Australia and other countries of the world, the oceans and the skies. The Library's cartographic collections are diverse in their format, and include maps, atlases, charts, globes, aerial photographs, satellite imagery and spatial data. The maps range from early manuscript maps showing the extent of the known world and beautiful seventeenth-century editions from celebrated European cartographic publishers, to familiar contemporary products such as street directories and tourist maps which aid our daily lives.

Australia in Maps aims to introduce readers to the range and richness of the National Library's map collections. It also tells the stories behind these maps: the dangers of traversing uncharted territories; the intrigue associated with competition for economic and strategic ascendancy; technological changes in mapmaking and dissemination; and, above all, changes in human knowledge and representation of the world around us.

If the foundation of the Library's rare and historic Maps Collection is based on the efforts of the four great private collectors, E.A. Petherick, Sir John Ferguson, Rex Nan Kivell and R.V. Tooley, the Library's Map Curators can claim credit for the subsequent development of this extraordinary collection. Tom Knight, the National Library's first Maps Curator (from 1962 to 1976), and Dorothy Prescott, Curator from 1979 to 1983, played important roles in the development of Australian cartographic collections. Maura O'Connor, Maps Curator from 1988 to 2005, was a great collection builder and without her advocacy this book would not have been published. In her twenty-six year career in the National Library's Maps Collection, Maura introduced many readers and visitors to the world of historical cartography and the wealth of information that can be discovered in maps. She pioneered the digitisation of the Library's rare map collections and today more than 7000 maps can be viewed from the Library's website. With Dr Terry Birtles, a geographer by profession and a great friend to the National Library, Maura selected the content for *Australia in Maps* and wrote much of the text. I trust their endeavours will lead to increased awareness and enjoyment of the delights of the National Library's Maps Collection.

Jan Fullerton AO
Director-General
National Library of Australia

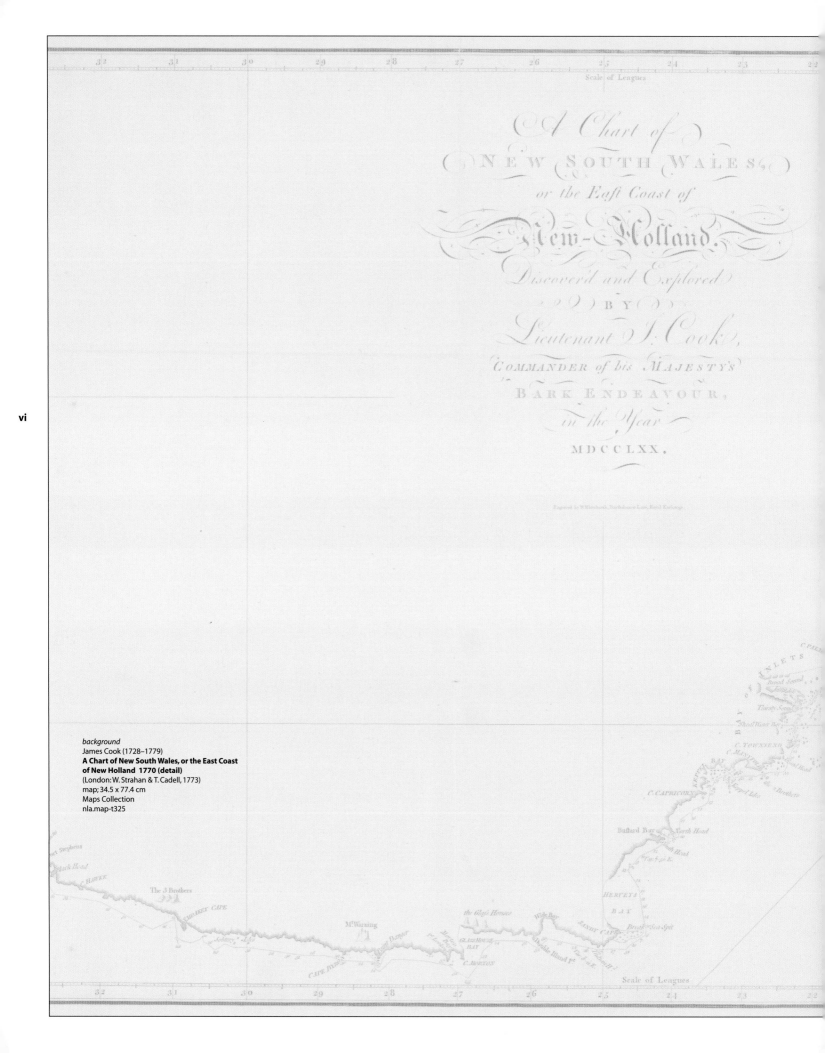

A Chart of
NEW SOUTH WALES,
or the East Coast of
New-Holland.
Discover'd and Explored
BY
Lieutenant J. Cook,
COMMANDER of his MAJESTY'S
BARK ENDEAVOUR,
in the Year
MDCCLXX.

Scale of Leagues

vi

Contents

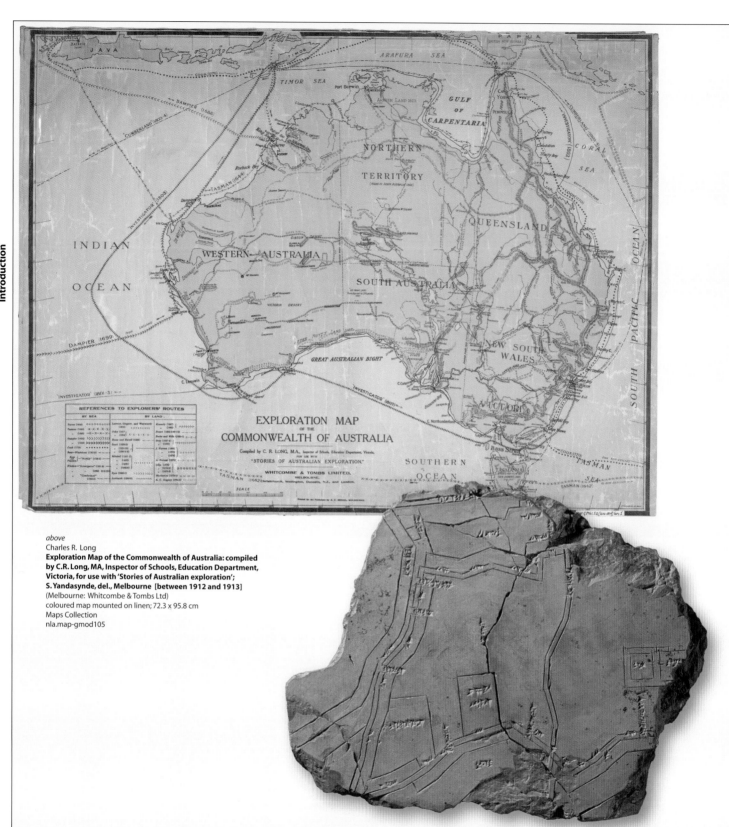

above
Charles R. Long
Exploration Map of the Commonwealth of Australia: compiled
by C.R. Long, MA, Inspector of Schools, Education Department,
Victoria, for use with 'Stories of Australian exploration';
S. Yandasynde, del., Melbourne [between 1912 and 1913]
(Melbourne: Whitcombe & Tombs Ltd)
coloured map mounted on linen; 72.3 x 95.8 cm
Maps Collection
nla.map-gmod105

above
City Map of Nippur
Babylonian Map 1500 BC
Hilprecht Collection,
Freidrich-Schiller-Unversität
Jena (Germany)

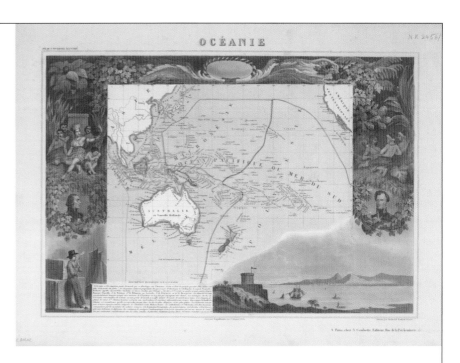

Introduction

What are maps?

Maps can range from the highly specialised, such as geoscientific maps requiring a high degree of accurate detail, to those that may be understood simply in terms of what they portray. Perhaps the best definition of a map is provided by Brian Harley and David Woodward in the first volume of their incomplete yet monumental work, *The History of Cartography* (1987):

> Maps are graphic representations that facilitate a spatial understanding of things, concepts, conditions, processes or events in the human world.

Maps provide a means to locate tangible items, such as roads and buildings within a landscape, or they may express less tangible thematic spatial relationships such as climate types. Maps can deal with complex relationships, and mapmakers are selective in the information they convey through symbols and their interpretation of data. Maps therefore reflect not only the practices and particular perceptions of individual mapmakers, but also their cultural and political assumptions.

It follows that maps can be revealing not only through what they include but also through what they exclude. They can be further limited by the skills of mapmakers and by the amount of information they include.

Maps provide us with the opportunity to seek further explanations of the world. As Peter Turchi succinctly puts it in his book *Maps of the Imagination*: 'Every map intends not simply to serve us but to influence us.'

Charting history and our understanding of ourselves

It is believed that maps in the form of wall paintings first appeared in the Neolithic period. One of the earliest known maps is the Nippur clay tablet, showing a Babylonian town plan dating from around 1500 BC. Incised into the clay, the map shows buildings, land boundaries and text graphics with clear spatial relationships. It was probably created for the transfer of land ownership or other legal or administrative purposes. The map embodies some of the important cartographic principles already outlined: the location of items and the spatial relationships between them.

In complete contrast, the Hereford *Mappa Mundi*—the largest surviving medieval world map—is a fascinating mixture of apparently divine timelessness and the obvious limitations of human time and space. This is reflected in the pictorial imagery surrounding, and incorporated within, the map surface. The ethnocentric map places Jerusalem at its centre, with east at the top, the Garden of Eden in a circle at the edge of the world, and Great Britain and Ireland at the north-western border, with the location of important Welsh and English castles and Lincoln Cathedral included. This map has many complex layers of meaning that are still to be fully identified.

When attempting to interpret early maps, we must be careful not to impose our own values on them. Maps represented, or were a response to, the communities that mapmakers served, to political and religious thinking, and to scientific knowledge at the time. The primary concern of early mapmakers was either to sell their product or, more often, to please a patron or employer. Consequently, the design of maps, particularly those with decorative features such as sea monsters and other fabulous creatures, was aimed at encouraging potential sponsors or customers through a combination of artistic beauty and geographical information. The Hereford and Nolin wall maps, despite their difference in age, are examples of maps designed to impress by their size and beauty. At the same time, their content was influenced

by the politics of the day and the need of the mapmakers' patrons to publicise their position and status through them.

For many centuries, Christian doctrine wielded considerable direct and indirect influence upon the design and content of maps. The Reformation and Counter-Reformation wars of the sixteenth century had a direct bearing on the printing trade, prompting the relocation of major printing presses from Germany to Flanders and Amsterdam—where map publishers fortuitously had access to the sea charts of mariners and traders. The religious beliefs of cartographers had a more subtle impact on map content—for example, with the Bible map of Montanus (reproduced on pages 24-25). Combined with speculation about the true geographical content of the lands they depicted, the resulting maps were complex productions, even from our modern perspective.

Wars also had another, more immediate, impact on mapmaking. They led to a flurry of map production, as the existing topographic and political maps did not always contain sufficient detailed information for military use. This was evident in England from the time of Henry VII, and was seen again, for example, at the outbreak of World War II, when the mapping of North Africa and the topographic mapping of Australia were notable projects.

A changing craft

One of the most fascinating aspects of the study of maps over time is to see how they have evolved, both as artefact and implement.

Perhaps the most significant change took place in the middle of the nineteenth century, when greater scientific precision and the search for accuracy led to the removal of the more decorative

content. Mapmakers could concentrate on refining their designs and providing the detailed information their customers required. Australia's coastal limits had been plotted, but its land had yet to be fully explored and settled. Both individual mapmakers and those working for government employers had considerable opportunity to create a range of maps detailing the results of exploration, gold discoveries, transport routes and other matters.

The twentieth century ushered in the greatest change in the way map data was gathered and presented to a more educated customer. Map production became concentrated in the hands of government agencies and specialist private companies. New forms of mapping appeared, including regularly updated series of topographic, geological and navigational maps, with uniform graphics and standards for map design.

New technologies for gathering and presenting data were employed, the most significant of which was aerial photography. Initially providing accurate data for paper-based topographic map sheets, aerial photographs later appeared in their own right as orthophotomaps (or corrected photographs), and included additional information via text and markings for roads and buildings.

By the end of the twentieth century, computerisation, satellite imagery (see pages 124-125) and the internet had had a significant impact on the way geospatial data was gathered and presented. The internet in particular has necessitated a whole new appraisal of map design and the cartographic profession. As an interactive medium, digital graphics allow the user not only to change the presentation and dimensions of maps but also to incorporate other forms of information.

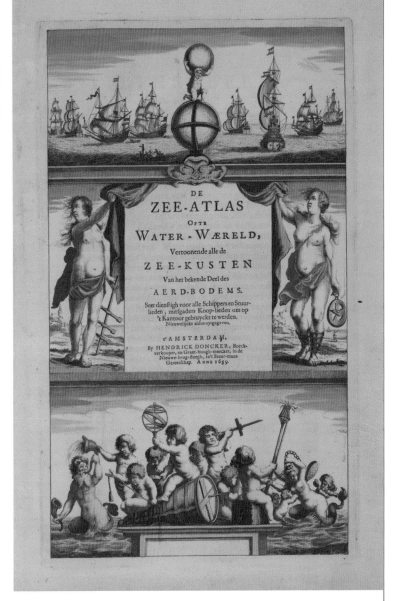

The Maps Collection at the National Library of Australia

Building the collection

Creating a map collection can be an exciting and daunting challenge. A successful collection requires time and persistence, and purpose. The aim of the collection at the National Library, according to the Library's Collection Development Policy, is to accumulate:

> … Australian and overseas cartographic materials, which form part of the documentary record of Australia and reflect its relationship to the rest of the world.

The National Library's Maps Collection spans more than 500 years, and it owes its strength and diversity to the activities of four individual collectors and the Library's first Maps Curator.

The Library's founding collector was British bibliographer and book collector, Edward Augustus Petherick (1847–1917), who migrated to Australia with his family in 1852. Employed by Melbourne bookseller George Robertson as his London agent, Petherick soon developed an interest in Australiana. He collected books, manuscripts and ephemera as well as maps, and in 1887 he founded the Colonial Booksellers' Agency.

The depth and breadth of Petherick's collection, which he first offered to libraries in the Australian colonies of Victoria and New South Wales in 1895, is reflected in its description:

> … the larger proportion comprises works on the geography, discovery, exploration, aborigines and natural history of Australia and Polynesia and works illustrative of the social, political, religious and literary history of the Australian colonies.

Petherick believed his collection could become the nucleus of an Australian national library, and he emphasised the need for continuing acquisitions after it had been deposited. His wish was granted with the establishment of the Commonwealth National Library in 1901 as part of the new Federal Parliament, and the related successful conclusion of negotiations to acquire Petherick's collection for the new library. Petherick's cartographic collection of 1200 maps and 300 atlases accounts for a substantial part of the National Library's Rare Map Collection which now numbers more than 4000 items. One of the great treasures acquired from him is the only surviving copy of the first edition of Hendrick Doncker's *De Zee-atlas ofte Water-waereld*,

published in 1659, along with maps by noted cartographers Abraham Ortelius, Nicolas Visscher and Pieter Goos.

The collection of Sir John Alexander Ferguson (1881–1969)—bibliographer, collector, and judge of the New South Wales Industrial Commission—was even more focused than Petherick's. Acquisition of the Ferguson Collection began in 1954 and continued through to the 1960s. Ferguson's cartographic interests lay in material relating to church and mission-station history in Australia and the Pacific, and in cadastral (land ownership) maps of New South Wales. Like Petherick, Ferguson believed that a carefully

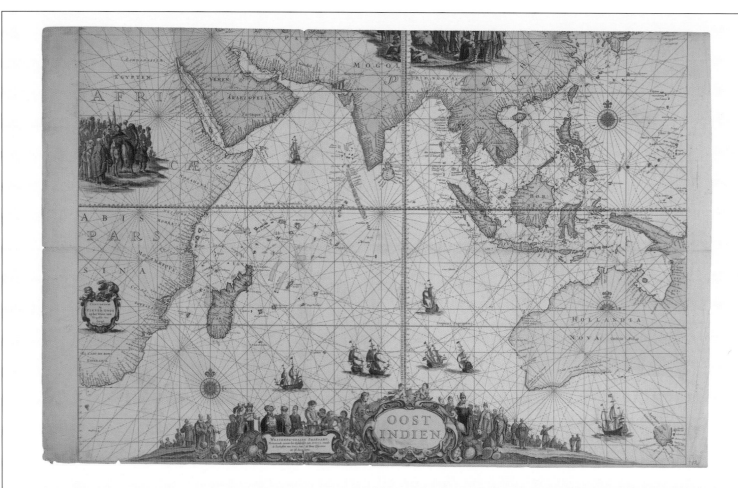

acquired collection of 'pamphlets, broadsides, pictures, maps, newspapers and manuscripts may throw important light on local events, social tendencies, the great men and movements of the past, parliamentary government, family history and the like'.

The Ferguson Collection of 911 maps and more than 7000 real estate sales plans reflects an interest in local and church history, and mining and industrial matters. Much of the collection consists of pencil tracings of original maps on butter paper (now often brown and brittle with age), recording land ownership throughout New South Wales during the nineteenth century.

New Zealander Rex Nan Kivell (1899–1977) was an art dealer based in London, where his collecting interests covered England, Europe and North Africa. In 1959, the Australian Government purchased Nan Kivell's collection of pictures,

manuscripts, pamphlets and maps—the latter material including about 1000 sixteenth- and seventeenth-century Dutch and French maps tracing the development of exploration in the Indian and Pacific oceans. About one-third of the collection outlines Australia's development during the nineteenth century, particularly through cadastral and electoral maps of Victoria.

A fourth important collector, Ronald Vere Tooley (1898–1986), who dominated the British antiquarian map trade for about 50 years, focused on maps. Tooley's Australian maps were acquired by the Library in 1973, but the Library's collection is not as complete as Tooley's catalogue suggests—several items were removed by an English dealer, then later by a Dutch dealer, and sold privately. Nevertheless, the collection still reflects one man's dedication to documenting the history of Australian cartography

to the turn of the twentieth century.

The National Library's first Maps Curator, Tom Knight, is credited with establishing the modern (post-1900) component of the Library's collection. A former secondary-school geography teacher, Knight found the collection lacked early topographic mapping of Australia and World War II mapping across Europe and Asia. He established the Maps Collection's long association with government mapping interests, such as the Australian Defence Force and the Division of National Mapping, and successfully acquired early topographic mapping and early aerial photography of Australia. He was also instrumental in the purchase of the Tooley Collection and early twentieth-century topographic mapping of Europe, Asia and South-East Asia.

Successive maps curators have built on this base and brought

to the Collection much-needed bibliographic control and, through the internet, off-site access to maps through digitisation and website links via the catalogue.

Memorable acquisitions

The acquisition of an item or collection for the National Library of Australia can have exciting consequences. In 1980, for instance, while preparing for an exhibition, Library staff became aware that a Petherick acquisition—the 1659 first edition of Hendrick Doncker's *De Zee-atlas ofte Water-waereld*—was the only known copy in existence, at least in a public collection. Petherick had acquired the item from Dutch dealer Frederick Mueller in the 1890s. From time to time, individual plates from the edition appear in dealers' catalogues, but no other intact

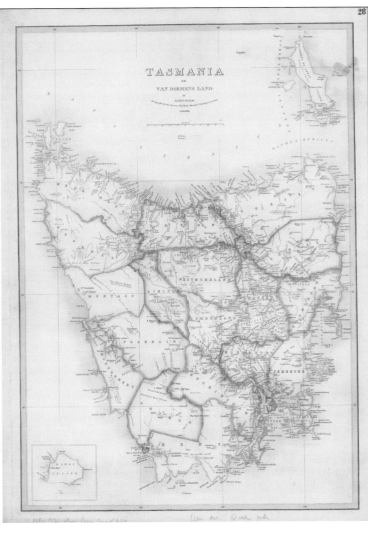

copy of the atlas appears to have survived.

Nearly two decades later, researcher Dr Jane Roberts, a Harold White Fellow, unearthed a unique collection of seven river pilot charts in the Budarick Collection, part of the Library's Manuscripts Collection. The discovery boosted the National Library's collection of the charts to nine, making it one of a handful of significant collections of this rare material in the country.

Over the years, government mapping interests such as the Australian Army and the Division of National Mapping have deposited large collections of maps which could not have been easily obtained from other sources.

Australia in Maps features unique maps, or maps typical of their time, to highlight significant periods in Australia's cartographic history. In the process we hope

to demonstrate the wide range of cartographic materials available for interpreting our world and to illuminate the National Library's role in recording Australia's documentary heritage.

Selection of items for *Australia in Maps*

Australia in Maps can provide only a tiny sample to whet the interest of map users. Because the Library has already published a range of facsimiles from the Tooley and Nan Kivell collections, few are presented here. Instead, the choice illustrates specific types of maps and other cartographic products, each supported by a commentary that places the item in a thematic and historical sequence to highlight its significance and particular features of interest. For some items, rarity has led to selection but age, function and design are also criteria for

particular maps to be prized and included. Several maps are valued for the information they exclude rather than for what they reveal. In this sense, they reflect not only the practices and particular perceptions of an individual mapmaker but also a range of cultural and political assumptions.

The selections have been grouped according to 12 themes, and the book opens in Chapter 1 with reference to Aboriginal Australia. Much Indigenous experience depicted as rock art and drawings in the sand or soil remains shrouded in religious ritual and sacred mythology. It is integrated within a system of restricted knowledge and, for that reason, very little can be revealed on paper as a published record to a non-initiate audience. Included here are discussions of the value of European cartographic

interpretations by Daisy Bates and Norman Tindale, and the comparatively recent legal recognition of Aboriginal title to land.

In Chapters 2 and 3, *Australia in Maps* utilises the oldest map in the Library's collection to demonstrate how ancient Greek theories about a vast southern continent were revived during the Renaissance and became a popular feature on sixteenth-century maps. European wars of the Reformation and Counter-Reformation influenced the balance of power, with the result that Dutch traders during the seventeenth century were the first to reveal specific cartographic knowledge of the 'South Land', leading to Abel Tasman's two voyages during the period 1642 to 1644. The Library possesses more than a thousand rare Italian, French, English and Dutch maps

right
Claes Jansz Visscher (c.1586–1652)
Nova Totius Terrarum Orbis Geographica
Ac Hydrograhica Tabula 1652
(Amsterdam: Hendrick Doncker, 1659)
coloured map ; 28.7 x 42.9 cm
Maps Collection
nla.map-ra10-1

that illustrate elements of this history in far greater detail.

Chapter 4 recognises the development of a more scientific approach to European cartography, but with reliance upon theory and conjecture for unexplored areas where data was absent. Guesswork about the shape of the east coast of New Holland produced a variety of maps until the 1770 'scientific' triangulation survey by Lieutenant James Cook, which is examined in Chapter 5.

Over the next few decades, French scientific excursions attempted to compete with British Admiralty charting. Three illustrations of coastal surveys after Cook are presented here: Flinders, Freycinet and Owen Stanley. In Chapter 6, transportation of British convicts to Sydney Cove is recorded by a selection of two charts by Raper and Fowkes. This was followed by hydrographic surveys of ports of immigration, and Stokes' 1841 chart of approaches to the Swan

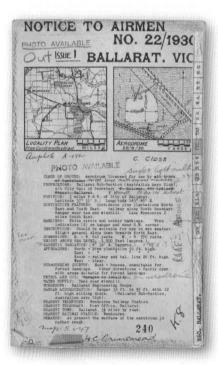

Notice to Airmen, No. 22/1930, Ballarat. Vic.
Department of Civil Aviation
(Melbourne: Government printer, 1930)
Byrne Goodrick Collection

River provides an example. Similar surveys of every other Australian port are available at the Library.

Chapter 7, on overland exploration and pastoralism, explores the shift from the development of port-oriented communities to the search for land resources. Selections in this book include Cunningham's chart of the Darling Downs, Hamilton Hume's map of a route to Port Phillip, Thomas Mitchell's map of the Nineteen Counties, Stuart's transcontinental crossing, a 1868 pastoral map of New South Wales and Forrest's West Australian Exploring Expedition of 1874. Opening up the land also relied on mineral discoveries and geological surveys. Significant fieldwork by Reverend W.B. Clarke and T.W. Edgeworth David is examined in Chapter 8. In addition, the chapter provides maps of the Barrier Ranges silver country and the Hannan goldfield to offer two instances of the industrial landscape of mining leases, lodes, shafts, dams,

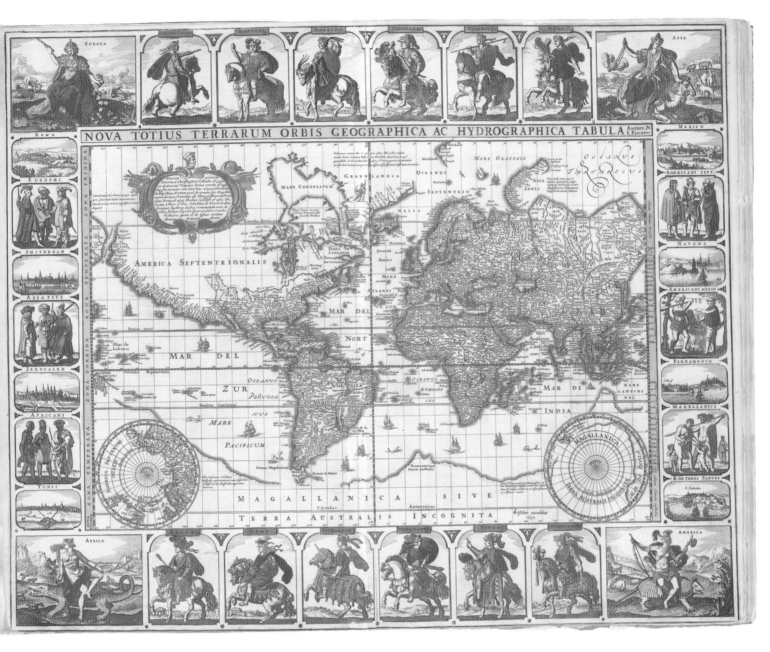

workings and tramways that became so common in many parts of Australia.

Land administration and management allows inclusions in Chapter 9 of cartographic information related to police patrol, oversight of Norfolk Island, high-country snow leases, planning of the Snowy Mountains Hydro-Electric Scheme and the charting of Antarctica. The urban concentration of Australia's population permits attention to examples of town planning ideas in Chapter 10, with reference to such selections as the 1836 Wedge survey of Port Phillip, William Light's survey of Adelaide in 1840, New South Wales real estate plans and Federal capital site selection. The two concluding chapters give attention to military mapping and transport mapping especially as a record of army field mapping and the application of satellite data to computer technology. The opening of inland Australia to stage coaches, trains and aircraft constitutes a vital historic theme.

The chapters address 12 themes through a series of examples. Each example, and its accompanying illustrations, has been sourced from National Library collections. We hope this book encourages and inspires an interest in maps and other cartographic items held in the collections of the National Library of Australia and in other collections throughout Australia.

**Native Gunnias [i.e. Gunyahs]
near Springwood [between 1820 and 1822]**
pen drawing; 25.6 x 31.2 cm
Pictures Collection
nla.pic-an6820643

1. Aboriginal Australia
Mapping the landscape

Aboriginal religious art has long portrayed cultural landscapes, though expressing spiritual and social relationships rather than strictly geographical ones. It is more ritual performance than cartography. Separately from this, however, Aboriginal people have also long used 'mud-maps': geographical depictions sketched out in the sand or dirt, typically with a stick, to convey topographic information to others less familiar with the local country. Unlike the religious depictions, these secular maps were almost always sketched in true alignment with the cardinal directions; they were meant to be relied upon at ground level.

The point of view of the Aboriginal mud-maps (as also with the religious depictions) is typically perpendicular to the earth's surface (in 'plan view'), although trees may be shown side-on (in 'section'). This perpendicular orientation, especially in the absence of aeroplane flight, has often surprised urban people.

However, the perpendicular mapping template is probably a human universal: we all consciously or unconsciously map our neighbourhoods, or homes, in the same way, rather than navigate solely by horizontal glimpses of landscapes. The plan view is also a feature of dreams, in which the dreamer flies over a landscape, as reported by many widely differing societies and cultures around the world, including Aboriginal ones.

Aboriginal people who have grown up with detailed knowledge of their local 'country' are typically proud of their independence of paper maps to find their way. From the early colonial era, new arrivals have sought to understand Indigenous knowledge and political geography and render it in field mapping. Since the beginning of the land rights era (beginning in earnest in 1976 and intensified with the High Court's Mabo Decision in 1992), the emphasis of this field mapping has moved from providing pure anthropological research to

providing evidence for tribunals, negotiators and courts. This kind of evidence addresses issues of site significance and history, but also issues of traditionally established boundaries between group territories, and traditional systems of land tenure.

European maps of Aboriginal territories were reasonably plentiful in the nineteenth century, and interest in attempting to map out Indigenous tribal boundaries and migration trails gathered impetus during the twentieth century. Amateur ethnographer Daisy May Bates (1863–1951) was one among many who tried to do so, mapping out what she could about Indigenous geographical knowledge, even though her methods and sources of information were to some extent unreliable or problematic. A number of other researchers, including Walter Baldwin Spencer (in anthropological expeditions in 1894, and further ones from 1899 to 1922, and aided by Francis Gillen)

had established that Aboriginal people had defined religion-based territories as well as constrained foraging areas. This concept challenged popular European acceptance of the *terra nullius* belief that Aboriginal people were non-territorial nomads. In 1940, anthropologist and entomologist Norman Tindale (1900–1993), with Joseph Birdsell, proposed a trihybrid theory of three waves of pre-European immigrants—a claim which was rejected during the 1960s in favour of different views of the ancient peopling of Sahul (the continent containing what are now mainland Australia, Tasmania and New Guinea). The mapping-out of ancient transcontinental trade routes has been spurred on by the finding of far-travelled artefacts —for example, trochus shell was carried from its point of origin on the north-east coast of the continent to Uluru and the coast of South Australia, while samples of melo shell from the Great Barrier

George French Angas (1822–1886)
Encounter Bay Women, Lubras, Roasting Trochus, Yankalilla, March 19th, 1844
watercolour; 19.0 x 24.3 cm
Pictures Collection
nla.pic-an2856782

Reef have been found near Tennant Creek, Bourke and Woomera.

Today, Indigenous Australians continue to guide ethnographers in transferring their knowledge of 'country' onto paper and digital maps, for both present uses and future generations. Large amounts of knowledge have already gone and continue to be lost with the passing of the last generations of those who lived off the land by foraging and 'footwalking'. Detailed bush knowledge is tending, even in the remotest regions, to become restricted to modern transport corridors.

Cartography creates history. Future students of the Australian landscape, including Indigenous descendants, may benefit from modern survey maps, recorded compass bearings, aerial photographs, and Global Positioning System readings used to record as accurately as possible the precise locations that have been the focal point of Indigenous traditions and life experiences.

Written by Peter Sutton,
Australian Research Council Professorial Fellow,
School of Social Sciences, University of Adelaide

The Daisy Bates Special Map Collection

Between 1900 and World War II, amateur ethnographer Daisy May Bates (1863–1951) amassed a large collection of material about Aboriginal people. Acquired by the Commonwealth before Bates' death, the collection (held in the National Library of Australia) also contains a striking series of annotated and manuscript maps that reveal important aspects of Aboriginal culture in Western Australia.

The Daisy Bates Special Map Collection contains three types of maps. The first type is published maps for Bates' reference or interest—some of these are on non-Australian subjects (maps 64–98, 104–116). The second type is published maps annotated by Bates as a record of her compilation of knowledge about aspects of traditional and contemporary Aboriginal culture, including social organisation, tribal areas, geographical distribution and totems (maps 1–16, 62–63, 99–103). And the third type is

manuscript maps attributed to Aboriginal informants containing representations of country (maps 17–61), including some of the earliest details of extensive areas of country recorded from Indigenous people. According to Phillip Jones, many of these maps appear to have been recorded in the decade after the production of the detailed Hillier map of placenames in central Australia.

The collection of Daisy Bates' 45 maps contains draft and final versions of the same information, so the number of regions represented is about half that number. The maps depict three areas in Western Australia: the mid Murchison River area, in the upper Murchison and Gascoyne goldfields, and places to the east; parts of the south coast of Western Australia in the vicinity of Albany, and areas in the vicinity of Eucla; and the Great Australian Bight and inland areas towards Ooldea in South Australia.

The map content is dominated by two elements: toponyms (placenames) and symbols to represent features. Most toponyms are Indigenous placenames, although each map has placenames in English for two or three locations—for example, Black Range, Murchison (river), Mount Aubrey and Rabbit-Proof Fence. Bates' map symbols are mostly dots or circles representing topographic features—particularly springs and waterholes, but also hills, ranges, sandhills and lakes—connected by lines that perhaps represent connections, associations or paths between the features. Where the name next to a symbol is a local language term for the topographic feature represented, Bates has included in brackets the English name—for example, '*ngabba* (water)' and '*warn* (creek)' (map 47).

On several maps, the lines are referred to as a 'road'—for example Lake Way Road (map 23) and Peak Hill Road (map 31)—but it remains

to be discovered whether Bates' informant referred to European stock routes or roads, or to long-trodden Aboriginal tracks. Several maps are arranged in a radial form, with a large circular symbol in the centre and many lines radiating outwards, along which smaller circles are placed and named. Map 46 is one of the few manuscript maps to place Aboriginal names in a topographically accurate sketch, in this case in relation to the path and scale of the Murchison River and its tributaries.

The topographic contents of Bates' maps are amplified by various annotations. For the most part, these annotations serve to connect Bates' informant to the country depicted. Map 25 contains 'Where Muri was caught', and map 50 notes 'Where Yingilit was born'. Similarly, other maps note the locations (by name or general area) where the informant took part in ceremonies such as initiation, where a particular person died, the location of their mother and

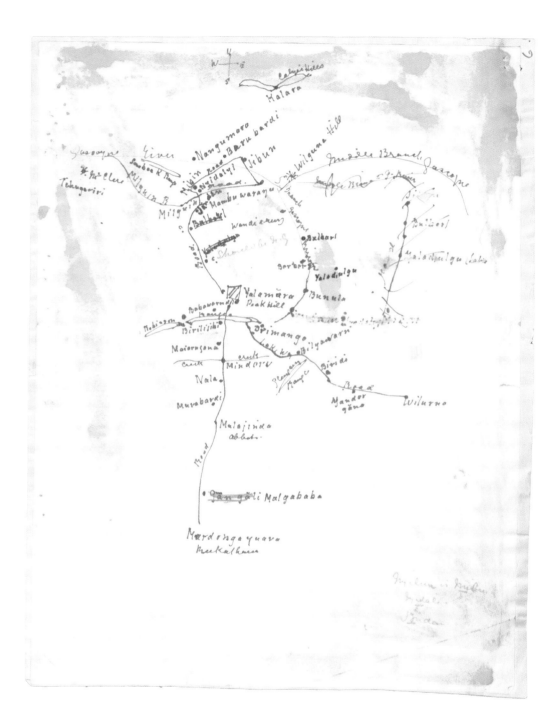

Group Areas of S. Bibbulmun [between 1910–1920]
manuscript map;
25.6 x 20.1 cm
Daisy Bates
Special Map Collection
Maps Collection
nla.map-db0
Courtesy University of Adelaide

father's country, and the nature of adjoining country. Infrequently, Bates' inference of the traditional owners or language group is noted—for example, 'Bardiwonga or Badimaia' (map 53). Overlaps with adjoining manuscript maps are occasionally noted.

Where and when the manuscript maps were recorded is a matter of conjecture, as Bates rarely noted such data on her materials. The names of many of the Western Australian map informants appear in notebooks she used at Rottnest Island prison during a visit in 1910 or 1911 (NLA MS 365 folio 67), and other informants were present when Bates visited the Meekatharra area in mid-1911 (NLA MS 365 folio 71). These notebooks contain data that also appear on the manuscript maps.

From Bates' notebooks, it seems that draft maps were sometimes constructed in the field—several show creases consistent with being folded to pocket size—but it is unclear when the final neat copies were drawn. Further research is needed to shed light on the context in which Bates' maps were created, and on the identity and cultural importance of the features they depict.

*Written by Michael O'Connor,
Postdoctoral Fellow,
Commonwealth Scientific and Industrial Research Organisation*

**N.B. Tindale Working in His Office at His Home
in Palo Alto c.1987**
Image reference AA338/6/
Biographical slide collection
Courtesy South Australian Museum Archives

right
Norman B. Tindale (1900–1993)
**Map Showing the Distribution
of the Aboriginal Tribes of Australia**
(Adelaide: Government Photolithographer, 1940)
coloured map; 64.0 x 76.0 cm
Maps Collection
nla.map-gmod91

Norman Tindale's *Aboriginal Tribes of Australia*, 1940

Controversy has raged for many years over the origins and future of Australia's first settlers, from 'doomed race' theories developed by church missionaries soon after European contact, to government policies of the late nineteenth century that promoted the removal of Indigenous people to exclusively Aboriginal reserves.

This map of Aboriginal tribal distribution before European contact marks a major contribution to a substantial change in official attitudes. Prepared in 1940 by anthropologist Norman Barnett Tindale (1900–1993), it has become a collector's item.

Tindale began his working life as an entomologist—an interest that dated back to a boyhood spent collecting butterflies in Japan, where his father worked on a Salvation Army mission from 1907 until 1915. In 1918, Tindale was appointed as an assistant entomologist at the

South Australian Museum. Just a few months later, however, an explosion in his father's photographic laboratory blinded him in one eye, and he subsequently changed careers and became an anthropologist.

In 1921, Tindale joined Sir Walter Baldwin Spencer's field expedition to Groote Eylandt and the Roper River. The expedition stimulated a lifelong interest in the concept of bounded tribal territories and, over the next 70 years, he confronted entrenched European adherence to a stereotype of Aboriginal people as aimless and landless nomads.

Tindale was also a pioneer of Australian archaeology. His analysis of a 4700-year-old *ngaut ngaut* (rock shelter) at Devon Downs on the Murray River in 1929 challenged the accepted belief that Aboriginal arrival in Australia had been recent.

With painstaking precision that confounded many critics, Tindale assembled high-quality empirical

data to demonstrate how Kartan stone artefacts, animal bones, shellfish and cultural remains could be linked together as a chronology of events dating back to before an ash eruption of Mount Gambier.

Tindale's experience of museum cataloguing had already underlined the importance of filling gaps in the record, and he linked his understanding of natural science to his belief that the legal definition of *terra nullius* denied the Indigenous reality of a strong religious and traditional connection with land.

Field studies among Aboriginal groups on Yorke Peninsula and in south-west Queensland and central Australia between 1930 and 1935 revealed Tindale's sense of social inquiry. As well as recording sounds on wax cylinders and taking a cinematic record of daily life and ceremonies, he discovered that several cat's cradle string games and sand drawings were geographically oriented. He also

pioneered European understanding of adult male Aboriginal art—by distributing brown paper and then documenting which crayons the artists chose, he revealed that Indigenous concentric-circle art constituted a cryptic and endlessly flexible reference to bounded space and time.

Tindale's 1940 map was controversial. Tindale was meticulous in his recording of data and bibliographic sources—for example, his evidence of distinct territorial boundaries and their local nomenclature in the heavily populated rainforest is supported by an 1897 police census of the Atherton district by William Parry-Okeden, observations of 'native' trails used by European explorers and early settlers of the 1870s and 1880s, and annual reports by the northern Queensland Protector of Aborigines, Walter Edmund Roth.

Tindale recorded tribal names on the map according to the alphabet of the International

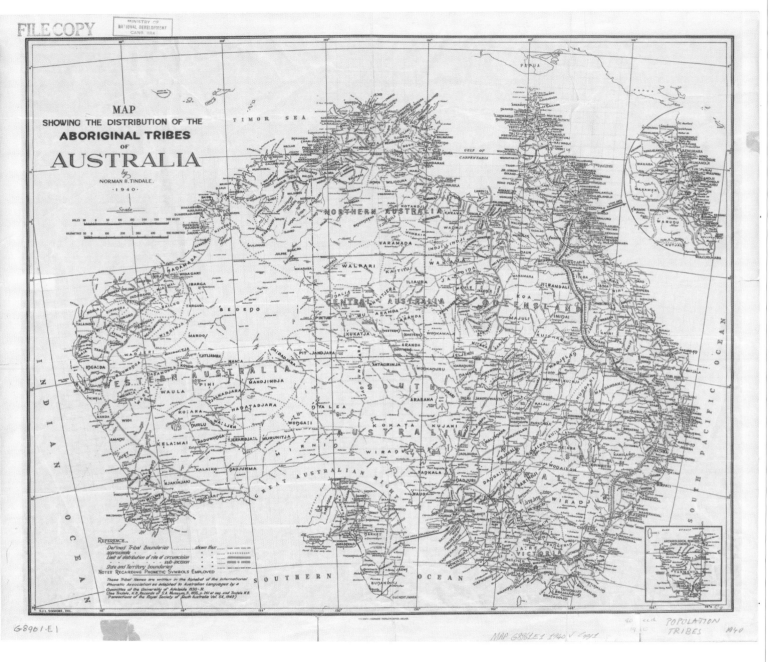

MAP
SHOWING THE DISTRIBUTION OF THE
ABORIGINAL TRIBES
OF
AUSTRALIA
by
NORMAN B. TINDALE.
·1940·

G 8961 · E 1

MAP G886LE1 1940

POPULATION
TRIBES
1940

Phonetic Association, adapted by a Committee of the University of Adelaide in 1930–1931. He also indicated geographical limits to the rites of circumcision and subincision. Regrettably, his map was edited before publication on the grounds that Australian Indigenous people were nomadic wanderers with no fixed abode or attachment to the land.

Ironically, Tindale's research received greater recognition in the United States than in Australia. The University of Colorado honoured him and the University of California (Berkeley) published his amended map of tribal distribution in greater detail on four sheets (1972), with updated *Geographic II* nomenclature.

By then, however, academic research in Australia suggested far greater complexity of Aboriginal social and territorial relationships. A more recent map on a scale of 1:47 000, compiled by David Horton in 1994, blurs all territorial boundaries with the disclaimer that it 'indicates only the general grouping of people, which may include smaller groups such as clans, dialects or individual languages of a group'.

14

right
William Westall (1781–1850)
**Views on the North Coast of
Australia 1802**
watercolour; 31.4 x 44.2 cm
Pictures Collection
nla.pic-an4564978

right, below
William Westall (1781–1850)
**Murray Isles, Natives Offering
Goods for Barter 1802**
drawing; 19.4 x 27.0 cm
Pictures Collection
nla.pic-an4577514

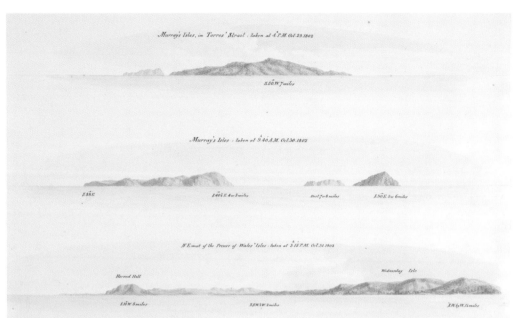

The Mabo maps
and native title

A historic decision by the High Court of Australia in June 1992 determined for the first time that Australian common law recognised the earlier, or prior, land rights of Aboriginal people. The Mabo Decision, as it became known, overturned a 1971 ruling that Aboriginal title to land had not survived British settlement of the Australian continent.

Instrumental in bringing about this momentous decision was Eddie Koiki Mabo (1936–1992), a member of the Murray Island people, inhabitants of part of the Torres Strait Islands. In 1974, Mabo had been told that land he believed he owned on Murray, or Mer, Island was regarded as Crown land and that he therefore held no legal claim to it. At a land rights conference at James Cook University in 1981, Mabo outlined native land ownership and land inheritance on Murray Island. A lawyer present suggested a test case could claim land rights through the courts.

Over the next 10 years, Mabo pursued the right of Indigenous title through the Queensland courts and, finally, the High Court. The Court rejected the earlier British declaration of *terra nullius* over Australia and accepted that, under British common law, the previous rights and interests in land possessed by the Indigenous inhabitants had survived the change in sovereignty.

The decision extinguished native title where there had been inconsistent use of the land, such as by grants of freehold, but not necessarily by the grant of lesser interests, such as permission to mine for minerals. Similarly, native title was also extinguished where the Crown had validly and effectively appropriated land for its own use, such as for roads, railways, post offices and so on, and it was wholly or partially inconsistent with a continuing right to native title.

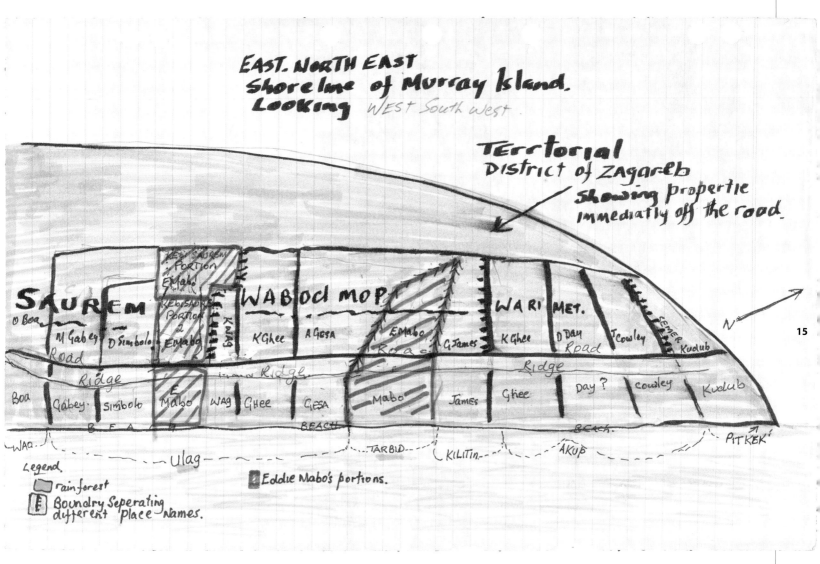

EAST. NORTH EAST
Shoreline of Murray Island.
Looking WEST South West.

Territorial
District of Zagareb
Showing propertie
immediatly off the road.

SAUREM

WABODC MOP

WARI MET.

Legend.
rainforest
Boundary Seperating
different place names.

E Eddie Mabo's portions.

15

Native title to particular land, events and persons is today determined by the laws and customs of the Indigenous people who have a connection with the land, irrespective of whether the laws and customs have changed. Such was the case of Murray Island, where the Meriam people retain a strong affiliation with their forebears, society, culture and land. In his findings in the case, Justice Moynihan said:

> Communal life based on group membership seems to have been the predominant feature of life … The people lived in groups of huts strung along the foreshore or strand immediately behind the sandy beach. They

still do although there has been a contraction of the villages and the huts are increasingly houses … organised in named villages … Garden land is identified by reference to a named locality coupled with the name of relevant individuals if further differentiation is necessary. The Islands are not surveyed and boundaries are in terms of known land marks such as specific trees or mounds of rocks.

The Commonwealth *Native Title Act 1993* provided mechanisms for dealing with the implications of the Mabo Decision, such as handling claims and retrospectively validating the interests of non-Indigenous landholders.

In 1996, a High Court claim by the Wik people concerning pastoral leases in Queensland resulted in a judgment that settled an issue left unresolved by the Mabo Decision—the Court determined that native title could coexist with other rights on land held under a pastoral lease. Two years later, the *Native Title Act* was amended to resolve complications created by the Wik case over pastoral leases, and to provide the states and territories with more opportunities to negotiate alternative options on individual claims. In September 2006, the High Court brought down a judgment in favour of Noongar Native Title over the Perth metropolitan area.

Sebastian Munster (1489–1552)
Cosmographiae Universalis lib. VI
(Basileae: apud Henrichum Petri, 1550)
atlas; 32.0 cm
Maps Collection

16

2. European theories of
Terra Australis Nondum Cognita
The heritage of an ancient Greek theory

The idea of a large southern continent dates back to the time of Pythagoras, in the fifth century BC.

Followers of Pythagoras were the first to document an astronomical theory in which a spherical earth revolved on its own axis and moved in an orbit. They reasoned that, to maintain the equilibrium of the sphere, there must be landmasses in the Southern Hemisphere acting as counterweights to the known lands of the Northern Hemisphere. The theory, one of the most persistent ever advanced, was supported during the Renaissance by European exploration of the South American continent and, later, of Australia.

Ancient Greek knowledge of the world (*oecumene*), however, was limited to the lands surrounding the Mediterranean Sea. Nevertheless, they calculated the circumference of the earth and allocated global 'climes' or climatic zones, from 'frigid' at both poles, through 'temperate' to 'torrid' at the equator. Calculation of the earth's circumference is attributed to Eratosthenes, the librarian of the museum at Alexandria, who in the third century BC also made a map of the stars. Much of Eratosthenes' theory was converted into practical application by the mathematician Klaudios Ptolemaios, known today by his Latinised surname, Ptolemy.

According to Ptolemy, the task of the cartographer was to survey the world 'in its just proportions'—that is, to scale. He created a method of depicting the spherical earth onto a plane surface, with equidistant parallels on a conical surface, developed around the axis of the earth.

Drawing on extensive astronomical observations made between 127 and 141 AD, Ptolemy included calculations of the equinoxes, careful plotting of Mediterranean landmarks, and his confirmation of the length of the tropical year as three-hundredths of a day less than 365-and-a-quarter days. His major work, *Geographia*, issued in eight books around 141 AD, provided the longitudinal and latitudinal coordinates for 8000 locations— the data for constructing the world map or some 26 regional maps, according to scale. Ptolemy's map projection proved invaluable to the Roman military and administrative command.

Ptolemy devised instructions on how to create maps of the inhabited world, but he was well aware that he knew about only a quarter of the globe, and he thus described only that part of its surface that was then known. Ptolemy's depiction showed the known inhabited Roman world, bounded on the south by an unknown land that enclosed the Indian Sea.

Ptolemy's manuscripts did not survive and the oldest known copies date from the fourteenth century. European knowledge of his work might have vanished if it had not held practical application for Arabic trade. Islamic mathematicians, such as al-Khwarizmi (ninth century), and Abu'l Wafa, Mansur and al-Biruni (tenth century), improved on Ptolemy's database for east Africa and India, including some borrowings from Jewish and Hindu sources. By the thirteenth century, Ptolemaic map projections were reconstructed from Arab sources for Greek manuscript editions of *Geographia* prepared in Byzantium.

In the late Middle Ages, Latin became the universal language of European scholarship, and Latin copies of *Geographia* were issued as illuminated manuscripts in several Italian cities—from about 1400 they were of increasing interest to a renewed European scientific community. The development in 1455 of moveable type and a market for printed translations of classical scholarship also stimulated European interest in a wider world open to overland and maritime discovery and trade.

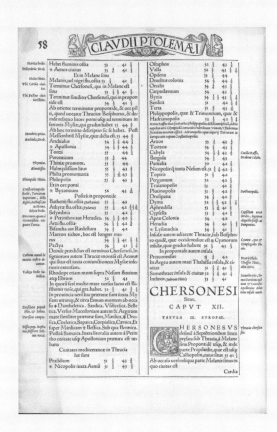

Included in *Australia in Maps* are two Renaissance maps illustrating continuity of the Greek idea of an unexplored *Terra Australis* based on printed forms of Ptolemy's projection.

From the early fifteenth century, European ships sailed around the world in search of new trading routes and partners to feed burgeoning capitalism in Europe. A revised Ptolemaic projection was constructed by the mathematician Gerardus Mercator in 1569, further aiding navigation. The science of cartography became an indispensable tool in the search for trading goods such as gold, silver and spices and, in the process, Europeans encountered new peoples and mapped previously unknown lands.

Portugal, under Prince Henry the Navigator, launched the first great wave of expeditions, and soon Portuguese colonies were established from the west coast of Africa all the way to India.

Meanwhile, Portugal's rival, Castile, began exploring the Atlantic, and in the fifteenth century the Spanish decided to fund Christopher Columbus' expedition. They hoped that by travelling west to Asia, Columbus would bypass Portugal's hold on Africa and the Indian Ocean.

But Columbus did not reach Asia. Instead, his discovery of a new world triggered the decline of the theory of *Terra Australis*. In 1500, the Portuguese navigator Pedro Álvares Cabral landed on the coast of what is now Brazil, and in 1519 an expedition led by Ferdinand Magellan became the first to enter the Pacific from the south Atlantic. In 1578, Sir Francis Drake, in the course of his circumnavigation of the world, passed through the Strait of Magellan into the Pacific Ocean, and travelled well to the south of Tierra del Fuego. The expanse of open water he encountered led Drake to guess that, far from being another continent, as previously believed, Tierra del Fuego was an island with open sea to its south.

Although the link between the Americas and a southern continent was now broken, cartographers continued to express belief in the existence of a vast southern continent well into the eighteenth century. The mega-continent, which can be seen in maps by Ortelius, Montanus and others, was a means of making sense of a rapidly changing geographical world, using and expanding cartographic theories inherited from the ancient Greeks. It was not until Abel Tasman rounded Australia in 1644–1648 and James Cook charted the continent's east coast in 1770 that the theory of *Terra Australis* was finally abandoned.

left and right
Secunda Etas Mundi
(Nuremberg: Hartmann
Schedel, 1493)
map; 31.0 x 43.0 cm
Maps Collection
nla.map-nk6074

Hartmann Schedel's *Secunda Etas Mundi*, 1493

Published just as news of Columbus' discoveries began to spread, the *Secunda Etas Mundi* was one of the last noteworthy world maps to be produced without any indication of the New World. The oldest printed map in the National Library's collection, it was part of a six-volume work known as the *Nuremberg Chronicle*, a survey of the history of the world from the Creation to the year 1493.

A product of Judeo–Christian belief concerning the creation of the world and the birth of man, the *Chronicle* was one of the most remarkable books of its time. Its many illustrations included this depiction of the ancient world surrounded by 12 windheads, and supported and held at three corners by the Old Testament figures of Ham, Shem and Japhet.

The *Chronicle* led the reader through five historical ages, from Genesis to the birth of Christ. The sixth and largest volume took

a world view, from the life and passion of Christ to the missions of the Apostles, reigns of emperors, papal history, and astronomical and astrological events. It also featured well-illustrated townscapes that accompanied a detailed study of city development and urban wealth.

Financed by the physician Hartmann Schedel (1440–1514) and the wealthy local businessmen of Nuremberg, the *Chronicle* contributed enormously to the spread of historical scholarship — at least 800 copies were published in Latin and 400 in German. Anton Koberger, one of Europe's foremost publishers, used 24 presses and employed more than 100 people to print the book. Among the designers were Michael Wolgemut and his stepson Hans Pleydenwurff, master painters of the Nuremberg workshop where Albrecht Dürer served his apprenticeship.

Schedel, who owned one of the largest manuscript and printed book collections in Europe, remained faithful to church orthodoxy by borrowing from earlier compilations, especially the *Supplementum Chronicarum* published in 1483 by Brother Jacobus Philippus Foresti, of Bergamo. The text contains much legend and fancy, contemporary medieval learning and admiration of holy biblical content.

The map is an updated version of the ancient Ptolemaic map projection. Christopher Columbus had been inspired by Ptolemy's exaggerated size of Asia and his considerably undersized dimension of the Earth's circumference. By 1493, Columbus had returned from the discovery of what he thought were eastern islands of India when Schedel's *Chronicle* appeared, although news of his stunning voyage had yet to reach Nuremberg. The world map, however, reveals knowledge of Portuguese explorations along the

west coast of Africa to Cape Verde, and appears to have been copied from a 1482 edition of Pomponius Mela's *De Chorographia*.

Schedel's map does not show that Bartolomeu Dias had rounded the Cape of Good Hope in 1488,

citur a rota τ est q̈libet figura sperica τ rotunda. Et d° orbis dr̄.q̄ rotūd° ēr̄ dr̄ orb terre vl orbisterra if āt bm̄ vince. filij sem obtinuisse asiā.filij chā affrī europā. Isid.in li.Etby.asserit cp orbis diuisus ē in eq̄liter. Nā asia a meridie p orientem vscp ad septē Europa vo a septētrione vscp ad occidentē ptingit. occidentem p meridiez se extendit. Sola quocp Asia

continet vnam partem nostre habitabilis.s.medietatem:alie vo ptes.s.affrica τ europa aliam medietatez sunt sortite. Inter has autem partes ab occeano mare magnū progreditur.eascp intersecat:quapropter si in duas partes orientis τ occidentis orbem diuidas in vna erit asia in alia vo affrica τ europa.Sic autem diuiserunt post diluuiū filij Noe:inter quos Sem cum posteritate sua asiam. Japhet europam:cham affri cam possederunt.vt dicit glo.super Gen.x.τ super libro Paralippo.primo. Idem dicit Crisostomus Isi torius τ Plinius.

possibly due to Portuguese secrecy before Vasco da Gama arrived at Calicut, India, during 1498 to open the first all-sea trading route with Europe. Schedel follows Ptolemy by suggesting an enclosed Indian Ocean bounded by a hypothetical Antarctic continent.

Before long, interest in backward-looking representations of this kind was overtaken by even more remarkable discoveries in the East. Da Gama returned to Portugal with enough spices to make a 3000 per cent profit on the voyage. The money smashed the Venetian

monopoly held with Arab traders and provided da Gama with funds to conquer the Indian Ocean as 'Admiral of the Indies'. In 1502, with a fleet of 20 well-armed ships, da Gama led his second voyage to India, paving the way for future Portuguese expeditions to land the

first Europeans in Malaya, China, Korea, the Spice Islands (now the Maluku Islands, formerly the Moluccas), Timor and New Guinea.

Johann Honter's *Astronomia,* 1545

This small woodcut (opposite) showing a simple world map is the oldest known map to use the name 'Australia'. The name is derived from the Latin, *australis*— 'southern'—and there has long been conjecture about the first use of the Latin word-ending '*ia*', meaning 'land'. The first use of the word 'Australia' deliberately to mean the charted landmass may be attributed to Matthew Flinders, although the term had appeared during the Renaissance.

According to ancient Greek theory, *Terra Australis* was located at the southern margin of the Indian Ocean (*Indicum Mare*). This 1545 'planigob'—a diagram showing the four main winds and the main compass points—is a crude upside-down representation of Ptolemy's original global projection.

The design is linked to the work of Johann Honter (1498–1549). Nicknamed the Luther of Transylvania because of his Protestant leadership, Honter introduced the first printing press to Kronstadt (now Brasov). The source of a steady stream of Lutheran publications flowing out to ethnic German Saxons in the rest of Transylvania (in eastern Hungary), the press became the lifeblood for the Saxon Evangelical Church, for Honter provided theological and organisational foundations in his most famous work, the *Kirchenordnung* (1542).

It is against a background of an emerging Transylvanian Protestant theology, as it shifted from Lutheranism to Unitarianism then Calvinism, that Honter emerged as a Saxon prophet. Born in Kronstadt, the son of a wealthy tanner, it is believed that Honter studied astronomy at the university in Vienna from 1520 until the Turks besieged the city in 1529. He fled to Regensburg, where he assumed the non-Saxon name of Honter, and in 1530 he briefly joined the University of Krakow, a Catholic stronghold, where he published *Rudimenta Cosmographica* in two volumes—one on astronomy, the other on geography. He then learned the craft of woodblock etching and printing as a printer's reader in Basle, before returning to Kronstadt, where he established the printing business that promoted his name throughout Protestant Europe. Honter began to preach, and a swarm of Reformation pamphlets followed.

In 1542, Honter printed an influential geography manual, in verse, entitled *Rudimenta Cosmographica*. He believed that verse would help students remember the information contained in the book. The maps of all known parts of the world were so popular that no less than 39 editions were printed across Europe.

In 1544, Honter opened a Saxon school as a humanist centre for transforming the Saxons into a new *Volk* through understanding the gospels, poetry and classical traditions. Known as the Coetus Honteri and organised by the pupils, this school survived until 1941, when it was considered contrary to Nazi doctrine. The heavy demands of the Kronstadt printing press required Honter to open a paper mill in 1546. A year later, Honter funded the opening of the Kronstadt Library as a repository for European publications.

For his Saxon readership, Honter applied his skills to various updated editions of Ptolemy's *Almagest* (1541–1551), a document traceable back to 151 AD. For 1400 years, the *Almagest* had promoted Greek and Arabic belief in a geocentric universe. Honter, aware of the recent European updating of Ptolemy's world map, borrowed from the source for the planigob that appeared as a single page in the 1545 *Teutsch Astronomie* (German Astronomy)—possibly in use as a textbook. The actual design of the planigob appears to be a poor copy from Albrecht

Dürer, once apprenticed to illustrate Schedel's *Nuremberg Chronicle*. While in Basle, Honter had printed two star maps drawn by Dürer (1532).

By 1545, the geocentric theory presented in *Teutsch Astronomie* had become outdated. In Poland to the north, Nicolaus Koppernigk (Copernicus) (1473–1543) had worked for many years on telescopic observations as dramatic new evidence of a solar planetary system (the heliocentric theory: that the planets, including the earth, rotated around the sun). Published in Nuremberg during 1541, but not widely available to scholars beyond the influence of the Catholic Church until six years later, Copernicus' *De Revolutionibus Orbium Coelestium* provided the means for more accurate global navigation.

Abraham Ortelius' world map, 1570

In 1570, *Terra Australis Nondum Cognita* appeared as a gigantic Antarctic continent on a new world map published by Abraham Ortelius (1527–1598). Ortelius' imaginative depiction of the mysterious South Land stretched northward beyond the Tropic of Capricorn, and this depiction was to influence European maritime exploration over the next two centuries.

Ortelius began his lifelong association with maps as a map engraver in his hometown of Antwerp in 1547 (he is listed in the Antwerp Guild of Saint Luke as an *aftsetter van Karten*). He was also associated with his father's trade in antiquities, books, prints and maps.

As a member of the influential Ortelius family of Augsburg, he travelled extensively on business throughout Europe with his Antwerp friend, Gerardus Mercator. Along the way, he became expert in Latin and Greek, and proficient in French, German, Italian and Spanish. As a map editor and publisher, he also acquired the rudiments of mathematics and cosmography.

In 1564, probably as a result of Mercator's influence, Ortelius published his first map—an eight-sheet *mappemonde* (world map). Publication in 1570 of his monumental work *Theatrum Orbis Terrarum*—the world's first 'atlas'—brought Ortelius instant success and made Flanders rather than Italy the centre of the European map industry. Ortelius developed the idea of binding together a set of charts while working on an assignment for the Antwerp merchant Gilles Hooftman, Lord of Cleydael and Aertselaer, a map collector who complained of the nuisance of unrolling and rolling up his many large maps.

Containing 53 maps, the *Theatrum* proved to be the most expensive and most popular work of the second half of the sixteenth century, with many maps derived from other cartographers but re-engraved to a uniform format. An addendum of 17 maps later appeared, followed by editions with 137 maps in 1593 and 166 maps in 1612.

The first map of the atlas, reproduced here, is unusual for its choice of an oval projection instead of the more usual twin hemispheres or the cylindrical (rectangular) form popularised by Mercator.

Ortelius obtained his geographical content from Mercator's large wall map of 1569. The sourcing resulted in a transfer of errors, the most obvious being the distorted shape of South America, some

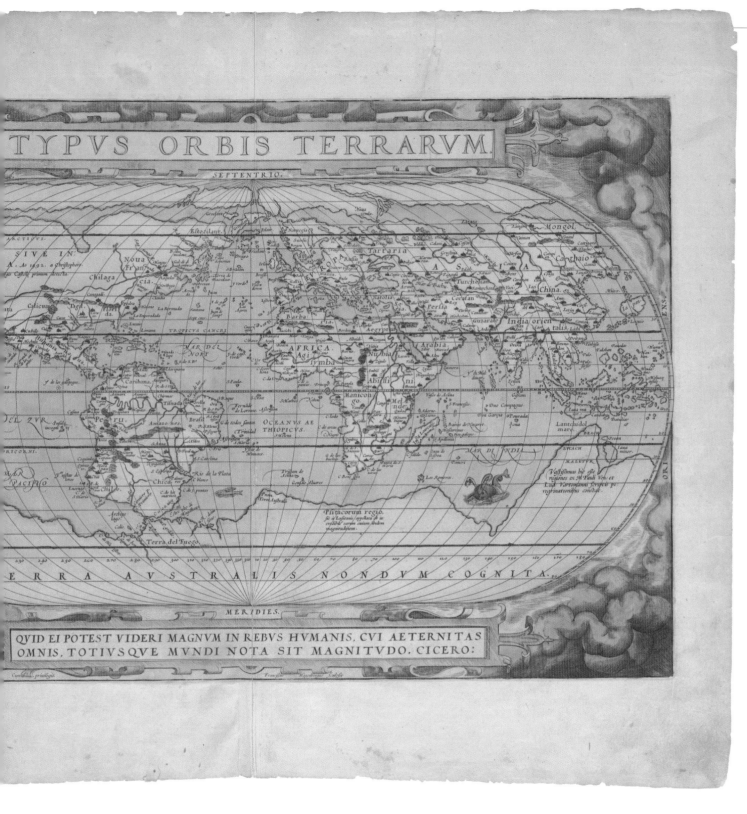

misrepresentation of northern Europe, and an extension of the Mediterranean Sea.

The Ortelius map revealed the lack of European knowledge of northern and eastern Asia but recognised the recent charting of New Guinea by the Spanish. The southern continent had changed little from the Ptolemaic concept, but Ortelius named prominent features (for example, Land of the Parrots, Cape of the Good Signal, River of Islands and the Sweetest River) to suggest that parts of *Terra Australis* might have already been discovered.

After the initial printings of 1570, the first plate suffered extensive damage when it cracked in the lower left corner. A second plate engraved in 1586 repeated the South America error with some name changes, while the third plate, used for the first time in 1592, corrected the South American error and introduced a new border design. Ortelius dedicated the *Theatrum* to the Spanish King Felipe II, who honoured him with the title of Royal Geographer and later appointed him Royal Librarian.

24

Benito Arias Montano's world map, 1572

In 1571, a curious 'blob' (island) lying below what seems to be the Indonesian Archipelago— suggesting to some a portion of northern Australia—appeared on a world map.

The map is attributed to Benito Arias Montano (1527–1598) and was published in Amberes as part of the eighth and final folio volume of the *Antwerp Polyglot Bible* projected by Christophe Plantin (circa 1520–1589), with its parallel texts in Aramaic, Hebrew, Greek and Latin. Plantin, a Huguenot, had fled to Antwerp to escape persecution in Paris.

Born in Fregenal de la Sierra, Spain, Montano's career covered a diverse range of interests, including religious poetry, humanism, philosophy, architecture, physical and medical sciences, 11 classical and oriental languages (including Arabic, Chaldean, Hebrew and Syrian), biblical scholarship and theology.

In 1562, Montano accompanied the Bishop of Segovia as consulting theologian to the Council of Trent, where he won great distinction (and some enemies) for his erudition. Four years later, King Felipe II of Spain appointed him Royal Chaplain and Confessor, and sent him to Flanders to supervise preparation of the *Complutensian Bible Poliglota.*

Montano showed great interest in maps, geography and mathematical instruments and became a close friend of the great Flemish cartographer Abraham Ortelius (see pages 22-23), who supported and encouraged Montano in the composition of his maps. While in Flanders, Montano enriched the Escorial Royal Library of Felipe II by judicious book collecting on a grand scale, paying particular attention to Jewish antiquities.

Montano, who may be described as a scriptural geographer, used maps to interpret his understanding of the sacred scriptures. Much information displayed on the map came from the Bible and was intended to show the distribution of the tribes of Israel across the world, thereby demonstrating its repopulation by the descendants of Noah. The use of Hebrew for placenames and tribes, and the interpretation of biblical gold-bearing regions in the New World,

indicated the map's devotional origins and material purpose.

Montano reflected the conventional geography of the day, leading to speculation on the distribution of the southern continents. A series of world maps produced in the French port of Dieppe during the mid sixteenth century claimed unnamed Portuguese sources, and some

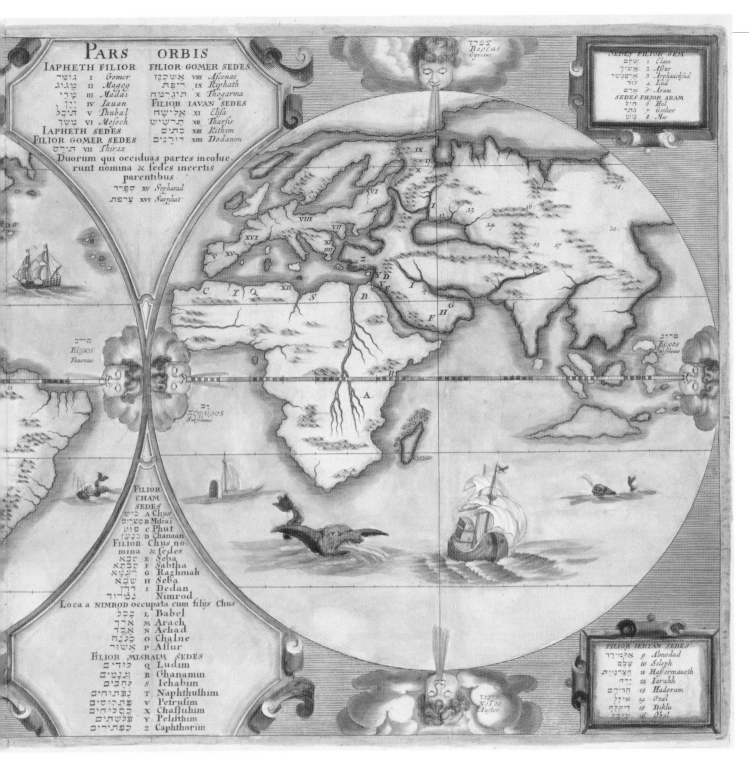

supposed evidence of Portuguese exploration of Australia. The curious 'blob' (island) roughly in the position of Australia in the Library's 1572 edition of the map reflects the Dieppe school of map rendition for the Southern Hemisphere, with an undefined southern boundary. Similarly, the undefined landmass south of the Americas seems to be influenced directly by Ortelius. Both may also be vestigial remnants of the Ptolemaic and ancients' concept of a southern landmass balancing that of the north.

After publication of the polyglot atlas, Montano took it to Rome for the approval of Pope Gregory XIII. He was, however, denounced at the Inquisition by supporters of the Vulgate (i.e. Latin) Bible for changing the original Hebrew text and for relying on Jewish rabbinical sources. Despite the protection of Felipe II, Montano was not freed of these charges until 1580. Felipe then persuaded him to take up the post of librarian of the magnificent Escorial Royal Library. Montano retired to Seville in 1594, where he lived until his death.

George Smirnoff
To the Indies 1944
oil on canvas;
65.7 x 76.8 cm
Pictures Collection
nla.pic-an2310308

3. Recorded European knowledge of the South Land

European arrival in Asia and the South Pacific

By the late 1500s, Portuguese and Spanish explorers had opened a sea-route to India, Asia and the East Indies (now South-East Asia), and charted much of present-day Indonesia, the northern New Guinea coastline and several islands in the South Pacific.

At the same time, considerable experimentation was taking place in cartographic circles. In the French port of Dieppe, chartmakers imagined a rich and vast southward-reaching Java, and before long a so-called 'Java la Grande' began to appear on world and regional charts. The Dieppe maps are thought by some to provide clues to the Portuguese exploration of Australia's coasts in the 1520s, but no documentation of such visits has ever been found. Numerous versions of the imagined South Land were depicted, and for many years coexisted with recorded knowledge.

Spanish explorers in the South Pacific expected to find a second Peru or India. According to the terms of the Treaty of Tordesillas, which divided the newly discovered lands outside Europe into an exclusive duopoly between the Spanish and the Portuguese, the Spanish viceroy of Peru had authority over much of the Pacific. Spain commissioned voyages to discover and colonise the unknown lands west of South America, and, without realising it, sailors began rounding in close to Australia's north-east. In 1606, a Spanish expedition landed on New Hebrides, declared the islands the long-sought-after South Land and named them *La Austrialia del Espiritu Santo.*

Further to the north, scientifically trained Jesuit missionaries exposed Chinese scholars to new astronomical and surveying theory and, in turn, Chinese navigational skills opened the way for new sea-routes in the east. In response to the spread of Protestantism across

Europe, the Catholic Counter-Reformation sent its missions into the New World and Asia, especially China. For a time the scholarly zeal of the Jesuits achieved great influence in the new Ch'ing (Qing) Court, after the overthrow of the Ming Dynasty (1644). The best-known Jesuit missionary, Father Ferdinand Verbiest (1623–1688), a Flemish missionary, led missions in Shansi (now Shanxi) and Peking (now Beijing). In addition to his work in astronomy and cartography, Verbiest supervised the construction of cannon when the Ch'ing was threatened by a rebellion in South China.

But it was the Dutch who achieved the greatest inroads into Asia, particularly in the south. The Spanish conquest of the Netherlands, also called the Dutch war of independence, had begun in 1568, and conflict between the two nations would last for 80 years. In 1580, Dutch access to the lucrative spice trade was curtailed when the harbour of Lisbon was closed to

Dutch ships. Without an income from spices, the Dutch were severely hampered in their ability to fund the war.

Impelled to seek new routes that skirted Spanish and Portuguese strongholds around the Cape of Good Hope and along the southern Asian coasts, Dutch sailors arrived in Bantam (now Banten) in 1596 to establish a foothold in the booming spice market. Dutch merchants banded together to form the Vereenigde Oost-Indische Compagnie (VOC), or Dutch East India Company, and in 1602 the Netherlands States-General granted the charter that established the VOC and its monopoly of navigation between the Cape of Good Hope and the Strait of Magellan, with its total monopoly over the spice trade.

The company grew rapidly, and in 1602 the ships of the VOC's Moluccan fleet broke a Portuguese blockade in the Bay of Bantam. By the mid-1600s, the VOC fleet

boasted 150 merchant ships, 40 warships, 50 000 employees, a private army of 10 000 soldiers and a network of trading posts that extended from the Persian Gulf to the China Sea.

Between 1570 and 1670—the years leading up to the formation of the VOC, and the subsequent decades of Dutch exploration along Australia's shores—a series of mapmaking families merged art and science in printed maps that were unsurpassed. In the workshops of Hondius, Blaeu, Jansson, Danckert, van Keulen and others, cartographers represented the rapid growth in geographical knowledge, while a flourishing trade in published maps and atlases centred on Amsterdam.

With a monopoly to Australia's north, the Dutch sought new trading partners and markets, improved cartographic and navigational techniques, and extended sea-routes. Through a series of accidental and deliberate expeditions, from the voyage of the *Duyfken* to northern Australia in 1606, the Dutch charted many parts of the Australian coast in the north, west and south, and by the time Abel Tasman completed his chart of the northern coastline in 1644 the continent had become known as New Holland.

British and French interests in the East Indies were still in their infancy and voyages to the southern continent were rare. In 1699, William Dampier was given command of HMS *Roebuck* with a commission to explore Australia and New Guinea. Dampier reached Shark Bay, in the north-west of Western Australia, and foreshadowed a new European understanding of the South Land. Like the French scientist and writer Melchisédech Thévenot, Dampier helped create a popular view of the continent that held sway until the coming of the British, in 1770.

28

Ferdinand Verbiest's *Kunyu Wanguo Quantu*, 1674

Flemish Jesuit priest Ferdinand Verbiest (1623–1688) arrived in Macao in 1659 soon after Portuguese mariners established this trading post. Here he served at the Catholic mission before being called on to help missionaries in Peking (now Beijing).

After winning a three-part astronomical debate and imperial favour from Emperor K'ang Hsi, Verbiest was appointed as Chair of the Board of Mathematics. He immediately suggested major revisions to the 13-month Chinese calendar and, despite bureaucratic opposition to the cost and inconvenience to millions of users, Verbiest triumphed.

Verbiest's most enduring work remains the construction of astronomical instruments for the Peking Observatory, originally built in 1279 and rebuilt by Verbiest in 1673. Using contemporary European technology, he also supervised the manufacture of 132 cannons for the Chinese army.

Verbiest taught geometry, European philosophy and music, compiled 30 books in Chinese on astronomy and religious teaching, and devised a steam engine to propel small ships.

Verbiest accompanied the Emperor on several expeditions throughout the Empire—journeys that formed the basis for his numerous maps of China. His cartographic output included the magnificent *Kunyu Wanguo Quantu* (or world map), issued in two hemispheres, each about 1.6 metres in diameter. The map is drawn from a number of sources, but principally from that of his predecessor and fellow Jesuit, Matteo Ricci (1552–1610), whose map of the same title was compiled in 1602. Another Jesuit, Father Giulio Aleni, corrected Ricci's map in 1623. Verbiest also drew on the work of Dutch cartographers of the day, notably Jean Blaeu and Abraham Ortelius.

Each hemisphere is drawn as a stereographic equatorial projection,

with the prime meridian centred on Peking. Two circles surround both hemispheres: the inner circle shows the latitudes and the outer circle the duration of the longest days for 18 different zones, moving away from the equator.

The most distinctive feature of the map is the remarkable blend of two advanced cartographic cultures—Western (Flemish) and Chinese. While the shape of continents and other landmasses reflects Western knowledge, Chinese technique is strongest for the topographic pictorial element, placenames, and the use of text panels to explain the geography of various areas, with illustrations of a number of the native animals.

The National Library's copy of Verbiest's map is an outstanding example in its own right. It comprises two scrolls, representing the eastern and western hemispheres. Each hemisphere of the Verbiest map consists of woodblock prints printed on silk,

now laid down on a supportive backing of stiffened silk panels. Pictorial elements, notably the animals and birds, were hand coloured, as were the topographic features, and the extensive text panels were boxed. Although there is some loss of clarity of the map surface, with careful scrutiny the text panels and cartographic details can still be interpreted.

The map shows Australia, based on contemporary Dutch knowledge. Sinologist and architect Hardy Wilson purchased the map in Peking in 1921 and donated it to the National Library in 1949.

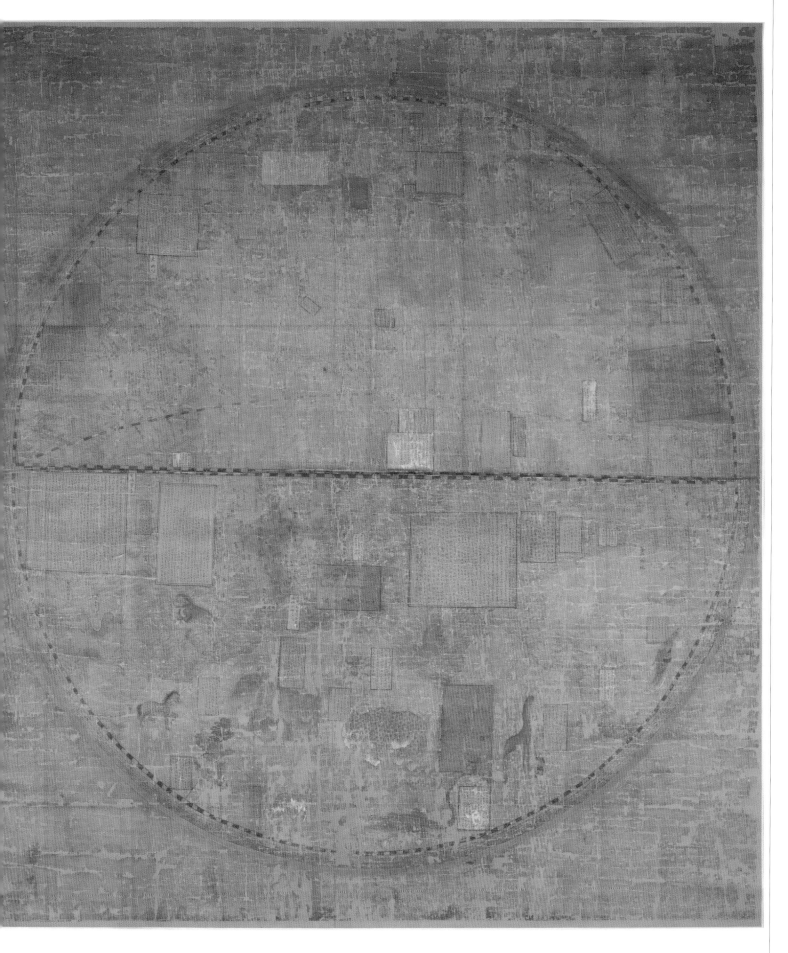

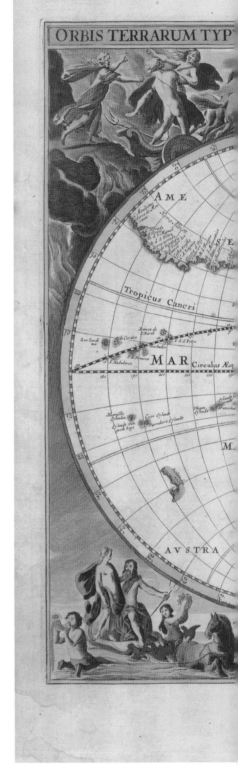

Cornelis Danckert's record of Tasman's 1642–1644 voyages to Australia

The success of Dutch exploration along Australia's northern, southern and western coastlines, beginning in 1606, encouraged further exploration of the southern waters.

In 1642, the Dutch theoretical geographer Franz Jacobszoon Visscher prepared a 'Memorandum concerning the discovery of the South-land' for the Governor-General of the Dutch East Indies, Anthony van Diemen.

Visscher suggested to van Diemen that the search for the South Land should track eastward from Mauritius to New Guinea along 52°S or 54°S latitude. The memorandum not only provided extensive direction concerning the area to be surveyed but also required that crews seek information on trading prospects.

Abel Tasman (circa 1603–1659), an experienced sea captain of the Dutch East India Company (VOC) was given two ships—the *Heemskerck* and the *Zeehaen*—to undertake the task. Accompanied by Visscher as his chief adviser and a council of officers, Tasman left Batavia for Mauritius on 14 August 1642.

This map is the earliest known world map to illustrate the results of Tasman's two voyages.

Following repairs to the *Zeehaen* in Mauritius, Tasman headed to 50°S latitude, where he encountered snow and hail. Returning to 44° S, he sailed east and, in late November, sighted the south-west coast of Tasmania (named, till 1855, 'Van Diemen's Land'). Sheltering from bad weather, he made anchor in Storm Bay and on 1 December moved on to Green Island, where he landed at Blackman's Bay. The Dutch flag was raised as Tasman claimed possession.

Seeking good water, Tasman sailed north on 4 December and after encountering bad weather headed east. On 13 December, he sighted the west coast of the South Island of 'Zealandia Nova'. Sailing north, he anchored in Murderers Bay, where four of his crew were killed by Maoris. Prevailing winds forced the ships west and north to the tip of the North Island, which Tasman named Cape Maria van Diemen. Believing that he was among the islands named in 1615 by Jacob Le Maire, Tasman named the island Staaten Landt as a Dutch possession.

After consulting with his committee, Tasman tracked to the north-east to locate Le Maire's islands and, on 19 January 1643, sighted four islands. Part of the Tonga group, they were later named the 'Friendly Islands' by James Cook. Sailing further north-east, Tasman located the then uncharted Fijian islands. The discovery caused confusion—Tasman did not know precisely where he was, nor could he determine his whereabouts in relation to the more northerly islands of Tonga, previously charted by Le Maire. At this point, he decided to return to Batavia (now Jakarta) via a safe and well-established route north of New Guinea. He reached his destination on 14 June, 10 months after the journey began.

INTEGRO IN PLURIMIS EMENDATUS, AUCTUS, ET ICUNCULIS ILLUSTRATUS

The VOC deemed Tasman's voyage unsuccessful: no trading partnerships had been made, no new resources or treasures had been found and no passage from the southern ocean to Chile had been discovered. Another expedition mounted during 1644 also failed to determine the route, but succeeded in establishing the relationship between Australia's northern coastline and New Guinea.

Cornelis Danckert's previously unrecorded double hemispherical world map, showing the results of both of Tasman's voyages to Australia, is believed to have been published in 1648. Danckert (1603–1656) was from a well-known Amsterdam family of print and map sellers who had immediate access to information gathered by Dutch seafarers and explorers.

Melchisédech Thévenot (c.1620–1692)
Hollandia Nova Detecta 1644; Terre Australe Decouuerte l'an 1644
(Paris: De l'imprimerie de Iaqves Langlois, 1663)
map; 40.2 x 52.9 cm
Maps Collection
nla.map-rm689a

TERRE AVSTRALE

découuerte l'an 1644.

Melchisédech Thévenot's chart of New Holland, 1663

32

The first person to publish a French chart of New Holland (now Australia) with an almost complete western coastline appears to have been Melchisédech Thévenot (circa 1620–1692), a wealthy traveller, an avid book collector and the inventor of the spirit level.

Thévenot copied from the 1645–1648 charts and globes published by Jean Blaeu, mapmaker for the Dutch East India Company in Amsterdam, and included details of Abel Tasman's 1642 survey of *Terre de Diemen's*, named by Tasman after the Governor of Batavia (now Jakarta).

Thévenot's map does not include *Zeelandia Nova*, which the Dutch still hoped to settle as a distant colony, but the War of Devolution (1667–1668) and the Dutch War of 1672, during which French troops occupied Lorraine and almost invaded Amsterdam, put paid to such plans.

Very little is known about Thévenot's early life—his first

name suggests that his family was Jewish and, possibly for business reasons, he is known to have been multilingual, speaking French, English, Greek, Hebrew, Latin, Italian, Arabic and Turkish.

At the age of 27, Thévenot returned to Paris to enter the service of the Royal Court, where he served as envoy to Genoa in 1647 and to Rome from 1653 to 1655. Back in France he set up an academy at his country house at Issy, and he frequently attended informal Parisian meetings of scholars interested in diverse fields such as mathematics, astronomy, mechanics, physics, chemistry, anatomy, medicine and navigation.

Thévenot advocated and undertook several experiments and scientific observations but was not qualified to enter the Académie Royale des Sciences, founded in 1666. His personal interest in translating accounts of maritime exploration as he expanded his library led him to publish four

volumes of *Relations de Divers Voyages Curieux* (1663–1672), a document renowned throughout Europe, especially for its up-to-date strategic detail of the Low Countries, which Thévenot toured extensively during 1668.

Thévenot's popular map of the 'Kingdom of the Great Mogul' (based on an earlier map by William Baffin) reinforced European conjecture about the Orient. In 1684, Louis XIV appointed Thévenot Keeper of the Royal Library, to which Thévenot donated his considerable book collection. A year later he was elected to the Académie Royale des Sciences.

Thévenot was inspired to write about 'The Disastrous Voyage of the Vessel *Batavia*' in the first volume of his *Relations*. His chart of *Nova Hollandia* was taken from one done in inlaid work on the pavement in the Stadt-House, Amsterdam. He did not follow the cartographic convention of

colouring the coastline blue. Instead he used pink and green, with the landmass shaded in blue. A vertical scale indicating latitude across the centre is borrowed from Blaeu's cartography. The chart is a tribute to the accuracy of Dutch navigational observation—several Dutch placenames remain in use today, for example, 'Arnhem Land', 'Groote Eylandt' and 'Carpenteria', and there is a suggestion of a channel shown for the Torres Strait.

It is not surprising that the British Admiralty took note of Thévenot's chart during the eighteenth century, particularly after the prolific English publisher Emmanuel Bowen reprinted the map (or possibly copied it from Blaeu) in 1744, with the addition of *Zeelandia Nova*. At a time of British–French competition to reap the rewards of colonial expansion, Bowen would have whetted

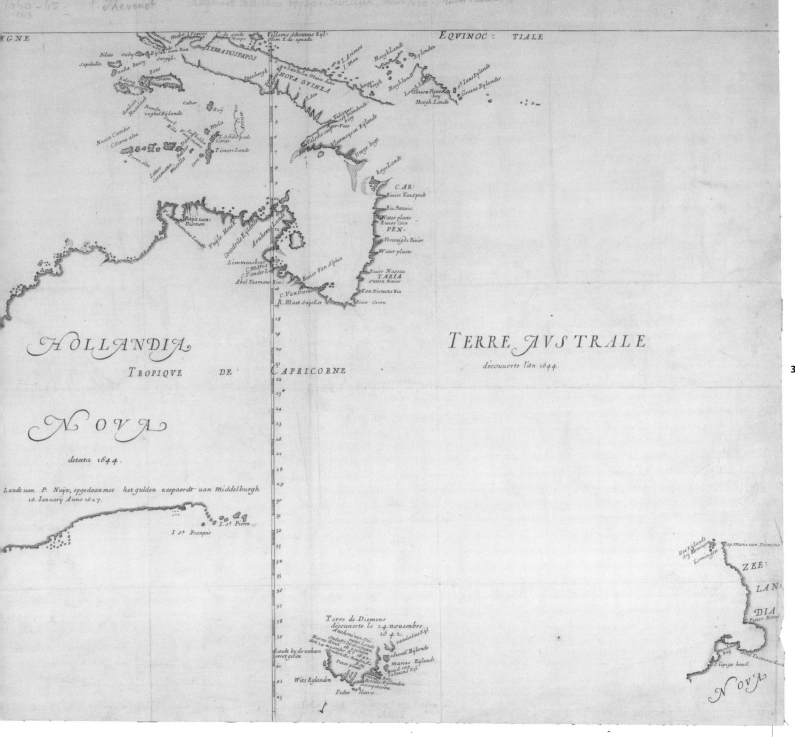

imperial appetites by printing the following speculation over the unmapped eastern coastline, identified as *Terra Australis*:

It is impoſsible to conceive a Country that promises fairer from its Scituation than this of Terra Auſtralis; no longer incognita, as this Map demonstrates, but the Southern Continent Discovered.

It lies Precisely in the richest Climates of the World. If the Islands of Sumatra, Java & Borneo, abound in Precious Stones and other valuable Commodities; and the Moluccas in Spices; New Guinea and the Regions behind it must by a parity of Reason be as plentifully endowed by Nature. If the island of Madagascar is so Noble and plentiful a Country as

all the Authors speak it, and Gold, Ivory and other Commodities are common in the Southern part of Africa, from Melinda down to the Cape of Good Hope, and so up again to C. Gonsalez; here in the same Latitudes in Carpentaria, New Holland, and New Zealand; If Peru overflows with Silver, if all the Mountains of Chili are filled with Gold, and this precious Metal, &

stones much more precious are yᵈ. product of Brazil, this Continent enjoys the benefit of the same poſition and therefore whoever perfectly discovers & settles it will become infalliably professed of Territories as Rich, as fruitful, & as capable of Improvement, as any that have hitherto found out, either in the Eaſt Indies, or the West.

right
Samuel Thornton (d.1715)
**A Draught of the Coast of New Holland,
and Parts Adjacent**
(London: [Mount & Page], c.1743)
coloured map; 39.7 x 19.9 cm
Maps Collection
nla.map-t1262

**Dampier & His Companions in Their Canoe
Overtaken by a Dreadfull Storm c.1777**
engraving; 10.5 x 16.5 cm
Pictures Collection
nla.pic-an9406669

34

William Dampier's survey of Shark Bay, 1699

William Cecil Dampier (1652–1715) ranks as one of Britain's most widely read seamen during the seventeenth century. Orphaned during his early teens, Dampier made the sea his career before the age of 20 and took part in several buccaneering voyages along the Spanish Main (the Caribbean coast of mainland South and Central America).

Dampier's account, *A New Voyage Round the World* (1697), relates to the English privateer, *Cygnet*, which was captained by Charles Swain (or Swan) until he was deposed by mutineers in the Philippines in January 1687. Early in January 1688, with Dampier aboard as a crewmember, the *Cygnet* was beached somewhere near King Sound in Western Australia. While the ship was careened (beached for cleaning or repairs), Dampier took detailed notes. His journal, with its careful observations of the Caribbean, rounding the Horn, visits to the Philippines, New Holland and the Nicobar Islands

(where he left the *Cygnet*), and small-craft excursions across the Indian Ocean to Sumatra and Batavia (now Jakarta), established his credibility with the British Admiralty.

Dampier's *A New Voyage* was published three years after the appearance of Tasman's journals had excited English interest in *Terra Australis Incognita*. Although Dampier is associated with the English landing on New Holland, earlier instances of English contact include the wreck of the *Tryall* in 1622 and a sketch of the Abrolhos Islands by the captain of the *London* in 1681.

In 1699, the British Admiralty commissioned Dampier to explore the east coast of New Holland via Cape Horn. HMS *Roebuck*, a somewhat unreliable leaky barque with an inexperienced crew of 50 men, was outfitted to undertake the voyage. A delayed winter departure caused Dampier to divert to the traditional Dutch

route around Africa and across the Indian Ocean.

On 16 August 1699, HMS *Roebuck* entered Shark Bay and remained in the harbour while the crew searched for fresh water on Dirk Hartog Island. Dampier took the opportunity to conduct not only a survey of the bay but also a detailed assessment of the native flora and fauna that he found so striking and unusual. Dampier provided accurate botanical records and his name is commemorated in the herbaceous plant genus *Dampiera*.

The ship headed north in search of water, making two further landings on Australia's northern coast before scurvy forced the crew to sail to Timor to replenish supplies. Dampier explored the northern coast of New Guinea and the islands on its eastern edge, and named them New Britain. He intended sailing south to chart the east coast of New Holland but the unseaworthy condition of his

ship and his own illness forced him west to Batavia. On the return voyage, HMS *Roebuck* fell apart off the coast of Ascension Island and most of Dampier's papers were lost.

Dampier finally reached England in 1701, where he faced court martial over his earlier imprisonment of an insubordinate officer in Rio de Janeiro. He was fined all his pay and banned from any future naval command. Despite this, publication of the journal of his second voyage, *A Voyage to New Holland* (1703), which included the Shark Bay survey, brought a measure of fame. It was, however, the last time that Dampier maintained a journal, even though he led two further world voyages. In 1719, Daniel Defoe published *Robinson Crusoe*, a story based on the exploits of Alexander Selkirk, a member of Dampier's crew, abandoned at his own request on the Juan Fernández Islands in the South Pacific in 1703.

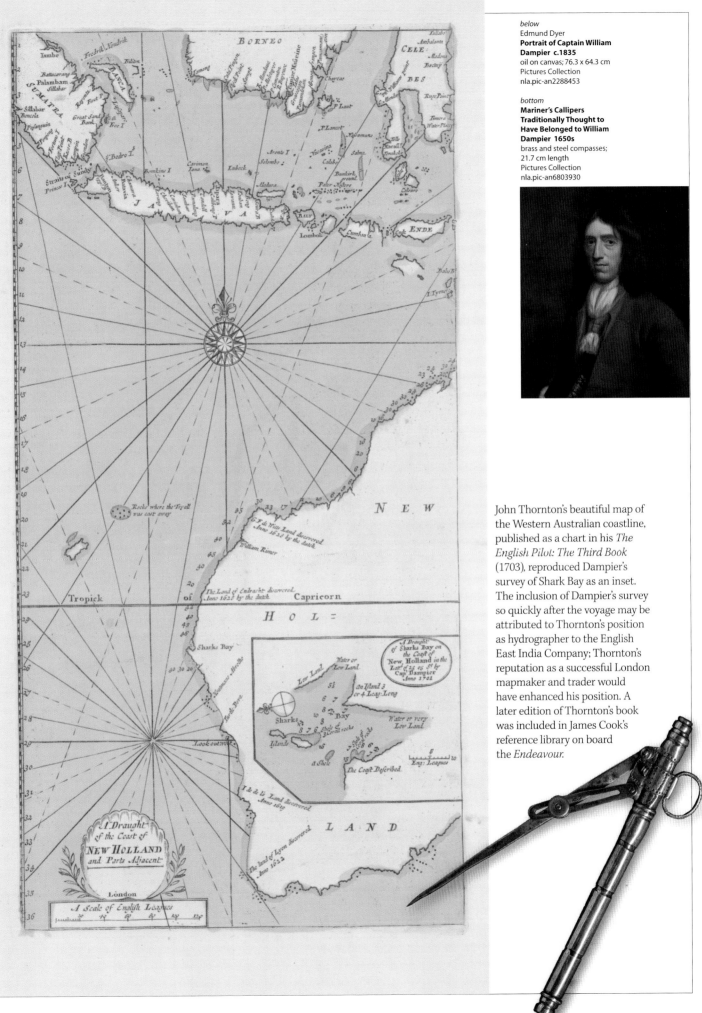

below
Edmund Dyer
Portrait of Captain William Dampier c.1835
oil on canvas; 76.3 x 64.3 cm
Pictures Collection
nla.pic-an2288453

bottom
Mariner's Callipers Traditionally Thought to Have Belonged to William Dampier 1650s
brass and steel compasses;
21.7 cm length
Pictures Collection
nla.pic-an6803930

John Thornton's beautiful map of the Western Australian coastline, published as a chart in his *The English Pilot: The Third Book* (1703), reproduced Dampier's survey of Shark Bay as an inset. The inclusion of Dampier's survey so quickly after the voyage may be attributed to Thornton's position as hydrographer to the English East India Company; Thornton's reputation as a successful London mapmaker and trader would have enhanced his position. A later edition of Thornton's book was included in James Cook's reference library on board the *Endeavour*.

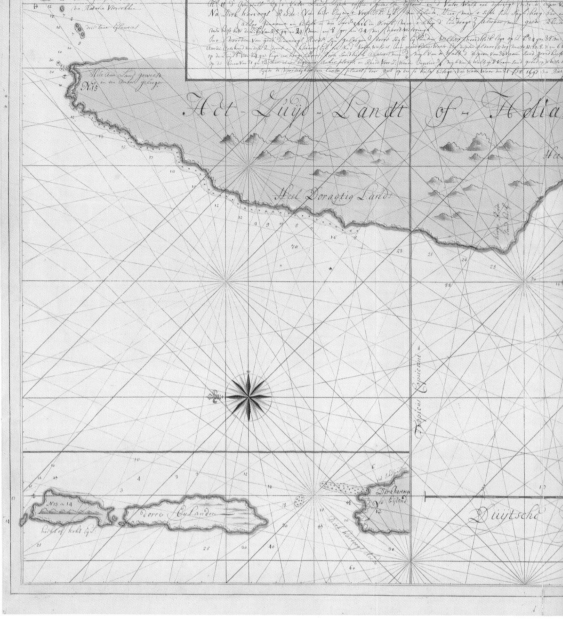

far right
Johannes van Keulen (1654–1715)
**Chart of Houtman Abrolhos, WA /
in't Ligt Gebragt door
Joannes van Keulen**
(Dordrecht: Joannes van Braam;
Amsterdam: Gerard Onder de Linden,
1726)
coloured map: 25.5 x 22.5 cm
Maps Collection
nla.map-nk2110

right
Gerard van Keulen
**T Zuijd landt Ontdeckt door Willem
de Vlaming in den Maande van Jan
an February 1697 met t Yagt de
Geelvink de Hooker de Nyptang ent
Galjoot t Weseltje**
[between 1697 and 1726]
coloured manuscript map;
57.0 x 96.8 cm
Maps Collection
nla.map-rm751

36

Gerard van Keulen's manuscript charts of New Holland, circa 1700

Despite Abel Tasman's comprehensive surveys, much of the west coast of Australia remained poorly charted or uncharted until the end of the century, an omission that resulted in shipwrecks, with many lives lost.

In 1656, the *Vergulde Draeck* (Golden Drake) sank at about 30°10′S with the loss of 118 men. Seven of the 68 survivors navigated a small boat to Batavia (now Jakarta), but two Dutch East India Company (VOC) rescue ships found no trace of the remainder. A coastal profile prepared from a rescue ship commanded by Aucke Pieters Jonck, and later reworked in Batavia by VOC cartographer Johan Nessel, is one of the oldest extant views of the coast. The map, depicting an Aboriginal camp, is housed in Algemeen Rijksarchief at The Hague.

Early in 1694, an enormous VOC capital ship, the *Ridderschap van Holland*, carrying 325 passengers and crew vanished without trace after sailing from Cape Town for Batavia. The disappearance caused VOC directors in Amsterdam to finance a thorough coastal survey eastward from Cape Town.

In May 1696 three newly built vessels sailed from Amsterdam under the command of Willem de Vlamingh, charting the island of Tristan da Cunha on the way. The crew of Vlamingh's flagship, the frigate *Geelvinck*, included Victor Victorszoon, a *cranckbesoker* (consoler of the sick) and an artist who sketched coastal profiles and features of this and later sightings.

At Cape Town, four local multilingual speakers were taken aboard in expectation of making contact with the residents of *t'Zuyd Land* (the South Land). Vlamingh's expedition then entered the southern Indian Ocean and charted the islands of St Paul and Amsterdam. Finding no trace of the lost *Ridderschap van Holland*, the three ships eventually pushed north to an island that Vlamingh named *Rottenest* (Rat-Nest, now Rottnest Island), because of the abundance of rat-like animals (quokkas).

Good drinking water there suggested that it might be a suitable watering place for later shipping. Traces of a shipwreck were also found. Following exploration of a river named *Zwaanenrivier* (or Swan River, named after the black swans seen there) and coastal landings to the north, Vlamingh decided that the hot and dry country was not suited to European cattle or settlement. He did, however, find Dirk Hartog Island and Hartog's pewter plate, left on the island

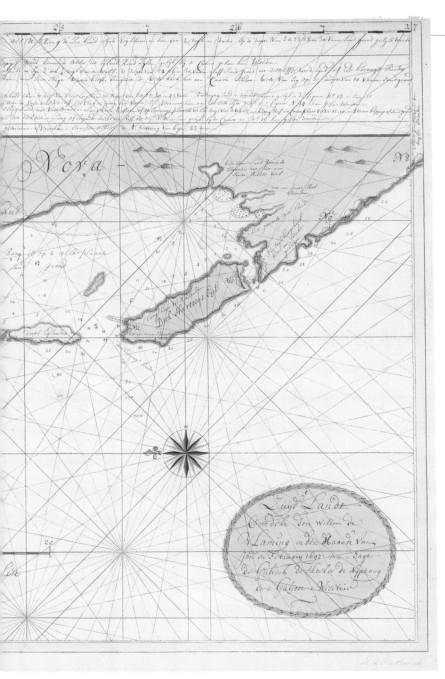

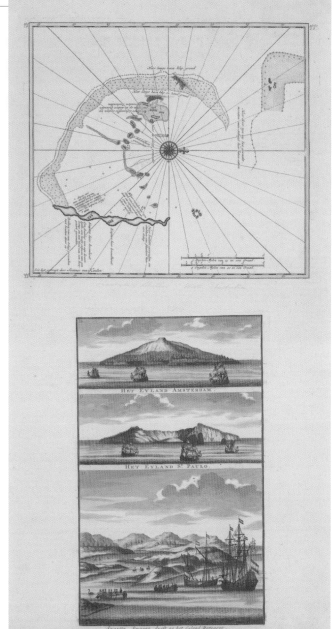

in 1616. The plate was later sent back to Amsterdam, along with specimens of flora and several black swans, which died en route.

Vlamingh left a replacement pewter plate on a pole as a record (it is now in the Maritime Museum in Perth) before sailing to Batavia, having completed a survey of the island of Mony (now Christmas Island).

An accomplished cartographer, Vlamingh produced detailed charts of the voyage. The charts were lost, however, on his return to Batavia. An outline chart and careful journal entries by Vlamingh allowed Victor Victorszoon to prepare a map of the South Land from 20°S to 32°S. Victorszoon painted at least 15 watercolour profiles of the coast (which are held in the Prins Hendrick Maritime Museum in Rotterdam).

Later, in Amsterdam, leading VOC cartographer Gerard van Keulen carefully constructed a manuscript chart on two sheets from these observations. These charts are among the oldest manuscript maps depicting part of Australia. Acquired by the National Library in 1911, the charts were discovered to be van Keulen's original drawings by the eminent cartographic historian Professor Gunter Schilder, following a research visit to the Library in 1981.

Van Keulen's chart of 'Dirck Hartog' Island and coast applied the name 'Het-Zùÿt-Landt of Hollandia Nova' to claim Dutch ownership.

Replica of the Vlamingh Plate
c.1950
copper plate; 37.1 cm diam.
Pictures Collection
nla.pic-an7743326

4. Theories of the east coast of New Holland

The struggle for maritime supremacy

Throughout much of the seventeenth century, European trade with South-East Asia remained a Dutch monopoly based in the northern port of Amsterdam, a major financial centre on the river Amstel that had developed international ties, particularly after the fall of Antwerp to Spain in 1585 drove many Protestant and Jewish merchants north.

Amsterdam interests were varied, extending to Caribbean and Latin-American plantations, the African slave trade, Baltic grain and timber markets, North Sea fishing, and French wine and brandy production. The united provinces of Holland held maritime supremacy and boasted

Europe's first industrial zone, the innovative shipbuilding centre of Zaandam. Goods freighted in Dutch barges and ships to their home ports gave Dutch merchants considerable control. Maritime prosperity ushered in a golden age, and Amsterdam became a world leader in technology, producing ships, printing presses, military equipment, charts and atlases.

Rival cities, such as Paris and London, could not match Amsterdam's shipping capacity. The English lost trade to the Dutch in Spain and Portugal, and Dutch traders from the New Netherlands on the Hudson River infiltrated English colonies in North America.

At the same time, the Dutch monopoly in the east inhibited French and British attempts to support their merchants in the East Indies. Following three disastrous naval battles between 1652 and 1752 that had attempted to establish British sovereignty over the Channel and the Irish Sea, the British navy was left in tatters.

With the French navy weakened by invasion attempts and Spain exhausted by fruitless ventures to regain Portugal and its former colonies, the installation of the Dutch William of Orange as English monarch in 1688 provided

unrivalled opportunities for a Dutch–English alliance.

Against this background of shifting maritime supremacy, the Dutch lost interest in the South Land. With little new cartographic information forthcoming on South-East Asia and the Pacific, the map-printing industry fell back on guesswork, although Dutch mapmakers, particularly the hydrographers of the Dutch East India Company, regularly updated illustrated manuals for maritime navigation, with careful attention to recorded sightings.

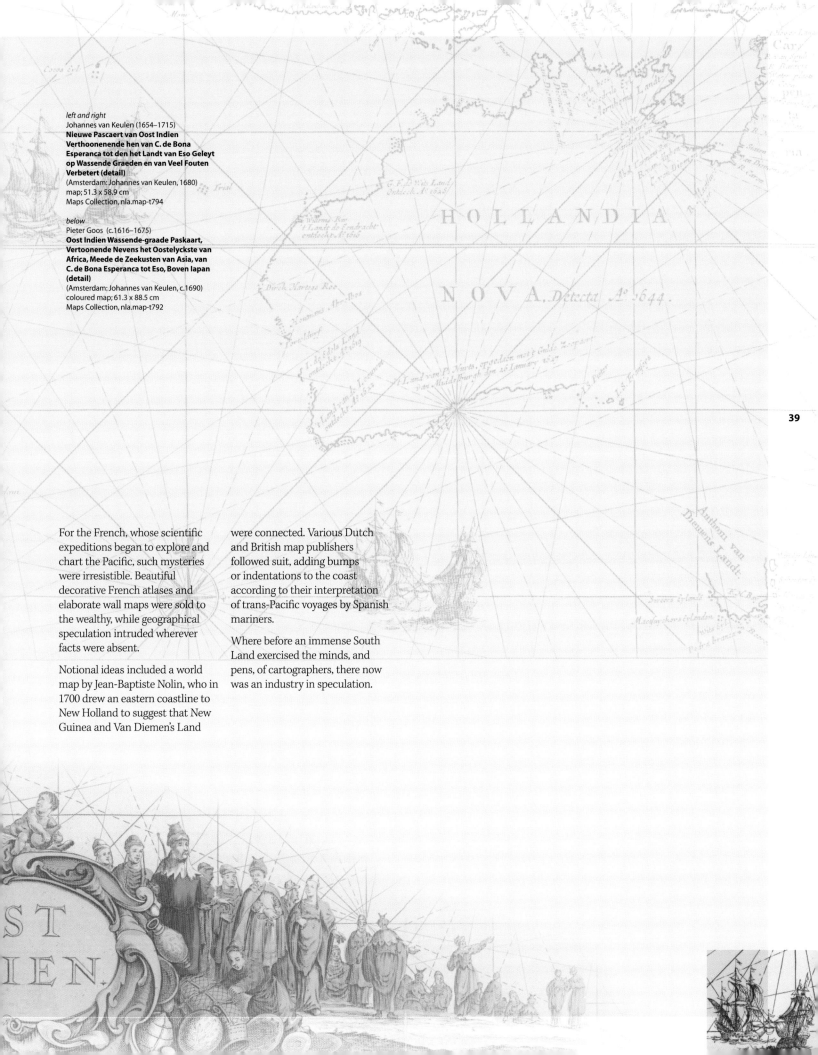

left and right
Johannes van Keulen (1654–1715)
**Nieuwe Pascaert van Oost Indien
Verthoonenende hen van C. de Bona
Esperanca tot den het Landt van Eso Geleyt
op Wassende Graeden en van Veel Fouten
Verbetert (detail)**
(Amsterdam: Johannes van Keulen, 1680)
map; 51.3 x 58.9 cm
Maps Collection, nla.map-t794

below
Pieter Goos (c.1616–1675)
**Oost Indien Wassende-graade Paskaart,
Vertoonende Nevens het Oostelyckste van
Africa, Meede de Zeekusten van Asia, van
C. de Bona Esperanca tot Eso, Boven Iapan
(detail)**
(Amsterdam: Johannes van Keulen, c.1690)
coloured map; 61.3 x 88.5 cm
Maps Collection, nla.map-t792

For the French, whose scientific expeditions began to explore and chart the Pacific, such mysteries were irresistible. Beautiful decorative French atlases and elaborate wall maps were sold to the wealthy, while geographical speculation intruded wherever facts were absent.

Notional ideas included a world map by Jean-Baptiste Nolin, who in 1700 drew an eastern coastline to New Holland to suggest that New Guinea and Van Diemen's Land were connected. Various Dutch and British map publishers followed suit, adding bumps or indentations to the coast according to their interpretation of trans-Pacific voyages by Spanish mariners.

Where before an immense South Land exercised the minds, and pens, of cartographers, there now was an industry in speculation.

right
Jean-Baptiste Nolin (1648–1708)
**Le Globe Terrestre Represente
en Deux Plans-hemispheres**
(Paris: Chez l'auteur sur le quay de l'Horloge du
Palais a l'Enseigne de la Place des Victoires vers
le Pont Neuf avec privilege du roy, 1700)
coloured map; 2 hemispheres, 60.6 cm diam.
Maps Collection
nla.map-rm3605

left
Jean-Baptiste Nolin (1648–1708)
Le Globe Terrestre (detail)

40

Jean-Baptiste Nolin's world map, 1700

The Rue St Jacques mapmaking outlet of Jean-Baptiste Nolin (1657–1725), which produced this large wall map of the world, was a product of the rise of Paris as Europe's largest city under Bourbon dynastic rule. Wall maps are the most endangered of all cartographic works, with less than 50 recorded from the hundreds produced during the seventeenth century.

The Treaty of Vervins of 1598 forced the withdrawal of Spanish troops from France, and royal bounties created a French merchant marine that, during the next century, would open trading posts with India and the North American colonial settlements of Louisiana, Quebec and Acadia. French charts provided new information, and French privateers began to compete with Dutch-Batavian and English shipping in the East Indies.

Political changes under Louis XIII and Louis XIV gave French mapmakers an element of royal support and patronage unknown elsewhere, marking a shift of geographical science to Paris ('New Rome') as Dutch maritime power declined.

At first, French mapping extended the cartographic knowledge centred in Antwerp, as they updated various charts by Mercator and Ortelius. But the marriage contract of Louis XIV to Maria Theresa then attached Habsburg Spain to France under the 1659 Treaty of the Pyrenees, a diplomatic coup that allowed French access to documents relating to Spanish colonisation and exploration of the Pacific.

Following the death of the powerful Cardinal Mazarin in 1661, Louis XIV developed his doctrine of 'natural boundaries' and encouraged French border expansion of his state to include the frontier features of ancient Gaul and his anticipated takeover of the Spanish (Belgian)

Netherlands. Topographic cartography blossomed, and Louis XIV employed Italian mathematicians and astronomers to establish scientific standards.

In 1669, Giovanni Domenico Cassini was appointed as the first director of the new Paris Observatory, with responsibility for introducing new astronomical methods to determine longitude according to eclipses of the satellites of Jupiter. For nearly two centuries the Cassini family developed the geometrical and geodetic triangulation survey techniques that revolutionised topographic mapping.

On the floor of the Observatory, Cassini prepared a gigantic scale planisphere map of the world based on observations filed by the Académie Royale des Sciences. Several French mapmakers drew on these observations, including Jean-Baptiste Nolin, who in 1696 published a world map as a single planisphere to demonstrate the

improved scientific accuracy of global cartographic positioning.

As evidenced by a 1690 world map prepared by Nolin as two planispheres, however, unexplored parts of the world required guesswork. Nolin repeated from Spanish sources the belief that California was an island, and the fiction of a *Mer de l'Ouest* (or North-West Passage) that for the next century would lure navigators to seek the fabled trading route to Hudson's Bay.

Similarly, in the region of Tahiti, Nolin misplaced the fabled gold wealth of King Solomon as the Spanish islands of Isabella and Guadalcanal. Access to Dutch charts allowed Nolin to provide an accurate shape of the western portion of New Holland, but he seriously distorted information from Tasman's surveys of Van Diemen's Land and an enlarged 'Nouvelle Zelande'.

Nolin's magnificent wall map of 1700, illustrated by Nicolas

Bouquet, supported the two hemispheres with mythological features surrounded by images of the creation of heaven and earth. The elaborately decorated border contains 16 vignettes of biblical events. The map is one of the rarest items in the National Library and shows the tracks of voyages by Magellan in 1520, de la Maire in 1626 and Tasman in 1642, as well as information recorded by Vasco da Gama, Mendana, Olivier and Chaumont. The most distinctive

feature by Nolin is a conjectured eastern coastline to 'Nouvelle Holland', shown in a provisional shade to link New Guinea to Van Diemen's Land. Other features are similar to his smaller 1690 map.

Pierre Mortier, who showed the hypothetical eastern coastline of New Holland, published a virtually identical copy of the Nolin 1700 wall map in London during the same year, but with Carpentaria shown south of the

Tropic. Mortier's edition may have triggered British Admiralty interest in the possibility of further French colonisation.

right
Fleming, London
Telescope c.1842
wood and brass; 36.7 cm length
Pictures Collection
nla.pic-an7880635

far right
Richard Cushee
**A New Terrestrial Globe Drawn
from the Best Authorities by Rd. Cushee
Containing the Latest Discoveries**
(London: Richard Cushee and Tho. Wright, 1731)
coloured globe mounted on wooden stand;
38.0 cm diam.
Maps Collection
nla.map-glob6

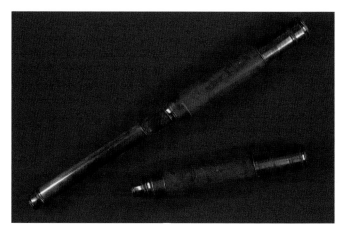

42

Richard Cushee's new terrestrial globe of the world, 1731

Globes are usually spherical models of the earth or heavens. The history of globes reaches back at least to Greek antiquity, and globes made of stone, metal or wood were described as early as 360 BC by Eudoxus of Cnidus (408–355 BC). Globes come in many sizes, sometimes as pairs (celestial and terrestrial), and they have been produced by a variety of methods and technologies. The first known English example dates from 1590: a silver and gilt globe highly prized by the wealthy, measuring 62 millimetres in diameter and handcrafted by Charles Whitwell of London, based on the 1541 and 1551 Mercator globes.

From 1710, however, 70-millimetre hand-coloured pocket globes made from papier-mâché, wood, varnish and sharkskin became more readily available through the London engraving shops of Charles Price (senior) and, a few years later, Herman Moll.

Following his apprenticeship in 1710 to Price as a map engraver and land surveyor, Richard Cushee (1696–1732) established a map-publishing and globe-making business in his own right in John Cogg's shop in Chancery Lane, London. As exponents of globe-making, the Cushee family specialised in the production of pocket globes, which were fashionable in eighteenth-century Europe. Both Price and Moll directly influenced Cushee's design of at least three variations of pocket globes.

Of more significant interest and rarity, however, is the much larger 38-centimetre globe, possibly made in 1731 for a special client, which is mounted on a wheeled mahogany stand for table display. It was acquired by the National Library of Australia in January 2005. As shown on its surface, plotted information was 'Drawn from the Best Authorities by Rd. Cushee Containing the LATEST Discoveries'.

Cushee's table globe of 1731 displays an impressive amount of maritime detail, much of it microscopic. North of 'Great Tartary or Siberia' the coastline of an Ice Sea is shown with an enormous entrance adjacent to 'Kamtschatka'. A multitude of new North American features include an enclosed Baffin's Bay, with Labrador named as 'New Britain', and a 'New South Wales' marked on the western shore of Hudson's Bay. The 'Falls of Niagara' are shown, along with such European colonies as Canada, New France, Acadia, New Scotland, New England, Newfoundland, New Jersey, New York, 'Pen. Sylvania' (and the town of Philadelphia), Maryland, Carolina, Louisiana and Florida.

All longitude was determined from London, and was to be used for plotting 'Adm Anſon's Tract', as well as Falkland Island and Falkland Sound, which were of longstanding interest to the British navy. Cushee followed Nolin's predecessors to

locate a bloated 'Salomon I.' (with the placenames St Christopher, St James and Guadalcanal) near present-day Tahiti.

Between 150°W and 160°W, Cushee positioned the 'Taberones I.', 'Ely I.', 'Waterland I'., 'Sonderyround' and 'St. Peters I.' Further west, he showed Tasman's discoveries of 'Cocos I.', 'Good Hope I.', 'Schouten I.', 'Rotterdam I.' and 'I. Imſedam' (Amsterdam Island). 'New Zeeland' is correctly positioned between 35°S and 45°S, with such landmarks as '3 Kings I.', Cape Van Diemen, 'Tasman's Road', 'Sand hills' and 'Rock Point'. Cushee did not suggest the existence of Antarctica.

It is of particular interest that Cushee borrowed from Dutch and French maps by Frederick de Wit, Jan Luyts, Nicholas de Fer, Aklexis-Hubert Jaillot and Cornelis Danckert for his conjectured eastern coastline of New Holland, only vaguely similar to that on the

Nolin and Mortier world maps of 1700.

More detail suggesting an eastward bulge in the vicinity of latitudes 17°S to 20°S is based on revived Dutch–French interest in a Spanish maritime discovery made in 1606 by Pedro Fernández de Quiros, who named his sighting 'La Austrialia del Espíritu Santo' in honour of the Habsburg house of Austria. His *Memoriael*—which claimed this discovery as a new continent with rich resources, such as gold, silver, pearls, spices and a great variety of crops, where Spanish colonists might find golden opportunities—was translated and published in Amsterdam in 1612 by Hessel Gerritz, who later became the chief cartographer of the Dutch East India Company.

Without access to a map scale, French (and Cushee's) rendition of Quiros' 'Land of the Holy Ghost' became enlarged, and drifted close to Cape York and New Guinea. Cushee's globe named this featured portion of eastern New Holland as 'Terra Australes de Spirito Sancto'.

Cushee reduced the overblown size of Van Diemen's Land to the scale plotted by Tasman and, by sketching three European sailing vessels in the south-west Pacific, he suggested more active shipping than was the case.

left and right
John Bowles (1701–1779)
A Map of the World or Terrestrial Globe in Two Planispheres
(London: Black Horse, 1740)
coloured map mounted on linen;
97.9 x 118.8 cm
Maps Collection
nla.map-rm3874

Thomas Bowles' world map, 1740

For much of the eighteenth century the talented Bowles family dominated the London print market. From the late 1600s, Thomas Bowles the elder produced beautiful hand-coloured etchings of city scenes, including a 1666 plan of London after the Great Fire.

His sons, Thomas (1697–1767) and John (1701–1779), each set up a sales outlet that revealed unusually high standards of engraving and map-printing. Their opus was the joint output of Herman Moll's shire and county surveys (1724–1739), Moll's *Atlas Minor* of European maps, art prints, portraits, scenes of naval battles and a rapidly developing market for prints of London's tourist attractions.

Together they printed a 1724 Gentlemen's Pocket Companion edition of Ogilby's *Britannia Depicta* (1675) as a strip map guide to roads of England and Wales. From his shop at 69 St Paul's Churchyard, Thomas the younger re-issued the guide in about 1732

as *Thomas Bowles' Traveller's Companion*. Thomas and John jointly published a 1737 map of the New England colonies.

The 1740 Bowles world map, acquired by the National Library in 2005, can be attributed to Thomas and John, who seem to have borrowed from the Nolin map of 1700 (see page 40) or, possibly, from Mortier's London copy of the same year, with an enlargement of Van Diemen's Land and with Carpentaria shown south of the Tropic.

Like the Cushee globe of 1731 (see page 43), the Bowles map recognised California as a peninsula, with the written comment 'California was always thought an Iſland till a Spanish Jesuit in 1701 discover'd it was joined to the Continent of which the Royal Society received information in 1708'.

The Royal Society clearly served as the authority for a wealth of information panels, including

identification of the earth's shape as an oblate spheroid, a diagram to show the two motions of rotation and revolution, details of sightings and predicted sightings of two comets, the plotting of a 'point as Opoſite or Antipodes to London', and reference to monsoon vagaries west of New Holland.

The Bowles map depicts a South Atlantic 'Icy Sea' and its seals: 'In this Sea are many Animals partly reſembling a Fiſh partly a Fowl having a Neck like a Swan which they often thrust above Water the reſt being always under'. From classical sources, the map suggests Africa had been rounded before the Portuguese:

> Herodotus the Hiſtorian relates that Necus King of Egypt (2200 Years since) furniſh'd certain Phoenicians with Ships. Theſe setting sail from the Red Sea and Coaſting along Africa doubled the Cape of Good Hope and after 2 years spent in the Voyage entered the Streights of Gibraltar in the 3d. Herod.: Lib 4th.y

Demonstrating contemporary research, the authors updated placenames used by Cushee, including names of the additional North American colonies of Saguenay, New Denmark and Georgia.

Drake's routes and portions of the routes followed by Dampier are shown, with the naming of an 'I. Discover'd by Sir F. Drake', St Peter's Island (found by Dampier) and Island of Dogs (named by de la Maire, and now Pukapuka). As part of the highlighted importance of Pacific voyages, recognition is given to the 'Marquis of Mendoce's Iſles' and 'Land discover'd by Mendan(a)' (the Solomons). Tasman's survey

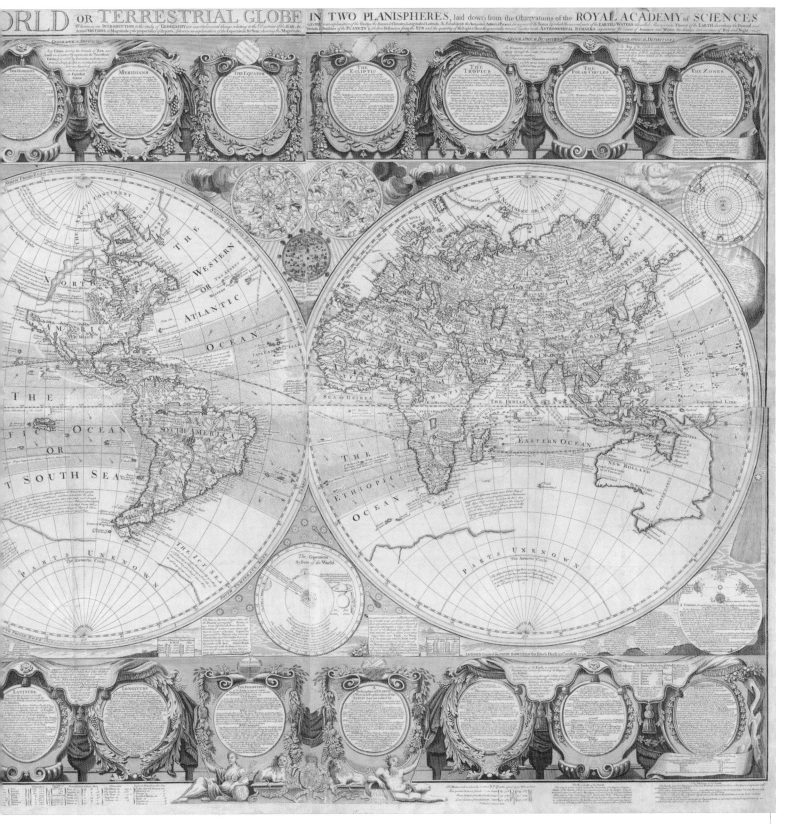

of New Zealand is shown close to a hypothetical but incomplete Antarctic Coast labelled 'Parts Unknown'—it would be easy for map-readers to assume the connection of the two.

Speculation about a New Holland east coast with a waist seems to have been influenced by Mortier's 1700 world map, particularly because of similar placement of the name 'Carpentaria' south of the Tropic, but there is no inclusion of Quiros' 'Espiritu Santo'. Instead,

the hypothetical coast is drawn out further eastwards from New Guinea, which is separated from an enlarged New Britain. Like many French cartographers, Bowles exaggerated the size of Van Diemen's Land ('New Land of Diemen's') but added features

such as the Island of Vanderlin, Schouten Islands, 'I. Frederick Henry', South Island and White Island. The cartographers do not appear to have referred specifically to the 1731 Cushee globe, but may have depended on Royal Society information.

right
Didier Robert de Vaugondy
(1688–1766)
Carte Réduite de l'Australasie, pour Servir à la Lecture de l'Histoire des Terres Australes 1756
map; 21.9 x 27.1 cm
Maps Collection
nla.map-t1002

Didier Robert de Vaugondy's chart of Australasia, 1756

A chart taken by James Cook on the *Endeavour* during his search for the east coast of New Holland reveals that much contemporary French cartographic knowledge of the day was an attempt to correct the fictional east coast suggested by the Nolin and Mortier world maps of 1700 (see pages 40-41). British dominance of the seas, however, limited French exploration of the Pacific until the 1760s.

In 1730, the Vaugondy family inherited the prestigious business of the Nicolas Sanson family, the most prolific Parisian mapmaking firm of the seventeenth century. Through the work of Gilles Robert de Vaugondy (1688–1766) and his son Didier (1723–1786), the Vaugondy family maintained a prodigious output throughout the Enlightenment.

The elder Vaugondy, a mathematician, also inherited the title of *premier géographe du roi*, which attracted an annual emolument of 1000 *livres* for life and ensured the comforts of Bourbon court luxury, as well as close communication with the source of the latest astronomical and navigational information, the *philosophes* (intellectual leaders) of the Académie Royale des Sciences.

The detail given to the fine engraving on copperplate and the carefully compiled geographical information illustrate the Vaugondy principle that maps, atlases, globes and texts should always be *bel et utile* (beautiful and useful). Vaugondy maps were sold throughout Europe until well into the nineteenth century and were copied by English and Italian printers.

The *Carte Réduite de l'Australasie* shown here was prepared in 1756 to illustrate a lecture by Charles de Brosses, a distinguished Académie member. De Brosses had earlier commissioned a general map of the Atlantic, Indian and Pacific Oceans from Vaugondy to accompany his extremely influential book, *Histoire des Navigations aux Terres Australes* (1756). The book, compiled from his study of the records of 65 European voyages into the Pacific, concluded that the island discoveries could be classified into three groups: 'Polynesie', identified by its multiplicity of islands; 'Melanesie', where its people were black skinned; and 'Micronesie', for the tiny size of its atolls. De Brosses' long and detailed digest of travel reportage proved extremely useful to James Cook during his 1768–1771 voyage.

The signature of 'Robert de Vaugondy' identifies both 1756 charts as designed by Didier, son of Gilles. Didier accepted the Académie results of expeditions to Peru and Lapland, which led to the scientific conclusion in 1744 that the earth was slightly flattened at the poles.

To support the de Brosses lecture, Didier drew on a chart of the same name published in 1753 by Jacques Bellin, hydrographer to King Louis XV. Clearly influenced by the 1700 Nolin map, Bellin had interpreted an eastern coastline to 'Nouvelle Hollande' with a completely misplaced and enlarged 'Terre du St. Espirit', with its fictitious 'River Jordan' and 'River St Saviour'.

Bellin qualified his fancy by putting the following words on the map: 'I suppose that the land of Diemen can join the land of the Holy Ghost,

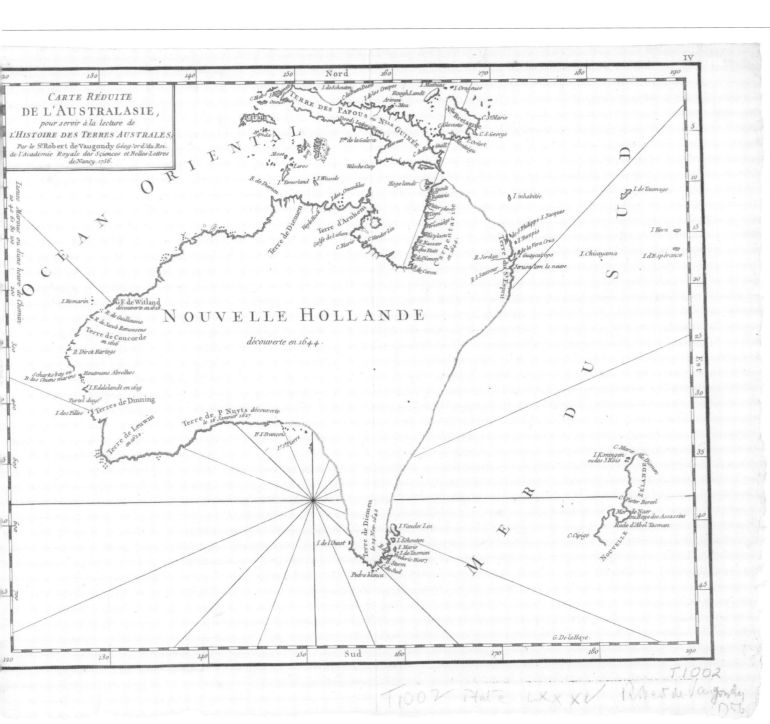

but this is without proof'. On his 1756 coastline, Didier Robert de Vaugondy placed the enlarged 'Terre du St. Espirit' further east, closer to its correct location, and he also featured a mythical city of 'New Jerusalem'.

A gift of the de Brosses' work, along with the Bellin and Vaugondy charts of Australasia, was presented to Baron Louis Antoine de Bougainville by his brother, before Bougainville's Pacific voyage with two privately funded ships. Bougainville located and correctly identified the true position of Quiros' 'Espiritu Santo' and the Solomon Islands, before heading west in 1769 towards his sighting of seas breaking on coral reefs.

Bougainville, although certain that New Holland lay beyond the horizon, was forced, because of shortage of food, to sail northwards around New Guinea and then to Batavia (now Jakarta).

Bougainville's report in 1771 popularised 'Nouvelle-Cythere' (Tahiti) as the true Garden of Eden, where the hospitality of its people continued to lure European shipping. Concerned about limited detail on Pacific charts, Bougainville wrote of 'geography as a science of facts' but containing 'many great errors, which can often only be corrected at the expense of the navigators'.

48

5. European coastal surveys of Australia

British and French hydrographic surveys 1770–1850

Britain's interest in the possible commercial prospects of an unexplored South Sea continent was revived after the conclusion of the Seven Years War with France (1756–1763) in its favour.

British attention turned toward consolidating gains and expanding trade, especially in the Pacific. The nature and extent of New Holland were unfinished business and an important part of Pacific ambitions. Acting under Admiralty orders, Commodore John Byron reached the Falkland Islands in 1764 before sailing through the Strait of Magellan and west to Batavia. Byron's circumnavigation of the globe returned little that was tangible. South of the 'Disappointment Islands' (the Tuamotus, in French Polynesia), however, he became convinced of the existence of *Terra Australis Incognita*. Adverse winds, however, prevented him from confirming his belief.

In 1766 and 1769, two more British ships were sent to investigate. Meanwhile, in France, Louis Antoine de Bougainville assembled a large scientific expedition (1766–1769) to follow in the wake of the British. South of the Tuamotus, both the British and French found Tahiti—the British named it 'King George Island' and

took possession, and Bougainville brought an islander back to Paris.

The next British voyage, commanded by Lieutenant James Cook RN, in HM Bark *Endeavour* (1768–1771), was also a scientific venture. Cook stopped at Tahiti before exploring Tasman's New Zealand, which he mapped for six months before surveying the east coast of New Holland. Cook's journal, edited by Dr John Hawkesworth and published in 1773, became an immediate bestseller. It was reprinted twice in that year and was immediately translated into several languages, including French, German and Italian.

French efforts to emulate Cook's voyages in the Pacific were unproductive, partly because most French expeditions did not yet adhere to the theory that asserted the curative properties of citrus fruits for scurvy. In 1769, Jean François Marie de Surville, of the French India Company, sailed to

the Solomon Islands and New Zealand, arriving within weeks of Cook but having lost more than half his crew to scurvy and desertion. Three years later, Marion du Fresne visited Van Diemen's Land and landed for a time at Marion Bay. He was later killed by Maoris at the Bay of Islands.

In 1772, while searching for 'Australe France', Yves Joseph de Kerguelen–Trémarec took possession of the islands in the southern Indian Ocean at latitude 49°15′S. Convinced this was part of *Terra Australis*, in 1773 Kerguelen led a second colonisation expedition, but was subsequently imprisoned by Louis XV for his gross overestimation of the desolate islands.

From 1785 to 1788, Jean-François Galaup de La Perouse sailed two vessels in an extensive scientific survey of much of the north Pacific. The frigates *Astrolabe* and *Boussole*, with a complement of 114 men, including 10 scientists,

investigated Easter Island and Hawaii, visited Spanish settlements in South America, crossed the Pacific and inspected the Philippines and Japan. La Perouse subsequently recrossed the Pacific to investigate British plans to establish a settlement in New South Wales. Tragically, after exploration of the eastern, southern and western coasts of Australia, the expedition was lost on its return to France. From 1791 to 1794, Chevalier D'Entrecasteaux led an unsuccessful search for La Perouse and mapped parts of Van Diemen's Land, but stopped short of a detailed survey of Bass Strait.

While civil revolution terminated French voyages for a time, the outbreak of the War of American Independence in 1775 curtailed the aspirations of many British merchants and forced them to turn their attention to India and East Asia. The Admiralty, meanwhile,

considered the strategic role of Botany Bay as a Pacific base.

Within three decades of establishing a penal colony in New South Wales, local coastal mapping had added details to Cook's initial survey. The most notable work was the circumnavigation of *Terra Australis* by Lieutenant Matthew Flinders, from 1801 to 1803. The voyage was prompted by the British Admiralty after it learned of preparations under way for a French voyage to New Holland under the command of Nicolas Baudin. The Admiralty sought to forestall any French claims to unexplored parts of the continent by placing Flinders in command of the *Investigator*, with orders to produce a detailed survey of the coast of the entire continent. Flinders' use of the term 'Australia' for the newly charted continent in his publication is widely considered to be the first

time it was used, and it certainly popularised the name.

Clearly, the French intended to stake their claim: from 1800 to 1804, Baudin's ships examined the western coast before venturing to Van Diemen's Land and the D'Entrecasteaux Channel, where coastal mapping resumed. Mapping of the southern coastline proceeded in direct competition with Flinders. While both the Flinders and Baudin expeditions succeeded in producing maps of Australia, subsequent French efforts did not consolidate their early successes.

For the next half century, the British Admiralty supported further detailed hydrographic surveys. The National Library possesses a large collection of British Admiralty charts, from the early work of Flinders and Bass, to the surveys of Phillip Parker King and later Admiralty

officers who paved the way for Australian coastal shipping. The Library's collection includes many charts from what is considered the 'Detailed Survey' (from 1837 to the 1860s), which corrected much erroneous information. The charts provide a valuable record of the British Admiralty's earliest contributions to the maritime charting and safe passage of Australian waters. One mid-century hydrographic chart, based on a voyage commanded by Captain Owen Stanley in HMS *Rattlesnake* from 1846 to 1850, reveals the vastly improved knowledge of Torres Strait, first sighted by Luis Vaez de Torres in 1606.

Samuel Atkins (fl. 787–1808)
***Endeavour* off the Coast of New Holland c.1794**
watercolour; 38.0 x 50.8 cm
Pictures Collection
nla.pic-an5921609

Portrait of Cook 1800s
oil on canvas; 97.8 x 134.6 cm
Pictures Collection
nla.pic-an2291508

50

James Cook's chart of the east coast of New Holland, 1770

Cook's chart of the east coast of New Holland was not only the culmination of a voyage of knowledge and discovery but also a demonstration of navigational and cartographic excellence. This chart exhibits the new and more accurate method of coastal surveying that accompanied a major expansion in British exploration, commerce and scientific interest.

The history of science as a modern discipline is intertwined closely with the story of the Royal Society, formerly known as the Royal Society of London for Improving Natural Knowledge. Increased government interest in science during the eighteenth century accompanied Britain's position as a leading world power. The Society forged a union between science and government, and promoted numerous scientific enterprises. Expertise in natural science was paramount, in terms of both the prestige and the practical

advantages it could garner for new markets and industries.

In 1766, the Royal Society appointed Lieutenant James Cook RN (1728–1779) to lead a scientific voyage to the 'South Sea' to observe a solar eclipse of Venus from Otaheite (now Tahiti). Cook was also instructed to 'make discovery' of the southern continent, to 'employ yourself diligently in exploring as great an Extent of the Coast as you can', and to observe its natural and human resources.

Cook proved to be an excellent choice. In October 1757, he had been appointed deep-sea pilot and master aboard HMS *Pembroke* and sailed to Canada with a fleet of 19 British ships. Charged with surveying the mouth of the St Lawrence River, he applied plane-table mapping techniques borrowed from army surveyors to produce an unusually accurate chart vital to the British siege of Quebec. The Admiralty upgraded Cook to the position of

hydrographer and gave him the task of charting Newfoundland and much of the coast of Labrador. Cook came to the attention of the Royal Society following his observation of the eclipse of the sun from Newfoundland.

On Cook's recommendation, the Admiralty purchased a shallow-bottomed 600-ton Whitby sailing vessel, called a cat. It was renamed the *Endeavour* and fitted out for a three-year voyage.

After loading a scientific team at Plymouth, the expedition left England on 26 August 1768. The vessel's navigational aids included a theodolite, a plane-table, an astronomical pendulum clock, powerful telescopes, an astronomical quadrant, a sextant, an octant, a 1756 copy of Charles de Brosses' *History of Navigation* (with Vaugondy's chart) and a 1767 copy of Alexander Dalrymple's *An Account of the Discoveries Made in The South Pacifick Ocean, Previous to 1764*

(including a copy of Torres' 1606 chart of the strait captured during the British sacking of Manila). Astronomical tables by Nevil Maskelyne helped Cook improve the determination of longitude.

After three months in Tahiti, Cook sailed the *Endeavour* to

James Cook (1728–1779)
Journal of the *Endeavour*, 1768–1771
Manuscripts Collection
nla.ms-ms1-s223v

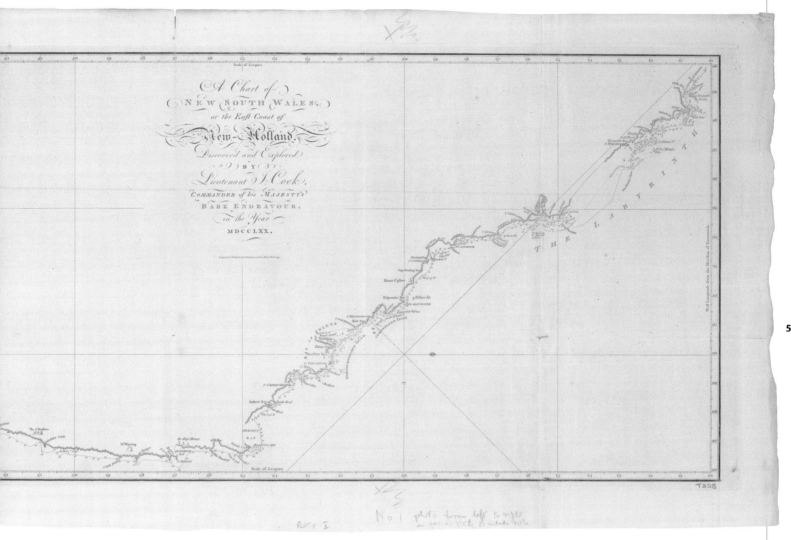

40°S in a vain search for *Terra Australis Incognita*. He then followed secret Admiralty instructions to circumnavigate and chart the main islands of Abel Tasman's New Zealand before heading west to New Holland. Cook intended to complete Tasman's map of Van Diemen's Land but was foiled by gales that drove him north to make landfall at Point Hicks (now Cape Everard) on 19 April 1770.

Cook carried out a running survey, spending the next four months taking bearings and observations, fixing points by triangulation and frequently referencing the ship's position to the shore by compass and theodolite. On Possession Island,

north of Cape York, he proclaimed the east coast of Australia for King George, giving the English Crown exclusive rights to negotiate future settlement sites as a treaty with the Indigenous people:

> … I now once more hoisted English Coulers and in the Name of His Majesty King George the Third took possession of the whole Eastern Coast [of New Holland] from the above Latitude down to this place by the Name of New South Wales …
> (*Cook's Journal*, 22 August 1770)

Many coastal placenames in eastern Australia date from Cook's original survey. Nomenclature on his chart followed several principles—honours to patrons,

recognition of observations by crewmembers (for example Point Hicks), images conveyed by landmarks (Ram Head, Cape Dromedary, Point Upright, the Glasshouses and Cape Bowling Green), significant dates on the church calendar (Cape St George, Pentecost Island and Trinity Bay) and particular events (Magnetic Island, Cape Tribulation, Smoky Cape, Weary Bay, Endeavour River, Shoalwater Bay and Possession Island).

The *Endeavour* returned to England in July 1771 with more than 1000 species of dried plants in its herbaria and seed collections, 500 preserved fish, a similar number of bird skins and mineral samples, countless insect

James Cook (1728–1779)
A Chart of New South Wales, or the East Coast of New Holland 1770
(London: W. Strahan & T. Cadell, 1773)
map; 34.5 x 77.4 cm
Maps Collection
nla.map-t325

specimens, ethnological material and more than 1000 detailed drawings.

Cook's survey of the east coast completed the outline of Australia, defining the continent's northern limits at Torres Strait. As a scientific venture, the voyage far exceeded the expectations of the Royal Society, and it changed forever the perception of the continent as a harsh and unrewarding land.

William Westall (1781–1850)
Wreck of the *Porpoise*,
Flinders Expedition 1802
watercolour; 31.2 x 46.0 cm
Pictures Collection
nla.pic-an4910322

right
Matthew Flinders (1774–1814)
General Chart of Terra Australis
or Australia
(London: G. & W. Nicol, 1814)
map; 63.1 x 91.7 cm
Maps Collection
nla.map-t570

52

Matthew Flinders' chart of *Terra Australis,* 1814

This 1814 chart, a summary of coastal surveys undertaken by Lieutenant Matthew Flinders RN (1774–1814) between 1796 and 1803, is the first published chart to use the name 'Australia' to describe the continent previously known as New Holland and *Terra Australis*. The chart accompanied Flinders' monumental book *A Voyage to Terra Australis*, the record of his circumnavigation of Australia.

Apparently influenced by Daniel Defoe's novel *Robinson Crusoe*, Flinders entered the Royal Navy in 1789 at the age of 15, and two years later served as a midshipman with Captain William Bligh RN on a voyage to Tahiti. After rising to the rank of lieutenant, Flinders first travelled to New South Wales aboard HMS *Reliance* in 1795 with Captain John Hunter RN, who succeeded Captain Arthur Phillip RN as governor of the penal colony.

During the voyage, Flinders formed an important friendship with the ship's surgeon, George Bass

who, like Flinders, was born in Lincolnshire. Bass was also keen to explore the coast of New South Wales, and Hunter offered his encouragement. In October 1795, Bass and Flinders, accompanied by a servant boy, William Martin, headed south from Port Jackson in the *Tom Thumb* on a mission to enter Botany Bay, chart George's River and advise Hunter on the merit of extending settlement. Taking a larger boat, also named *Tom Thumb*, in March 1796, the trio sailed as far as Lake Illawarra, 80 kilometres south.

During 1798, sailing in a whaleboat, Bass explored and named various coastal features as far away as Twofold Bay, Wilson's Promontory and Western Port. Later the same year, in the sloop *Norfolk* supplied by Hunter, Flinders and Bass made soundings and mapped the northern coast of Van Diemen's Land, located a site for future settlement (modern-day Launceston) and proved the existence of a strait (named after

Bass), before retracing Tasman's survey of the west coast and mapping the well-protected Derwent estuary.

Accompanied by his brother Samuel, Flinders then sailed *Norfolk* north to survey Moreton and Hervey bays. Flinders was also accompanied by Bungaree, an Eora man from Port Jackson, who later also assisted Phillip Parker King with his charting of northern Australia. Flinders' reports were published in London in the *Naval Chronicle*, where they were noticed by the influential president of the Royal Society, Sir Joseph Banks, to whom Flinders dedicated his Van Diemen's Land observations.

In 1800, Flinders sailed back to London in the *Reliance*. Aware of the absence of any good quality charts of much of the *Terra Australis*

coastline, he took his case to Banks and Earl Spencer, First Lord of the Admiralty. At the time, the French Republic had applied to Britain for a passport for two ships under the command of Nicolas Baudin to undertake scientific exploration in the South Seas and to carry out a survey of the south coast of New Holland, which France claimed as inheritance from the Dutch.

In January 1801, at the unusually young age of 26, Flinders was given command of HMS *Investigator*. Flinders' instructions were to show the British flag along the south coast of New Holland as priority of discovery to forestall French claims.

Robert Havell (1769–1832)
Panoramic View of King George's Sound, Part of
the Colony of Swan River 1834
Pictures Collection
nla.pic-an7404363-1

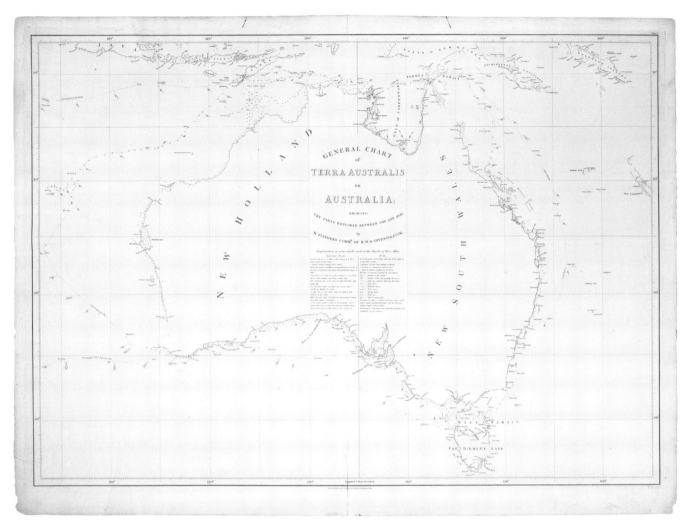

Eastwards from Cape Leeuwin, Flinders and his men charted and drew coastal profiles. Further east, on 8 April 1802, the crews of the *Investigator* and Baudin's *Geographe* met in Encounter Bay. A month later Flinders reached Port Jackson, where he reprovisioned before continuing north to Hervey Bay and Port Curtis, sailing past the Endeavour River and rounding Cape York to survey the Gulf of Carpentaria. By June 1803, the hull of the *Investigator* had deteriorated to such a degree that Flinders was forced to abandon his survey. Flinders did not actually

fully circumnavigate Australia: his *General Chart* included some elements of other cartographers' work, but he intended to return and continue the survey in a new vessel.

While attempting to return to England in 1803, Flinders was shipwrecked in HMS *Porpoise* north of Hervey Bay. Following the rescue of his crew, he sailed for Cape Town but was forced to divert to the French possession of Mauritius, where he was imprisoned until June 1809, as France and England were again at war.

Flinders finally reached England on 24 October 1810 in poor health, only to discover that French geographers from Baudin's voyage had claimed the New Holland south coast as 'Terre Napoleon', with Spencer's Gulf named 'Golfe Bonaparte', St Vincent's Gulf 'Golfe Josephine' and Kangaroo Island 'L'Isle Decre's'.

Aided by his wife Annette (Ann), and *Investigator* botanists Robert Brown and Ferdinand Bauer, Flinders spent his last years preparing his charts for engraving. Publication of the first copies of the record of his surveys, completed

the day before he died, provided evidence of the priority of English discovery of the parts of the continent previously uncharted by Europeans, to which Flinders gave the name 'Australia'. The work of Flinders paralleled the expansion of the British Hydrographic Service. His charts, published as an atlas of 18 map sheets and coastal profiles, began a detailed survey by the Service, confirmed by hydrographers such as Phillip Parker King, John Lort Stokes, and Henry Mangles Denham.

Flinders' legacy endured—many of his detailed navigational charts were used as base maps by the Admiralty well into the 1950s.

William Westall (1781–1850)
Seal Island in King George's [i.e. George] Sound, Western Australia 1802
watercolour; 14.4 x 44.4 cm
Pictures Collection
nla.pic-an6053421

I. Green
Entrance to Hobart Town, V.D.L. 1829
watercolour; 11.3 x 22.4 cm
Pictures Collection
nla.pic-an4828245

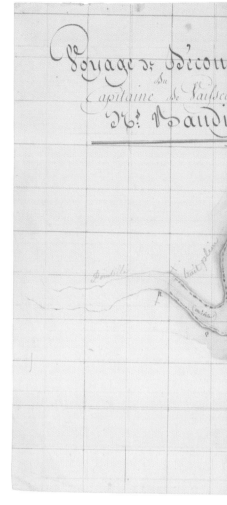

Louis-Henri de Freycinet's chart of the Derwent River, 1802

This chart is one of 13 manuscript maps compiled during the voyages of Baudin and the Freycinet brothers, Louis-Henri and Louis-Claude, in the years 1800–1804 and 1817–1820.

The significance of the scientific voyage of Nicolas Baudin (1754–1803) dates from the 1795 proclamation that allied the Dutch Batavian Republic with revolutionary France and ultimately led to British occupation of the Dutch colony at Cape Town.

Following the appointment of Napoleon Bonaparte as First Consul, French interest in Pacific scientific exploration increased. Baudin, a distinguished explorer, had already achieved outstanding success. Thanks to the large (and live) botanical collections he had collected during three voyages to the Far East and the South Seas, the holdings of the Museum of Natural History in Paris were unrivalled. He was the obvious leader for the new commission

to complete the survey of New Holland and report on British interests and settlements.

Napoleon appointed the largest maritime scientific team ever assembled (22 members), with the expectation that results would overshadow those of Cook's voyages. Among the crew that flocked to join were Louis-Henri de Freycinet (1777–1840) and his brother Louis-Claude (1779–1842). Both men were qualified in hydrographic surveying and cartographic drafting, and were appointed ensigns. No expense was spared in equipping two brand-new vessels, the *Geographe* and the *Naturaliste*, and the Mint struck a medal forecasting future success.

The *Geographe*, with Baudin aboard, and the *Naturaliste* sailed from Le Havre on 19 October 1800, and arrived at Cape Leeuwin, in Western Australia, in May 1801. The two ships became separated, and the *Geographe* sailed north to Rottnest Island and on to Shark

Bay, the North West Cape and Bonaparte Archipelago. After Baudin had reprovisioned in Timor the two ships were reunited.

The *Naturaliste*, under the command of Emmanuel Hamelin, conducted its own surveys of Rottnest Island and the Swan River, and boats under the supervision of Louis-Claude de Freycinet conducted a more detailed survey of Shark Bay. On Dirck Hartog Island (now Dirk Hartog Island) de

Freycinet discovered de Vlamingh's pewter plate (although he wished to take the memento on board, de Freycinet was persuaded to re-erect it on a pole). The expedition placed a second disc on the island as a record of their visit.

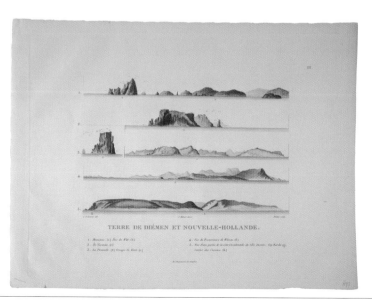

Claude-François Fortier (1775–1835)
Terre de Diemen et Nouvelle-Hollande
(Paris: de l'Imprimerie de Langlois, 1807)
hand-coloured engraving; 24.5 x 31.7 cm
Pictures Collection
nla.pic-an7573626

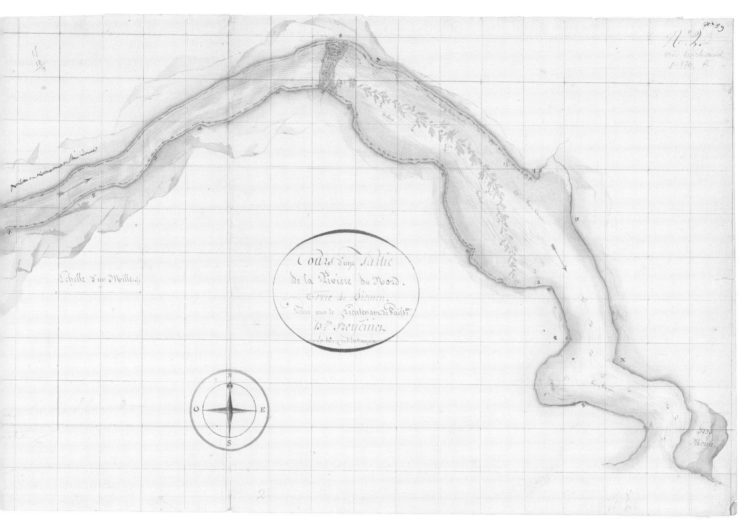

From Timor, the expedition sailed directly to Tasmania, reaching the D'Entrecasteaux Channel in January 1802. Over two productive months it augmented the surveys of Beautemps-Beaupre and Flinders—the chart of the Derwent River included depth soundings and recorded the strands of giant kelp that extended downstream. Such detail is excluded from the much-modified chart published in 1812 by Freycinet to accompany the account of the Baudin expedition, *Voyage de Découvertes aux Terres Australes*. Meanwhile, the expedition's ethnographers collected information from the people of Tasmania's western coastal rainforests—and the contact was reportedly amicable.

The expedition made running surveys of coastal Victoria, duplicating the work of James Grant in the *Lady Nelson* in 1800. After meeting Flinders at Encounter Bay, in Western Australia, Baudin charted South Australian waters before returning to Sydney. The *Naturaliste* returned to France with the expedition's records, while the *Geographe* and the newly purchased schooner *Casuarina*, under Freycinet's command, carried out further surveying of Tasmania, Bass Strait and the south. With British suspicion rising, Baudin set sail for France in March 1804.

The British formally seized Van Diemen's Land in 1803 and established settlements at Risdon Cove, on the Derwent River, in 1803, and at Port Dalrymple, on the Tamar River, in 1804.

Fifteen years later, Louis-Claude de Freycinet, accompanied by his wife, returned to Shark Bay in the *Uranie* as part of a scientific expedition that identified many new species of fauna. On this occasion Vlamingh's pewter disc was transferred to Paris for safekeeping.

Louis-Henri de Freycinet (1777–1840)
Voyage de Découvertes du Capitaine de Vaisseau Mr Baudin 1802
coloured manuscript map; 35.4 x 73.5 cm
Maps Collection
nla.map-rm3671

Antoine-Germain Bevalet (1779–1850)
Voyage de l'Uranie, Oiseaux, Cassican Fluteur, White-backed Magpie 1800s
watercolour and pencil; 26.8 x 18.8 cm
Pictures Collection
nla.pic-an24283548

Sesostris and *Morley* **Piloted through the
Torres Straits by the Little *Britomart*, Captn
Stanley c.1841**
watercolour; 13.3 x 22.9 cm
Pictures Collection
nla.pic-an23501541

56

Owen Stanley's chart of the Torres Strait, 1855

Published by the British Admiralty on 1 June 1855, this hydrographic chart acknowledges the 1848–1849 survey of New Guinea by Captain Owen Stanley RN (1811–1850) in HMS *Rattlesnake*.

The entire western portion of Stanley's chart reveals a maze of banks, shallows and coral reefs, and no possible passage for the 36 nautical miles north of Jervis Island. This explains why Willem Janz in the *Duyfken* in 1606 concluded that a land bridge connected 'Carpentaria' with 'Landt vande Papuos' (New Guinea). Soon after, the Spaniard Luis Vaez de Torres (a captain on the Quiros expedition, 1605–1607) found a way through the strait that now bears his name. During Quiros' landing at 'La Austrialia del Espíritu Santos' (Vanuatu) the crew experienced food poisoning, which led Torres to set course for the Philippines. The passage north around New Guinea proved too dangerous, so Torres' ships groped southward through the maze of

reefs to reach Ternate, in the Spice Islands (now the Maluku Islands). Torres may even have sighted Cape York, but his account remained generally unknown for over 150 years.

On an earlier chart, published in 1595 to show the Pacific routes sailed by Francis Drake from 1577 to 1580 and by Thomas Cavendish from 1586 to 1588, Jodocus Hondius the Elder (1563–1612) had surmised separation of 'Nova Guinea' from *Terra Australis*. Hondius lived in exile in London to escape religious intolerance in the Netherlands. Strong evidence to support Hondius materialised during 1623, when Jans Carstensz, commanding the *Pera* and the *Arnhem*, retraced the route of the *Duyfken*. Before storms drove him from the strait, Carstensz decided that the tides indicated the existence of a passage. (His report concluded that this portion of New Holland offered no commercial prospects.)

Jean Etienne Gonzal may have passed through the strait in the *Ridjer* in 1756, but the fusion of Cape York Peninsula and New Guinea remained the convention on charts until Cook's voyage in 1770.

British knowledge of the Torres Strait dates from 1762, when Alexander Dalrymple found a chart in the Manila archives during the occupation of Spanish Manila. Dalrymple named the strait after Torres from the Quiros expedition. He made copies of Torres' 1606 chart, one of which was used by Cook during the historic voyage of the *Endeavour* from 1768 to 1771.

Cook was determined to find a passage between Australia and New Guinea, and eventually navigated the Torres Strait's numerous shoals, landing on Possession Island on 22 August 1770.

In the years directly following Cook's voyage, few attempts were made to establish new shipping

routes to the north and to ensure the safety of emergent steamship commerce. From 1842–1846, Francis Blackwood and Joseph Jukes in the *Fly* charted a course through the outer Great Barrier Reef, and through Torres Strait.

The subsequent 1846–1850 voyage of HMS *Rattlesnake* captured the public imagination: the ship left Sydney carrying the Edmund Kennedy expedition, which was offloaded at Rockingham Bay in April 1848 with an intended rendezvous at Port Albany on Cape York. However, Kennedy's party was impeded by inadequate knowledge of the high coastal escarpment and tropical rainforest. The expedition ended in disaster when Kennedy was fatally speared.

The Stanley chart, which sold for four shillings through the Admiralty agent J.D. Potter of Tower Hill, London, shows several ship passages but recommends only two—Endeavour Strait (identified from James Cook's

Australia, Torres Strait, Western Channels
Surveyed by Captain O. Stanley …
(London: Hydrographic Office of the Admiralty, 1855)
MAP British Admiralty Special Map Col./81

Ellis Rowan (1848–1922)
Fruit, Northern Queensland c.1891
watercolour; 54.7 x 38.0 cm
Pictures Collection
nla.pic-an6764632

survey of 1770) and the preferred Prince of Wales Channel, of no less than seven fathoms (12.8 metres). Both passages show strong tides, with the Endeavour Strait experiencing ebb and flood flows of two knots, and a difficult narrow westerly approach as shallow as five fathoms.

The chart shows Stanley's meticulous attention to survey detail. Instructed to find country suited to British settlement and a safe anchorage at Cape York, he could only reinforce an earlier choice of a port with fresh water at Albany Island. Tuesday, Wednesday, Thursday and Friday islands, adjacent to Flinders

Passage, mark the survey by Captain Matthew Flinders in HMS *Investigator* in 1802. Hawkesbury Channel and Hawkesbury Island are named after Lord Hawkesbury, President of the Board of Trade. Stanley was careful to note local Indigenous nomenclature (for example 'Moorŏlug' for Prince of Wales Island, 'Naroŏpai' for Horn

Island, 'Badoo' for Musgrave Island and 'Eet Mooa' for Banks Island). Stanley named three shallow east-west channels after his three lieutenants, as well as the strait locations of Yule Point, Dayman Island and Simpson Bay. Kennedy River may have been named by the Admiralty to honour the victim of that fatal expedition.

6. British colonial settlement and port mapping

The importance of colonial seaports

During the early decades of European settlement, Australian ports were a lifeline for the new colonies relying on supplies and news from 'home'. The British colony of New South Wales dates from the arrival of HMS *Supply* at Botany Bay on 18 January 1788, a day ahead of a convoy of 11 ships carrying 1350 people (including 750 convicts), under the command of Captain Arthur Phillip RN.

Phillip was not impressed with James Cook's favourable report on the harbour and, soon after proclaiming the new colony on 26 January, he moved the enterprise to Port Jackson, eventually anchoring at Sydney Cove, 11 kilometres inside Sydney Heads. Phillip described Port Jackson as 'one of the finest harbours in the world, in which a thousand head of the line might ride in perfect security'. Within a few weeks HMS *Supply* was dispatched to found a second settlement on Norfolk Island, a strategic move in light of French interests in the Pacific.

Sydney and Hobart served as Australia's key immigration ports during the early penal era, largely because they both offered natural, well-protected, deep-water harbours. As agricultural and pastoral settlement spread to other Australian colonies, ports were established at other river mouths. De Vlamingh, Baudin and others had recognised the potential of the Swan River, on the western side of the continent, and on 2 May 1829 Captain Charles Howe Fremantle, of the *Challenger*, claimed the whole of Australia not included within the boundaries of New South Wales.

The first Governor of Western Australia, James Stirling, took a leading role in exploring the coastal districts near the Swan and other rivers. Fremantle's role as a port was for a long time distinguished by a rocky bar that blocked the entrance to the estuary. In preference, vessels headed 400 kilometres south to the safe deep-water anchorage of King

George Sound (Albany). During 1892 work began on the creation of a safe, deep and protected harbour at Fremantle, and the first migrant ships tied up at the new Victoria Quay in 1897. From then on, Fremantle replaced Albany on the Australian shipping route.

The founders of the South Australian colony in 1836 confronted an even worse predicament: the colony's first regular landing place was the aptly named Port Misery, a mile up the Port Creek (now the Adelaide River). Boats stuck fast in the mud flats and new arrivals had to wade through the mire to reach the shore. The site of the port was soon moved, and in 1845 the South Australian Government agreed to an Admiralty survey to be carried out under the supervision of Commander John Hutchison RN.

Similar decisions faced those seeking to establish a port in the north. Hutchison was still engaged in his coastal survey of South

Australian waters in 1864 when he was instructed to proceed to the Northern Territory to conduct survey work for a new settlement. Twenty years previously, Captain John Clements Wickham and Captain John Lort Stokes had surveyed the northern Australian coast, naming Port Darwin, among other features. When it was discovered that the initial site chosen, at Escape Cliffs, was subject to seasonal flooding, the settlement was relocated to Port Darwin, and detailed surveys were conducted of the port and Victoria River.

The first overseas immigrant ships to sail directly to Melbourne arrived in 1838. Unlike the small coastal vessels that had established the settlement four years earlier, the ships were too large to navigate the shallow Yarra River. Instead, people and goods were off-loaded into small boats and carried overland from Williamstown or Liardet's Beach (now Port Melbourne), creating costly and

inefficient double-handling of goods. With the discovery of gold in Victoria in the 1850s, thousands of hopeful settlers poured into Melbourne, placing enormous pressure on the already inadequate port facilities. During 1860, an extensive marine survey of the Victorian coast began, including Geelong Harbour and Port Phillip, on the scale of six inches to the mile.

Although Matthew Flinders had charted a large part of Moreton Bay, near Brisbane, and a penal settlement was established there in 1824, it was not until the 1840s that the Admiralty turned its attention to new shipping routes, and the safety of existing ones, along the northern and north-eastern coastlines. Shipping services for migrants intending to reach Moreton Bay and settle on the Darling Downs terminated at Sydney, with smaller coastal vessels given the task of transferring them further north. The frigate HMS *Rattlesnake*, under the command of Captain Owen Stanley, made detailed surveys of the approaches to Moreton Bay and surveyed the Queensland coast. Larger migrant ships began arriving there in the 1850s.

By the mid nineteenth century, hydrographic surveys of Australia's ports had become indispensable tools in the development of the fledgling nation's economy. Knowledge of sea-routes and hazards was recorded in a growing body of Admiralty charts. In 1830, the *Australia Directory*, predecessor to the *Australia Pilot*, was introduced to supplement information on the charts, and from 1833 *Notices to Mariners*, noting recent amendments, were produced.

The hydrographic surveyors who charted harbours and sea-lanes supported an expanding network of Australian settlements, and increasingly large ocean-going vessels. By the 1880s, steamers using the Suez Canal and Cape of Good Hope routes were regularly calling at Albany, and later Fremantle, and Port Adelaide. Over the years, port facilities were greatly improved and migrants found themselves stepping from their ship onto solidly constructed wharves, while the construction of railway and telegraph lines ensured the efficient transfer of cargo, mail and passengers.

Joseph Lycett (c.1775–1828)
Distant View of Hobart Town, Van Dieman's Land, from Blufhead
(London: J. Souter, 1825)
hand-coloured acquatint; 23.0 x 33.0 cm
Pictures Collection
nla.pic-an7691009

DISTANT VIEW OF HOBART TOWN.
Van Diemen's Land, from Blufhead.

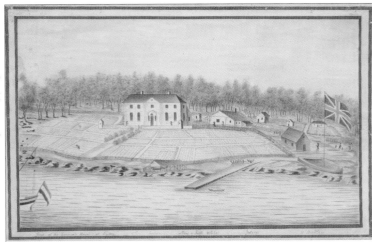

William Bradley (c.1757–1833)
View of the Governor's House at Sydney in Port Jackson New South Wales Jan'y 1791
watercolour; 21.6 x 36.0 cm
Pictures Collection
nla.pic-an3329075-1

right
Francis Fowkes
Sketch & Description of the Settlement at Sydney Cove Port Jackson in the County of Cumberland Taken by a Transported Convict on the 16th of April, 1788, Which Was Not Quite 3 Months after Commodore Phillips's Landing There
(London: R. Cribb, 1789)
coloured map: 19.0 x 31.1 cm
Maps Collection
nla.map-nk276

Francis Fowkes' survey map of Sydney Cove, 1789

Records of the first Middlesex court of the Old Bailey for 13 December 1786 reveal the simple grand larceny indictment of a former midshipman, Francis Fowkes, a five-year veteran of the War of American Independence (1775–1783).

Fowkes was accused of 'feloniously stealing on the 1st day of November, one cloth great coat, value 20s. and one pair of men's boots value 18d. the property of Joseph Inshaw', a customer of the Green Man Tavern, New Street, Covent Garden. Despite Inshaw's 'extreme unwillingness' to prosecute, the Bow Street police had other ideas.

Fowkes was one of thousands of former servicemen who found themselves wandering London looking for work at the end of the war. Like many of his fellow veterans, Fowkes, the son of a Strand businessman, was destitute.

Although employed occasionally as an amanuensis to lawyers

Lord Mountstuart and Sir James Erskine, he had been forced to sell his books and much of his clothing two months before his court appearance. Unfortunately, his captain was at sea and unable to testify on his behalf, but Fowkes presented an articulate written appeal to the court: 'I have therefore to request, that if it lies in your breast, I may be rather permitted to become a VOLUNTARY EXILE than leave my native country as a WRETCHED CONVICT'. His plea was unsuccessful. Fowkes was convicted for seven years and sent to a hulk to await transportation to Botany Bay. The Old Bailey issued 69 such transportation sentences that day.

Fowkes sailed from Portsmouth on the *Alexander* on 13 May 1787, part of the convict cargo on the First Fleet that ultimately established a penal colony on the shores of Sydney Cove. The *London Gazette* of October 1788 reported that 717 convicts, 180 of them

women, under the charge of 181 marines, arrived at Botany Bay under sentence 'by His Majesty's Judges to be sent to that part of New Holland known as New South Wales'. Someone in authority in the new colony appears to have recognised Fowkes' cartographic training and appointed him to the staff of the colony's surveyor, Augustus Alt.

Fowkes' survey map of Sydney Cove—'3 Leagues to the Northward of Botany Bay'— provides a snapshot of the emerging settlement on 16 April 1788. Published by R. Cribb, of 288 High Holborn, London, on 21 July 1789, it is the oldest record of the camp set up by Captain Arthur Phillip RN (1738–1814), the colony's foundation governor, after it was discovered that Botany Bay lacked adequate fresh water.

Fowkes' map, drawn on a scale of 1:55 000, set out the port settlement and the First Fleet at anchor, along with key

elements such as buildings, tents, observatory, hospital, smithy, sawpits, workshops and storehouses. The map also indicated early convict activities to convert the camp into a town, such as shingling parties for splitting wooden roof shingles and a 'Brick Field'.

The hospital tents filled quickly with patients suffering from dysentery and scurvy. Meanwhile, convicts in the new farm and gardens were busily supplying seamen's greens as a cure. To the west of the main stream stood the convicts' tents; on the other side was Governor Phillip's large canvas marquee, his temporary residence while stonemasons built the first Government House. The residence was officially opened on 4 June 1789, just in time to celebrate the birthday of King George III.

Little else is known about Fowkes, other than that he received a land grant from 19 November 1794 to 8 October 1799. It is probably

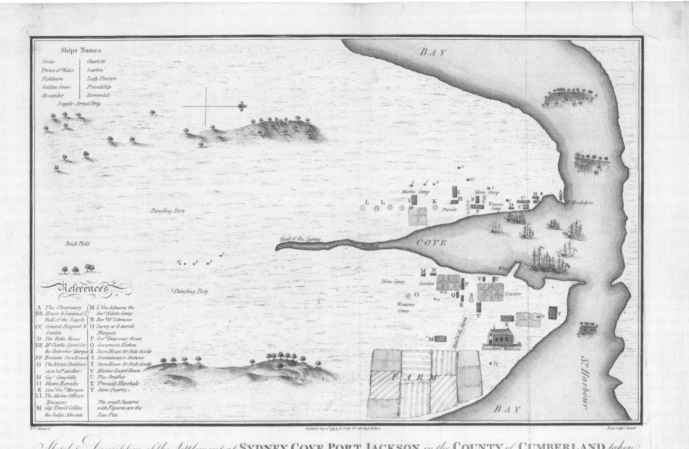

References

A   The Observatory
BB   House & Garden of Ld.
     Ball of the Supply
CC   General Hospital &
     Garden
D   The Bake House
EE   Mr Clarks Agent for
     the Contractor Marquee
FF   Provision Store Houses
G   The Master Builders
     now bel: another!
H   Cap.n Campbells
I   Marine Barracks
K   Lieut Govr. Marquee
LL   The Marine Officers
     Marquees
M   Cap.n David Collins
     the Judge Advocate

M L. Gov Johnsons the
     Gov.r Middle Camp
N   Rev.d Mr Johnsons
O   Survey or Generals
     Marquee
P   Govr Temporary House
Q   Governors Kitchen
R   Store House for Bale Goods
S   Commissary's Marquee
T   Store House for Bale Goods
V   Marine Guard House
U   The Smithey
X   Prevost Marshals
Y   Stone Quarry

     The small Squares
     with Figures are the
     Saw Pits

Sketch & Description of the Settlement at SYDNEY COVE PORT JACKSON in the COUNTY of CUMBERLAND taken
by a transported Convict on the 16.th of April, 1788, which was not quite 3. Months after Commodore Phillips's Landing there
Sydney Cove lies 3 Leagues to the Northward of BOTANY BAY which is situated in Lat.34 S: Long.151 E.

more than coincidence that
the same page of the Colonial
Secretary's register also shows
that a Susannah Fowkes received
a land grant on 8 October 1799.
Following his emancipation, it may
be assumed that Francis Fowkes
began a new life.

Thomas Whitcombe (1763–1824)
**Departure of the Whaler Britannia
from Sydney Cove, 1798**
oil on canvas; 82.0 x 122.5 cm
Pictures Collection
nla.pic-an2253068

George Raper (1769–1797)
**Entrance of Port Jackson When Close
under the South Head 1791**
ink and watercolour on paper; 23.2 x 18.5 cm
Pictures Collection
nla.pic-an21511990-3

George Raper (1769–1797)
Wa-ra-ta c.1789
watercolour; 40.0 x 31.1 cm
Pictures Collection
nla.pic-vn3579250

62

George Raper's chart of Port Jackson, 1791

The National Library's George Raper Collection provides a first-hand account of the voyage of the First Fleet and its arrival at Botany Bay and Port Jackson. Until it was acquired by the National Library in 2000, the collection of nine charts, five coastal profiles and a manuscript of naval observations had been held for two centuries by the descendants of Raper, who had sailed with the HMS *Sirius,* flagship of the First Fleet.

The son of a London insurance businessman, George Raper (1769–1797) joined the Royal Navy at the age of 13 as a 'young gentleman'. He was attached to HMS *Rose* as captain's servant, to be groomed as a possible officer. Promoted to able seaman, Raper was transferred on 22 November 1786 at the age of 17 to HMS *Sirius*, a 540-ton sixth-rate, 20-gun frigate which, under Captain John Hunter RN, was preparing to transport convicts to Botany Bay.

During the voyage, Raper was promoted to midshipman and, under the tuition of Hunter and Lieutenant William Bradley RN, was introduced to the regular naval training program of astronomy, navigation, cartography and topographic drawing. HMS *Sirius* also provided Raper with the latest navigational aid—a chronometer to help determine precise longitude.

Like the other young midshipmen, Raper was obliged to copy the charts prepared during the voyage. Later noted for his paintings of settlement scenes, landscapes, Aboriginal artefacts and native flora and fauna, Raper was one of four untrained but effective military artists by the time the fleet anchored at Botany Bay in January 1788. Items in the Library's Collection provide an insight into the work and life of eighteenth-century midshipmen in the British navy, demonstrating the practical skills required of naval officers.

Obliged to repair substantial damage to the lower decks and hull of HMS *Sirius* following a return voyage to collect supplies from Cape Town, Captain Hunter put the ship in at Careening Cove (now Mosman Bay), Port Jackson, on 17 June 1789, before relocating to Sydney Cove the following November after discovering that the damage was more serious than first thought.

During the period in port, Raper helped make detailed soundings for a hydrographic chart prepared by Hunter. As training for his personal record of observations, he made a copy of this chart in 1791. The chart shows the soundings and landmarks such as 'Roſs Farm' (established by Major Robert Ross, marine commandant of HMS *Sirius* and a Lieutenant-Governor), Farm Cove, Garden Cove, Keltie Cove, Blackburn Cove, Rose Bay, Camp Cove and Green Point on the southern shore (west is at the top of the chart). It also notes the location of important sources

of fresh water in the vicinity of Careening Cove. Raper's title to his copy, unlike the signature on Hunter's original chart, appears to be carved distinctively into a rocky sandstone headland.

Raper sailed with Hunter to Norfolk Island, where the *Sirius* was wrecked on 13 March 1790. Given the date on his Port Jackson chart, Raper probably made his copy after returning to Sydney Cove in February 1791. He arrived back in Portsmouth with his charts and watercolours in April 1792.

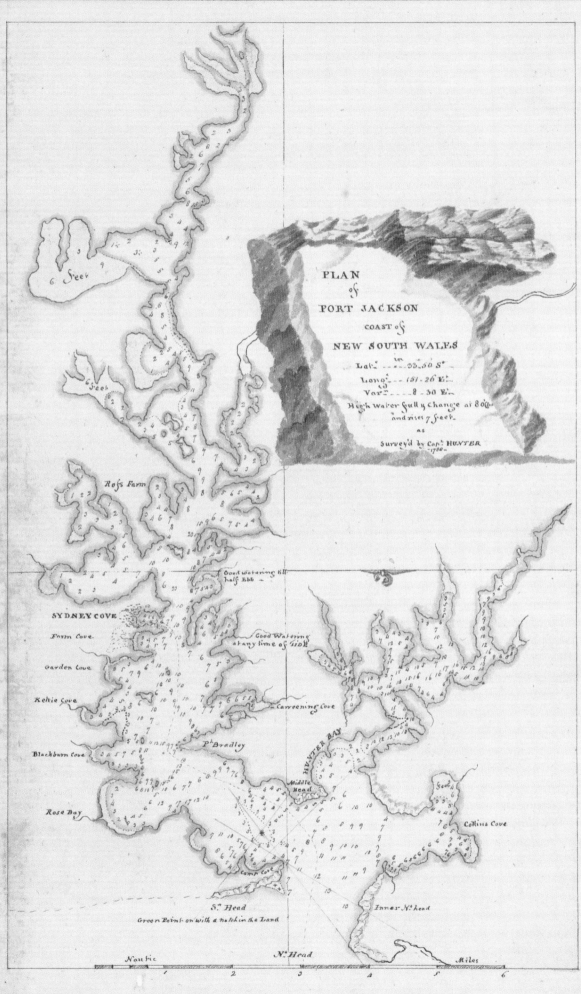

63

Richard Bridges Beechey (1808–1895)
Lt. J. Stokes Speared in the Lungs
While Discovering the Victoria River,
Australia, 1839 1863
oil on canvas; 64.6 x 91.6 cm
Pictures Collection
nla.pic-an2291837

John Lort Stokes' hydrographic chart of approaches to the Swan River, 1841

This rare chart is the work of First Lieutenant John Lort Stokes RN (1812–1885), who served aboard the famous HMS *Beagle* for nearly 18 years.

In 1837, the British Hydrographic Office commissioned Stokes to survey those parts of the northern Australian coastline that had not been mapped closely by Matthew Flinders in 1801–1802 (see page 52).

Stokes served as assistant surveyor on the *Beagle,* a survey barque initially under the command of Commander John Clements Wickham, whose name later became associated with the settlement of Brisbane. Stokes had sailed with the *Beagle* on its two earlier survey voyages, on the first as midshipman (1825–1830) and on the second as mate and assistant surveyor (1831–1836). The latter voyage, with the young naturalist Charles Darwin aboard, visited the Galapagos Islands and the Great Barrier Reef, and

proved to be a groundbreaking oceanographic expedition.

Due to Wickham's ill health, Stokes assumed command of the *Beagle* in 1841. By 1843, when the *Beagle* returned to England, the adventurous Stokes had surveyed the sandy beaches of Port Darwin (named by Wickham after Charles Darwin in 1839), located relics of Dutch contact with Houtman's Abrolhos Islands and a four-pounder gun at Gun Island, discovered traces of bitumen in wells dug for water on the banks of the Victoria River (where Stokes was speared in the lungs by an Aboriginal man—a scene painted by Richard Beechey in 1863), and narrowly escaped drowning and crocodile attacks.

Stokes excited public interest in the Gulf of Carpentaria after finding fresh water on Sweers Island and naming the 'Plains of Promise' (1841), the future goal of the transcontinental expeditions of first Leichhardt

and then Burke and Wills. Stokes circumnavigated Australia twice and was the last surveyor to hold a roving commission similar to that of Flinders and Phillip Parker King. Promoted to captain before he surveyed the New Zealand coastline between 1847 and 1851, Stokes later rose to the ranks of rear admiral (1864), vice-admiral (1871) and admiral (1877), before retiring from the navy in 1878.

Stokes' hydrographic survey of the dangerous approaches to Fremantle includes details of Rottnest Island and refers to intervening shoals as 'all foul ground within the five fathoms line the Sea breaking throughout bad weather'. Despite the warning, these approaches proved to be a graveyard for many ships. The chart shows the narrow Challenger Pass to Scott's Jetty at Fremantle, and identifies Garden Island and the relatively protected Cockburn Sound.

above
Swan River and Rottnest Island 1841
(London: Hydrographic Office of the Admiralty, 1845)
map; 61.2 x 91.5 cm
Maps Collection
nla.map-t34

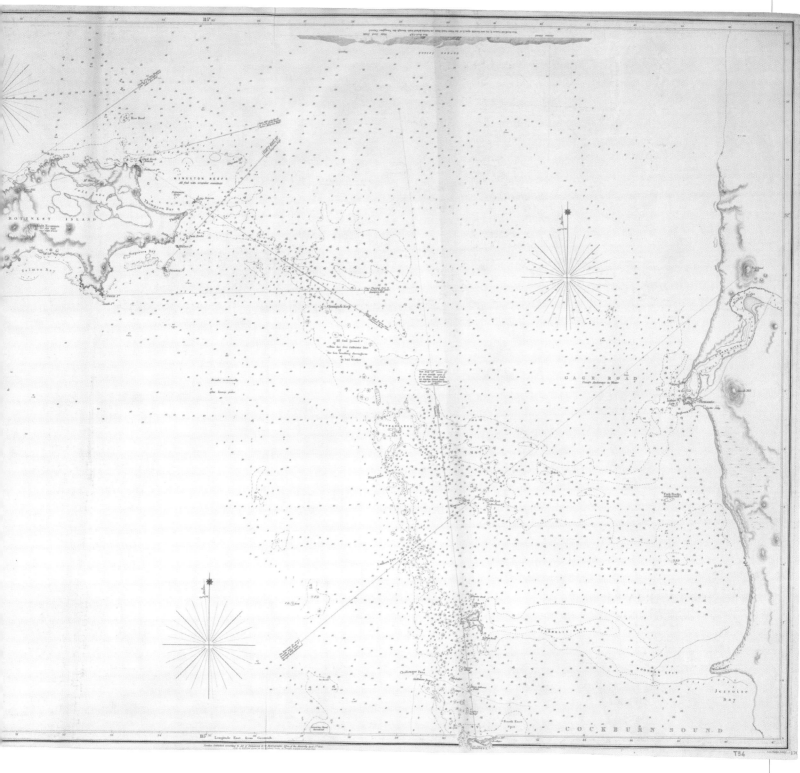

Charles Rodius (1802–1860)
**Convicts Building Road over the Blue
Mountains, NSW, 1833**
watercolour; 17.3 x 28.8 cm
Pictures Collection
nla.pic-an6332110

66

7. Overland exploration and pastoral land acquisition
Surveys to open Australia's interior to European pastoralism

Until the arrival of Lachlan Macquarie, early settlement at Sydney Cove remained port oriented. Governor Macquarie's term of office (1810–1821) coincided with a significant increase in the number of convicts arriving in the colony. To accommodate them, he launched a program of town planning and road construction in the County of Cumberland surrounding Sydney. As well as promoting free settlement, Macquarie offered opportunities to emancipated convicts and extended the practice of issuing tickets-of-leave to more trustworthy convicts.

Aware of the topographic constraints imposed by the Blue Mountains west of the settlement, Macquarie encouraged overland exploration. During 1813 three wealthy landowners—Gregory Blaxland, William Wentworth and William Lawson—achieved the first important goal: the blazing of a trail over the Blue Mountains to find more pastoral land.

Four years later the Surveyor General, John Oxley, explored the Lachlan River country west of Mount Blaxland. Oxley's journal records his general melancholy at the extremely flat monotonous landscape, the many anabranches, stagnant swamps and 'universally bad and small' timber, as well as the drought conditions that tested both the endurance and food supply of his party. As he proceeded with his cumbersome party of horses, carts, beasts and dogs, Oxley wrote of the unlikelihood that 'these desolate plains be ever again visited by civilized man'.

Allan Cunningham, a botanist accompanying Oxley, held a different view. His journal shows a keen observation of variations in the vegetation, friendly contact with 'natives' and daily details of his travels, including identification of his wayside collection of seeds and 450 plant specimens. Both Oxley and Cunningham turned their attention northwards for

several ventures, one of which resulted in Cunningham's reports of the rich soils of the Darling Downs in 1827.

To the south-west, Charles Throsby, James Meehan (Deputy Surveyor General) and Hamilton Hume undertook several explorations to open new farming and pastoral lands at Bong Bong, the Goulburn Plains, Lake Bathurst and Lake George. Between 1824 and 1825, Hume and William Hovell pioneered a route from the region of Lake George to the Australian south coast at Port Phillip. The return journey took just three months.

In 1827, Major Thomas Mitchell succeeded Oxley as Surveyor General of New South Wales. Mitchell led four major expeditions, each of which opened up new pastoral land: the Macquarie Valley (1831–1832); a portion of the upper Darling River (1835); the Lachlan, Murrumbidgee and Darling rivers, including

'Australia Felix' and Portland Bay (1836); and the Warrego and Barcoo rivers north of the Darling (1845). Mitchell also compiled a detailed map of the colony, published in 1834.

In 1829, Captain Charles Sturt travelled down the Murrumbidgee River, the upper reaches of which had been seen by members of the Hume and Hovell expedition five years earlier. During 1828, Sturt and Hume traced the courses of the Macquarie, Bogan and Castlereagh rivers and reached the Darling River. But the ultimate fate of the western-flowing rivers of New South Wales remained a mystery.

In January 1830, Sturt and George Macleay reached the confluence of the Murrumbidgee and a much larger river, which Sturt named for Sir George Murray, Secretary of State for the colonies. On 23 January, the party came to a large stream flowing in from the north. After rowing upriver for several miles Sturt was convinced it was

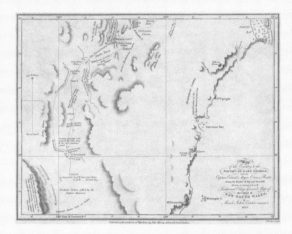

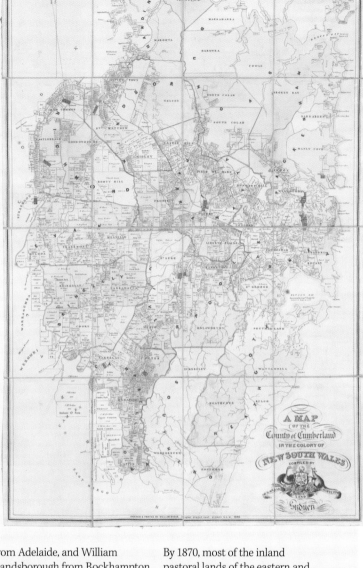

the Darling and returned to the Murray. In general, Sturt and the local Aboriginal people maintained friendly relations: there was a confrontation at the junction of the two rivers but hostilities were averted. The expedition eventually reached the channel where a lake (Lake Alexandrina, in South Australia) entered the sea, but Sturt was disappointed to find it unsuitable for shipping.

During the 1840s, considerable areas of land were mapped, and pastoral leases were extended into new regions. In 1842, a Prussian scientist named Ludwig Leichhardt led three major expeditions. The first, and most successful, began in October 1844 at Jimbour Station on the Darling Downs, and, after a 4800-kilometre overland journey, ended in Port Essington on 17 December 1845. Meanwhile, Thomas Mitchell's fourth expedition explored the river system north-west of the Darling Downs. A subsequent attempt by Leichhardt to cross the

continent from east to west was halted by monsoonal rain, and in March 1848 he set out again from the Downs to reach the Swan River. The disappearance of Leichhardt and his entire party on this expedition, although investigated by many, remains a mystery.

Twelve years later, with great fanfare, the Royal Society of Victoria persuaded the Victorian government to support an expedition to explore the Australian interior and cross the continent from south to north. Although the party led by Robert O'Hara Burke (1821–1861) reached the mangroves at the entrance of the Gulf of Carpentaria, they were too exhausted to continue and, without having gazed on the open sea, they began the long journey home. The loss of Burke and his second-in-command William John Wills (1834–1861) produced much mystery and misinformation, although subsequent search parties led by Alfred William Howitt from Melbourne, John McKinley

from Adelaide, and William Landsborough from Rockhampton, added considerably to recorded knowledge of the interior.

The Burke and Wills tragedy may be contrasted with the persistence and accomplishment of John McDouall Stuart, who achieved a return transcontinental crossing from Adelaide to near Port Darwin after several attempts between 1859 and 1862. Although he had uncovered little of apparent economic value, Stuart traced a sustainable route north, which led to the completion within 10 years of the Overland Telegraph Line, to connect Australia with the rest of the world.

By 1870, most of the inland pastoral lands of the eastern and southern mainland had been taken up. The large atlas maps published by William Owen in 1869 document the extensive pastoral settlements of New South Wales, Queensland, New Zealand, Victoria and South Australia. Soon after, the explorations by John and Alexander Forrest found good pasture lands and mineral resources in the west, and forged a link to the overland telegraph.

68

Allan Cunningham's map of the Darling Downs, 1827

This unique chart is the original record of a cross-country expedition undertaken in 1827 by Allan Cunningham (1791–1839), who discovered and named the rich agricultural pastoral lands of the Darling Downs. Cunningham plotted his course in pencil as an extension to an earlier chart published in 1820 by Lieutenant John Oxley RN, Surveyor General of New South Wales.

At the age of 25, Cunningham arrived at Sydney Cove as king's botanist and the protégé of Sir Joseph Banks to continue the taxonomic work of Robert Brown of the Flinders survey. As clerk to the curator of the Royal Gardens in Kew, Cunningham had spent the previous two years in Brazil assembling an impressive collection of dried specimens, live plants (especially orchids and bulbs) and seeds. Sailing from Rio de Janeiro to Port Jackson, he focused first on collecting native species at Woolloomooloo, before taking up a cottage at Parramatta.

Within months he had joined Oxley's first overland expedition in 1817 to explore the Lachlan River country west of Bathurst, first sighted by Europeans in 1813.

Cunningham's journal revealed a keen observation of variations in the vegetation, contact with 'natives' and daily details of his travels—including identification of his wayside collection of seeds and 450 plant specimens. As he did in his later travels, Cunningham scattered peach stones and seeds

collected in England, Brazil and Cape Town in favourable locations for possible regeneration.

Between December 1817 and April 1822, Cunningham sailed with Captain Philip Parker King RN on five coastal hydrographic surveys. Working from the tiny cutter HMS *Mermaid*, he collected botanical specimens from the south, west and north coasts of Australia from 1817 to 1818, Tasmania (1819), and the Endeavour River, Cape York and the Gulf of Carpentaria (1819), before returning to the Endeavour River in 1820. During Cunningham's fifth voyage, also with King, in HMS *Bathurst*, he spent much time along the north-west and south-west coasts of Australia, collecting botanical material for notes to accompany King's official record (1826) and his own publication (1827).

Cunningham then turned his attention to inland Australia, making botanical excursions in 1822 to the Illawarra rainforest

where settlers were taking up land, and to the Blue Mountains and Bathurst where he opened a route to the Cudgegong River. In April 1823, he left Bathurst on an expedition to the Goulburn River, but it took him three attempts to find a pass through difficult terrain to Oxley's Liverpool Plains. In 1824, he studied the botany of the Murrumbidgee headwaters and 'Monaro' district, before joining Oxley's survey of the suitability of settlement at Moreton Bay. Cunningham visited the Liverpool Plains again in 1825, this time from Parramatta, to prove accessibility to the pastoral district.

In 1827, a drought year, an expedition led by Cunningham left Segenhoe Station in the upper Hunter Valley with provisions for 14 weeks and crossed the Liverpool Plains, before traversing new country northward. Equipped with a chronometer for precise determination of longitude, he plotted his route carefully. Cunningham named the Namoi,

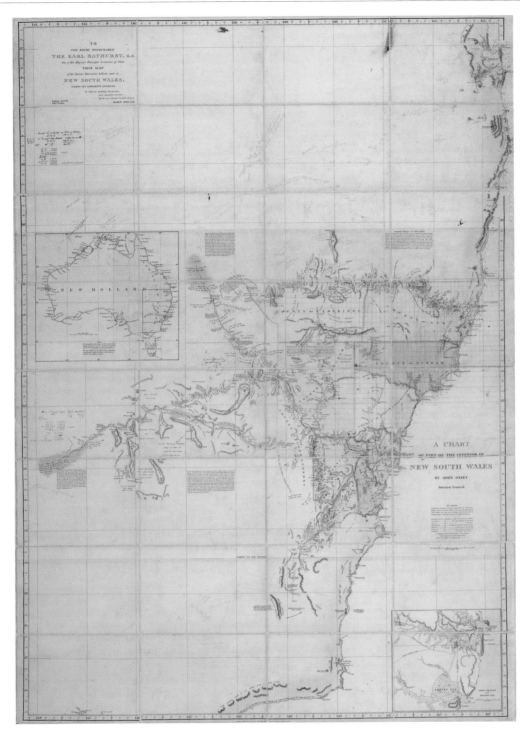

69

69

Ellis Rowan (1848–1922)
Cupania erythrocarpa
F.v. Mueller, *Diploglottis*
cunninghamii **W.J. Hooker,**
Johnstone River 1887
watercolour; 54.5 x 38.0 cm
Pictures Collection
nla.pic-an6723089

Gwydir and Dumaresq rivers before reaching 'open plains or downs of great extent', which he named the Darling Downs in honour of the governor. He also named the Condamine River, where his party found good fishing, but a shortage of provisions ended plans to explore westwards.

Cunningham's return to the Hunter Valley and Sydney with an encouraging report of agricultural

land excited the colony. In the following year, he sailed for Moreton Bay to open a shorter route to the Darling Downs. Although he mapped the Bremer River, the first squatters, led by Patrick Leslie, followed his route from the Hunter Valley and the Liverpool Plains. During much of 1829, Cunningham collected plant specimens in the upper Brisbane River valley.

On Cunningham's last botanical study—a visit to Norfolk Island and neighbouring Phillip Island in 1830—a convict stole his prized chronometer, tent, pistols and provisions. Without any compensation, Cunningham was forced to replace his belongings at his own cost. He returned to Kew in 1831 to sort his plant specimens before briefly visiting Sydney and New Zealand in 1837–1838. His

comprehensive manuscripts are preserved at Kew, along with the descriptions of many new plant species. An almost complete representation of his Australian botanical collections is housed in the Kew Herbarium.

Brendon Kelson (b.1935)
Cooma Cottage, Yass River (Property of Hamilton Hume), Yass District 1996
gelatin silver photograph;
16.5 x 21.6 cm
Pictures Collection
nla.pic-an12002934-37

right
Hamilton Hume (1797–1873)
Mr Hume's Sketch of a Tour Performed by W.H. Hovell and Himself from Lake George to Port Phillip, Bass's Straits 1825
Photo reproduction map; 44.5 x 55.6 cm
nla.map-f3
Royal Historical Society of Victoria

F.A. Sleap
Hume and Hovell Crossing the Murray in 1825 1880s
wood engraving; 18.1 x 14.8 cm
Pictures Collection; nla.pic-an8960228

70

Hamilton Hume's map of Lake George to Port Phillip, 1825

Australia's first colonial-born explorer, Hamilton Hume (1797–1873), was born at Toongabbie (now a suburb of Sydney) just 11 years after the First Fleet landed.

The son of a Parramatta superintendent of convicts, Hume spent his boyhood in the Appin district, south-west of Sydney. From the age of 17, he roamed the country to the south on horseback with his brother John, hunting kangaroos with his dogs and often following Aboriginal trails as he explored new land between Bong Bong and Berrima.

Two neighbours shared Hume's interest in exploration—Charles Throsby of Glenfield Park, near Liverpool, and James Meehan of Macquarie Fields, who was appointed Deputy Surveyor General in 1810. Recognising Hume's bushcraft and affinity with the Aboriginal people, the pair invited the 21-year-old Hume to accompany them on an expedition to the south-west, on orders from the NSW Governor, Lachlan Macquarie.

Hume and Meehan discovered the Goulburn Plains to be suitable for wheat farming and found pastoral land surrounding Lake Bathurst. As a reward, Hume received a land grant near Argyle Town (now Goulburn). In 1821, with the help of assigned convicts, Hume established a squatting run he called 'Collingwood' on the Fish River (now the Lachlan River), north of Lake George and next to a site later surveyed for Gunning village.

In 1824, the new Governor, Sir Thomas Brisbane, instructed Hume to accompany Captain William Hilton Hovell RN (1786–1875) on an expedition to blaze a road from Lake George to Spencer Gulf, in South Australia. Hovell, although an older Englishman with little bushcraft, was a capable navigator. The Government met the cost of a small amount of equipment, but the two explorers had to supply most of their materials.

The party that assembled at Collingwood included six servants, 16 weeks supply of food, two carts, five bullocks, three horses and several kangaroo dogs. They departed on 17 October 1824.

Hume's map of 1825, drafted after he returned, is oriented with south at the top and shows his station in the bottom left-hand corner. Borrowing Aboriginal toponymy, Hume named the 'Yass Plains', which he described as favourable pastoral land, and 'Mt. Buaning' to the west (now Bowning Hill). On 22 October, the explorers crossed the flooded Murrumbidgee River, '40 or 50 yards wide' as noted on the map, and passed through country with 'wombats numerous' and slopes so steep that they were forced to leave their carts behind. By this time they had abandoned their intended destination of Spencer Gulf and had begun marking out a track to

the settlement at Western Port, in southern Victoria.

Everything was loaded onto the bullocks. Keeping west of the snow-covered Australian Alps, they crossed the Medway River (possibly the Goodradigbee) and

Portrait of Hamilton Hume c.1860
b&w transparency; 11.9 x 9.5 cm
Pictures Collection
nla.pic-vn3060070

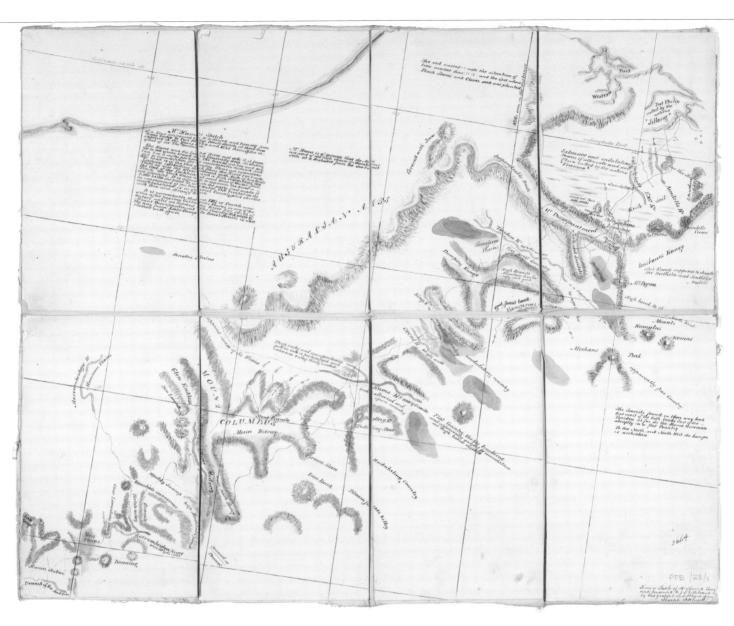

on 16 November reached the Hume River (now the Murray), where they carved their names on a tree near present-day Albury. The men made a boat from poles and a tarpaulin to ferry supplies across the river, and they led each animal across by rope. Hume wrote a favourable notation on his map:

> The Hume was the largest River met with, is from 80 to 100 yards broad and generally deep, its waters run 2 or 3 miles per hour. The Banks are low and subject to inundation for a considerable distance and the land is the best quality. There are numerous Lagoons extending back from the River 1 or 2 miles. There is also the River abound with Fish of two kinds the Cod of the Lachlan and a Fish resembling the Tench

the black Swan and most Kind of Waterfowl are plentiful. It is difficult to approach the River a little below the point at which the party first made it in consequence of the Back Water. The timber in its neighbourhood is in general Cacalyphis skirted with Box and Stringy Bark.

Hume and Hovell named rivers they crossed after Captain John Ovens, Hovell (now the Goulburn River) and Twisden. Forced to backtrack from 'impenetrable brush' during their first attempt to zigzag up the 'Brisbane Range' at 'Mt. Dissapointment', they found a track near Mount Macedon and crossed the Exe River (now the Werribee River). Hume and Hovell traversed a 'Plain called by the

natives "Tramoo"' to reach Corio Bay, Port Phillip, in the mistaken belief they were at Western Port to the east. Damage to the survey instruments during the journey had upset the men's longitudinal calculations.

The party arrived back at Collingwood on 18 January 1825, three months after it had left and without any loss of life. The return route is marked on the map.

Hume's map appeared in 1825 after drafting by Meehan or one of his staff. The expedition report encouraged pastoralists to move west immediately to the Yass Plains and the Murrumbidgee valley.

Four years later, Hume joined Captain Charles Sturt's party to explore by boat the Darling and Murrumbidgee rivers as a possible route to Spencer Gulf. The health of both men suffered from the hardships of food shortage and rowing upriver against the flood. Hume lost his hearing and Sturt much of his sight. Afterwards, Hume retired to a grazing property, 'Cooma', near Yass, and Hovell retired to Goulburn.

William Romaine Govett (1807–1848)
Major Mitchell Sketching the Entrance of the Caves in Wellington Valley, New South Wales 1843
pen drawing; 23.0 x 29.0 cm
Pictures Collection
nla.pic-an4700786

Thomas Mitchell's map of the Nineteen Counties, 1834

Outspoken, exacting and persistent, Major Thomas Livingstone Mitchell (1792–1855) had already distinguished himself as a surveyor and cartographer before immigrating to Australia in June 1827.

Born in Stirlingshire, Scotland, Mitchell entered the East Troop of Yeomanry Cavalry in 1809 following his withdrawal from university, and in 1811, aged 19, he volunteered for the British forces in the Peninsular War. He served for three years as a military surveyor, making topographic surveys in the Pyrenees, and was selected by Sir George Murray, the Quartermaster General, to produce plans of the Peninsular battlefields (a task he continued after the war).

Towards the end of 1826, Mitchell wrote to the Colonial Office regarding surveying positions in New South Wales. With Murray's support, he became Assistant Surveyor General, on the understanding that he would

succeed John Oxley, who had become unpopular with the governor, Sir Ralph Darling. In June 1827, Major Mitchell and his family set sail for Australia.

On appointment, Mitchell submitted a proposal to survey the colony and divide it into counties, hundreds (administrative divisions) and parishes, with reserves and tracts for clergy and schools (as part of this division parishes were to be separated by natural boundaries). The area to be mapped came to be known as the Nineteen Counties and defined the limits of settlement by which Crown land could be either purchased or granted.

Mitchell's task was made all the more daunting by the parlous state of the New South Wales Survey Department—poor techniques and lack of funds, as well as disputes arising about boundaries. Nonetheless, Mitchell planned a survey of such detail that it would allow a map to be

produced at a scale of about 8.5 inches to the mile, or 1:535 000. He provided written instructions with sketch maps detailing the survey requirements, and he was supported by 21 staff, mainly surveyors and draftsmen. In all, about 900 feature survey plans were prepared for the map base.

Working 'chiefly on Sundays when I ought to have been at Church with my family', Mitchell reduced the information to the proposed scale, determined the nomenclature and provided the map portion to his engraver, John Carmichael, who had previously been apprenticed to the distinguished British hydrographer and mapmaker, John Horsburgh, of Edinburgh.

Mitchell instructed his surveyors to record Aboriginal placenames wherever possible, and the map features such examples as Tuggerah, Gullongalong and the Minnamurra River. Some names, for example Madura, are transposed from the Peninsular War. Topography is indicated by hachuring and surveyed roads are marked. Three sheets of ship's copper were used to prepare the engraved map for printing.

On 25 March 1834, the map was completed and submitted to the Colonial Secretary in London for permission to publish. Approval arrived in Sydney on 14 July 1835, and a week later the first printed copy was available for the sum of £1. Mitchell originally planned

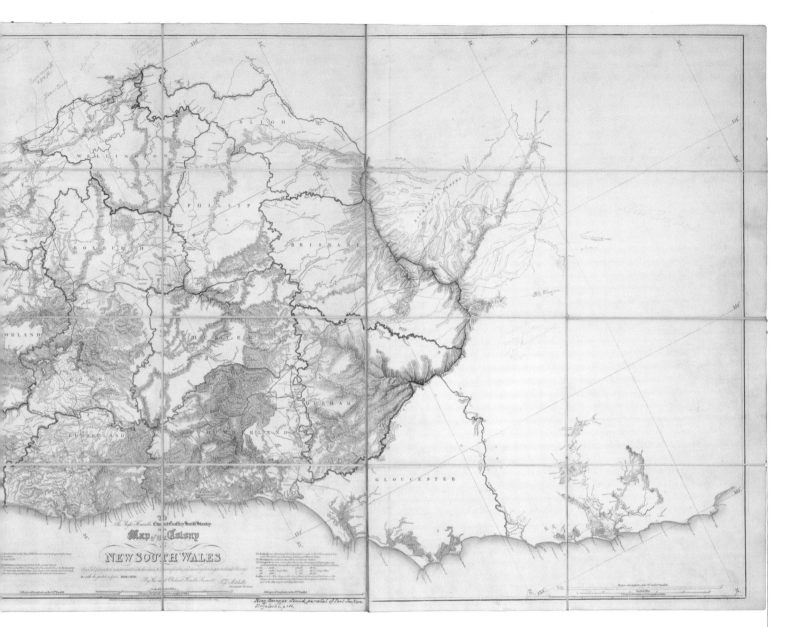

to produce 200 copies. From the condition of the plates, however, it appears that about 1000 copies were printed. In 1852, Mitchell offered the copper plates and 300 copies of the map to the Colonial Government for £300.

Major Mitchell's four principal expeditions of unsurveyed parts of inland eastern Australia opened new pastoral lands, with maps prepared by measuring a mile (1.6 kilometres) as 950 paces of a horse.

Mitchell returned to England in 1839 to be knighted for his services to surveying in both Europe and Australia. He served in New South Wales as Surveyor General from 1828 until his death in 1855.

Thomas Mitchell (1792–1855)
Part of New South Wales from the Summit of Jellore
(London: T. & W. Boone, c.1839)
hand coloured lithograph;
16.7 x 35.2 cm
Pictures Collection
nla.pic-an9941601

Thomas Mitchell (1792–1855)
To the Right Honorable Edward Geoffrey Smith Stanley This Map of the Colony of New South Wales 1834
coloured map; 59.8 x 129.4 cm
Maps Collection
nla.map-nk6228

R.B. Bate
Surveying Instruments Used by Sir Thomas Mitchell During his Three Expeditions 1831–1846 c.1830
brass and cedar instrument set in box; 55.0 x 55.0 cm
Pictures Collection
nla.pic-an6393476-1

J. Macfarlane (fl.1890–1898)
John McDouall Stuart Planting the Union Jack on Central Mount Stuart, 1860
(Melbourne: Geo. Robertson & Co., 1890s)
photoengraving; 52.5 x 69.0 cm
Pictures Collection
nla.pic-an9025855-5

George French Angas (1822–1886)
Chambers' Pillar c.1860
drawing; 10.0 x 16.0 cm
Pictures Collection
nla.pic-an2854523

74

John McDouall Stuart's central Australia expeditions, 1858–1862

British imperial expansion during the early part of the nineteenth century, along with continuing conflicts in Russia and India, resulted in increased interest in opening an overland route from Adelaide to the north coast of Australia. Realisation of the task relied on the courage and tenacity of one man, explorer John McDouall Stuart (1815–1866).

Born in Fifeshire, Scotland, the youngest son of nine children, Stuart arrived in Adelaide in January 1839 as a qualified civil engineer and surveyor. The two-year-old town consisted of little more than a collection of tents and wooden huts, and surveyors were in high demand. Stuart joined the restructured Survey Department as a draughtsman. Resources were stretched to the limit and life in the survey camp was harsh.

During 1844, the colony's Surveyor General, Captain Charles Sturt, invited Stuart to join his expedition to 'unfold the secrets of the interior'. It was hoped that an inland sea awaited as the end point of New South Wales' western rivers. Sturt surveyed a portion of the Darling River before turning to the Sturt Stony Desert and the impassable Simpson Desert, where both Sturt and Stuart experienced eyesight problems as a result of scurvy. Ten years later, after farming near Port Lincoln, Stuart joined William Finke's 1855 expedition to the Flinders Ranges, opening up land for pastoralists. The nature of the land further north, however, remained a mystery.

Finke financed the first of Stuart's six expeditions. In May 1858, accompanied by a European man and an Aboriginal boy, and equipped with only a prismatic compass, Stuart headed from Oratunga Station to the north-western tip of Lake Torrens in search of a strange land known to Aboriginal people as *Wingillpin*. By following Aboriginal trails to waterholes, Stuart found a direct route from the Flinders Ranges to central Australia, discovering Chambers (Stuart) Creek before the party, half starved, diverted south-west to Streaky Bay. Stuart discovered 100 000 square kilometres of potential sheep-grazing country for his sponsor, James Chambers, and was awarded the Royal Geographical Society's gold medal and a gold watch for his efforts.

In April 1859, Stuart left Adelaide on his second expedition to survey Chambers Creek where, as its discoverer, he had applied for land. He discovered more pastures and water supplies and, following a line of springs erupting from the Great Artesian Basin, pushed on a further 250 kilometres. Returning to Adelaide in July, Stuart encouraged the South Australian Government to offer a reward of £2000 to the first person to cross Australia.

Stuart's reports encouraged the Government Astronomer and Superintendent of Telegraphs, Charles Todd. Rivalry among the Australian colonies to become the first to find a transcontinental route was prompted by a pressing need to link the colonies to the international telegraph and by the economic advantages supposed to eventuate from such a route.

Stuart's third expedition began on 22 August 1859, when he left Adelaide for Chambers Creek to resurvey his claim and those of his sponsors. He established the northern limits and seasonal nature of Lake Eyre and, pushing north, found a pass through the MacDonnell Ranges, where his way was blocked by dense sand.

On his fourth expedition, following the next summer, Stuart left Chambers Creek to reach the centre of Australia, where he raised the Union Jack. Stuart continued north and named Tennant Creek on 6 June 1860. His most northerly point was Attack Creek, where a skirmish with Warramunga men forced his return.

above
George French Angas (1822–1886)
**Natives Frightened near Mount Kingston
[between 1859 and 1864] (detail)**
transfer lithograph; 12.4 x 18.9 cm
Pictures Collection
nla.pic-an22891586

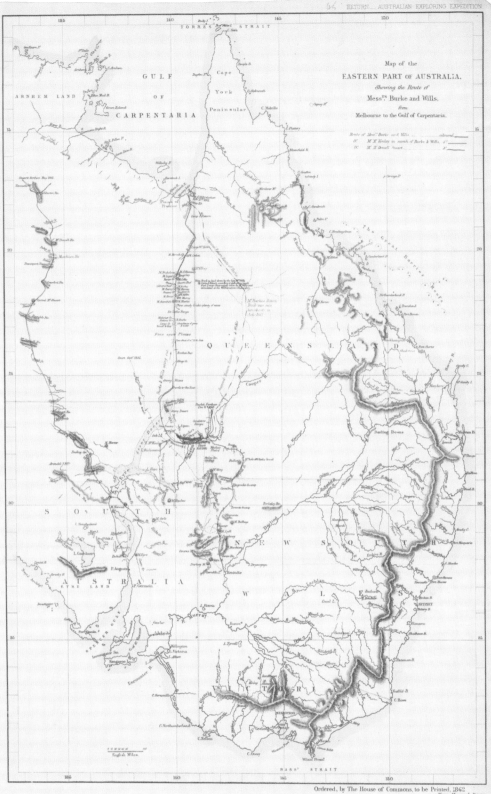

right
**Map of the Eastern Part of Australia Showing
the Route of Messrs. Burke and Wills from
Melbourne to the Gulf of Carpentaria**
(London: Henry Hansard, 1862)
coloured map; 48.5 x 30.9 cm
Maps Collection
nla.map-rm2840

75

Nevertheless, Stuart returned to Adelaide a hero, with the 'veil over the centre of Australia' removed; the feat at the time was equated with the discovery of the source of the Nile. Stuart was awarded the Patron's Medal from the Royal Geographical Society.

Rivalry with the Burke and Wills expedition, which imported camels from India and left Melbourne on 6 August 1860, ensured Stuart enough funds for a fifth expedition to try to reach the north or north-west coast of the continent. He departed on 20 October 1860. Summer drought conditions and poor horses meant a difficult journey to Attack Creek, but Newcastle Waters, which Stuart discovered on 23 May 1861, offered respite. Several forays east and west from this base failed to locate a secure way forward, and Stuart was forced to return to Adelaide.

Stuart immediately began preparations for his sixth journey and left on 6 November 1861.

This time a scientist, Frederick Waterhouse, joined the party, along with additional packhorses equipped with waterbags. On 23 May 1862, Stuart discovered Daly Waters and, moving north-east, he followed creek lines and watersheds to coastal swamps. The party sighted the sea east of Port Darwin and on 24 July raised the Union Jack. The return journey was slow, and Stuart almost succumbed to scurvy. He reached Adelaide on 17 December and began preparing his diaries for publication.

The Overland Telegraph Line, completed in 1872, followed most of Stuart's line-of-march and stands as the greatest testimonial to his expeditions.

Alexander Denistoun Lang
An Exploring Party Looking for a Sheep Run
(London: Mclean & Co., c.1847)
hand-coloured lithograph; 22.0 x 27.4 cm
Pictures Collection
nla.pic-an6016175

Eirene Mort (1879–1977)
A.A. House, Stroud, 17.9.34 1934
charcoal drawing; 17.6 x 22.5 cm
Pictures Collection
nla.pic-an3732224
Courtesy Timothy Thelander

76

William Owen's atlas maps of the Australian colonies, 1869

William Owen's *Atlas Maps of N. South Wales, Queensland, New Zealand, Victoria and South Australia*, published in Melbourne in 1869, provides the earliest record of the extent of squatting runs across the four mainland colonies of eastern Australia and New Zealand.

The maps, which comprise a set of five large linen-mounted lithographs, show the placenames of many small settlements that vanished without trace during the nineteenth century. The maps provide a treasure trove for historical research. Owen, however, remains an obscure author.

The Owen map of New South Wales—'including the Riverine District with Squatting Runs'— represents the 'settled districts' in colour as counties. By 1868 (the date on this map has been updated from 1864), the counties had doubled in number from the original 19 proclaimed for nine

million hectares within the Limits of Location of 1829.

Initially, official rejection of squatting in 1833 dealt only with trespass on Crown land inside the Limits. Such restriction, however, forced many pastoralists to cross the Limits. Legislation passed in 1836 and 1839 borrowed the British North American colonial practice of squatting (beyond the settled districts) as permissive occupancy for pastoral purposes, and identified 'pastoral districts' to be administered by Crown land commissioners empowered to police annual licences and administer stock censuses.

The *Imperial Waste Lands Act 1846* (Earl Grey's Act) created additional counties, many in a new category of 'intermediate districts'. The Act also identified 15 squatting districts in which squatting runs could be taken up as both legal and illegal assumption of pastoral rights, preferably with access to water.

The *Waste Lands Repeal Act 1855* transferred the administration of land policies from the British Government to the colonies. The Owen map shows the results of a process unsuccessfully challenged by passage of the *Crown Lands Act 1861*, a new measure intended to permit yeomanry farming as free selection 'side by side with pastoral tenants'. Instead, the *Occupation Act 1861* favoured pastoralists who used pre-emptive rights and dummying tactics to preserve pastoral runs.

Although the 1829 Limits of Location were initially considered the frontier of British settlement, during the 1840s squatters followed the Murrumbidgee route taken by the westward expeditions of Major Thomas Mitchell in 1836 and Charles Sturt in 1839 in search of suitable grazing land for sheep flocks. Sturt's track is marked on Owen's map as a significant lure into the Lachlan and Murrumbidgee districts.

Owen used the phrase 'the Riverine District' (now the Riverina) in the map title and highlighted the town of Deniliquin, suggesting that he was influenced by the Reverend Dr John Dunmore Lang who, in 1850, proposed an inland colony. In 1857, Lang encouraged separation of the Riverina as a consequence of a successful NSW legislative claim to use the Murray River as the southern border, instead of the Murrumbidgee River. The Riverina separation movement ultimately failed because of the sparse population. The arrival of telegraph links to Sydney after 1860 led to the establishment of new branches of Sydney banks in the larger towns, consolidating the role of the city as the colonial capital at a time of economic threat from Melbourne.

The map also shows the influence of gold discoveries following the separation of Victoria from the colony of New South Wales in 1851—the first discovery, on the 'Summerhill' pastoral run near Orange, is marked, together with

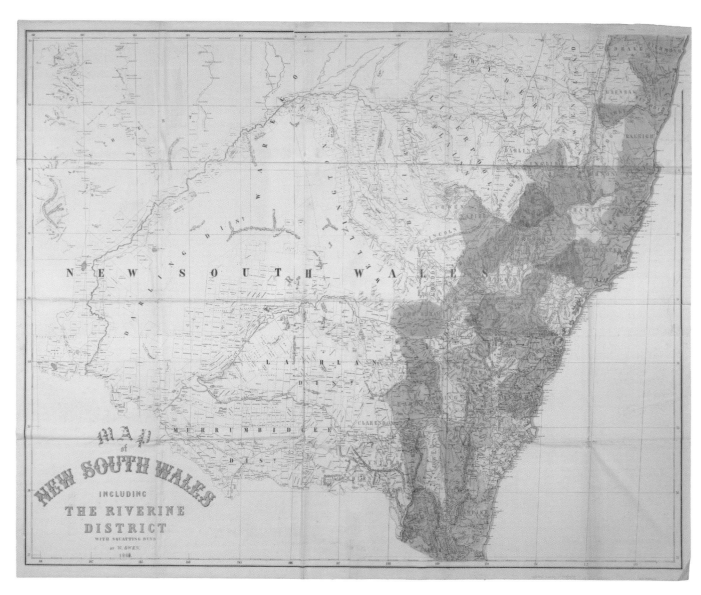

Frederick Town, Ophir, Sofal (now Sofala) and the goldfields of Hargraves, Merinda, Louisa Creek, Tamboroora and Burrendong.

Although Owen shows several roads branching from the western and southern roads, a regular coach service from Sydney did not run until 1857. Gold prospectors, ex-convicts and less privileged immigrants usually walked in search of employment, but during the 1860s Cobb & Co., with coaches imported from America, became the established passenger carrier. Slow bullock teams moved inland freight to and from Sydney,

Newcastle and Melbourne, and an erratic riverboat service from Adelaide reached the river ports of Albury, Gundagai and Wagga Wagga during the wetter years.

The track of the first railway from Sydney is shown by Owen to have reached Picton via Campbelltown by 1868, with a spur from Liverpool to Parramatta. Tracks of early roads are marked, with many radiating from centres such as Goulburn, Armidale and Deniliquin. By 1868, squatting runs had taken up virtually the entire Liverpool Plains and Macquarie valley areas, discovered by Oxley in 1818.

At the same time, new counties suitable for agricultural settlement had replaced many pastoral districts—for example, the map shows the giant Australian Agricultural Company Estate east of Tamworth and accessible from Port Stephens. The only road north of Kempsey heads inland to New England, suggesting that settlement of coastal land was limited to access from small ports.

William Owen
Map of New South Wales Including the Riverine District with Squatting Runs, 1868
(Melbourne: H. Bolton, 1869)
coloured map mounted on linen;
171.0 x 176.8 cm
Maps Collection
nla.map-rm3596-3

Backcountry Squatter, A.D. 1892
(Melbourne: McCarron, Bird & Co., 1892)
lithograph; 48.5 x 30.0 cm
Pictures Collection
nla.pic-an8488440

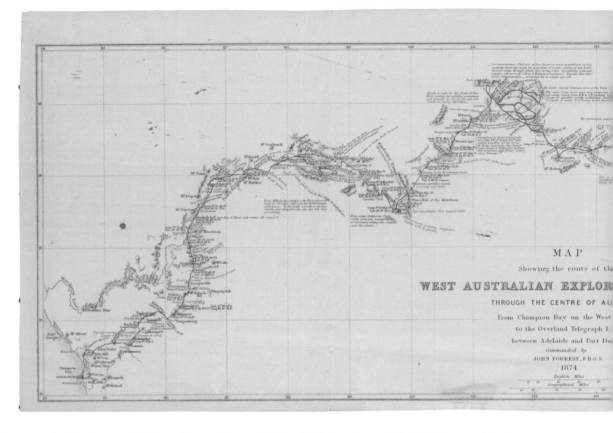

78

John Forrest's West Australian Exploring Expedition, 1874

Australia's first peer, John Forrest (1847–1918), was born at Preston Point near Bunbury, Western Australia, to Scottish immigrant farmers. John attended the government school at Bunbury, before following his eldest brother William to Bishop Hale School, where he excelled in mathematics. In 1863, John Forrest was apprenticed to T.C. Carey, the assistant surveyor at Bunbury, and he was appointed a temporary government surveyor in 1865.

Over the next few years, John Forrest and his younger brother Alexander (1849–1901) worked as surveyors in the south-west, including valuable experience with John Septimus Roe, the noted surveyor and explorer. In 1869, John was offered appointment as second-in-command and navigator to Dr Ferdinand Mueller on an expedition from Perth in search of clues as to the fate of Ludwig Leichhardt. When Mueller could not manage the trip, Forrest was chosen to succeed him and, from

April to August, with Alexander and Aboriginal tracker Tommy Windich, his expedition charted lands around Lake Moore and Lake Barlee, and inland almost as far as the later site of Laverton.

During the expedition, the men discovered mineral prospects and named Lake Barlee, Mount Ida, Mount Leonora, Mount Malcolm and Mount Margaret. The 3600-kilometre venture into the desert encouraged the Governor of Western Australia, Frederick Weld, to finance a second expedition. In 1870, the brothers—again accompanied by Windich—left Perth to find a suitable overland route to Adelaide via their supply links at Esperance and Eucla.

Like John Eyre in 1841, however, they found little country suitable for farming, with the exception of the region near Mount Hampton. From 1871–1872, Alexander Forrest led an expedition east and south of Hampton Plains.

The map held by the National Library relates to the 1874 West Australian Exploring Expedition, led by John and including Alexander and Tommy Windich, to link up with the Overland Telegraph Line, which ran from Port Augusta, in South Australia, to Port Darwin, near present-day Darwin.

The men found good pasture at the headwaters of the Murchison River (now the Meekatharra district). With hindsight, they recognised that camels would have been more useful than horses on the trek across the Gibson Desert—country that had earlier been reported by Warburton, Giles and Gosse as dry and desolate. The map records the sites of 106 camps along the route to The Peake Station (the digital version of the map allows the user to retrace the 4400-kilometre track the team followed). Windich Springs, at Camp 41, are described as 'immense pools of permanent water very deep, 300 y^{ds} long & 20 y^{ds} wide'.

The Weld Springs—'The Oasis in the desert' (Camp 46)—is described as:

> …a most magnificent spring running down the creek for a quarter of a mile, clump of tea trees close to camp, through which the springs runs. Beautifully grassed country all around–Emu & Kangaroo numerous. Pigeons and other birds innumerable.– ATTACKED BY ARMED NATIVES.

But the map shows no permanent water between Weld Springs and Alexander Springs (Camp 62). Beyond Weld Springs it records 'Miserable spinifex country to east'. With details such as 'clay holes' or 'rock water hole, 30 gallons', 'micaceous iron ore' and notations for each death of a horse, it is possible to reconstruct the hazards the party faced as well as the public acclaim it received on reaching Adelaide. A year later, at the age of 28, John Forrest was appointed Deputy Surveyor General.

In 1879, persuaded by Governor Ord to investigate the settlement potential of the Kimberley district, Alexander Forrest led an overland expedition from the De Grey River to the Overland Telegraph Line via the Fitzroy, Margaret and Victoria rivers. He suggested the availability of good pastoral land, but his report did not become public until 1883, when his brother John succeeded Malcolm Fraser as Surveyor General and Commissioner of Lands. John Forrest was elected unopposed in 1890 as the only Premier of Western Australia while it was a self-governed colony. During the decade of gold discoveries, he borrowed funds from London to improve water supply to the main towns, open new ports and extend the railway system.

Alexander Forrest was twice elected Mayor of Perth (1893–1895 and 1898–1900), and both brothers campaigned actively for Australian federation—John entered the Commonwealth Parliament in 1901 to serve as Minister for Defence, Minister for Home Affairs and Treasurer to five governments. 'Big John', as he became known, was the epitome of the self-made man—his papers were read to the Royal Geographical Society and his honours included a knighthood in 1891 and a peerage as Baron Forrest of Bunbury in 1918.

top
George French Angas (1822–1886)
Reaching the Overland Telegraph Line, 1874
c.1874
drawing; 10.8 x 16.7 cm
Pictures Collection
nla.pic-an2854561

above
J. Macfarlane (fl.1890–1898)
John Forrest's Party (His Brother, Alexander, Second in Command) Sight the Overland Telegraph Line, 1874
(Melbourne: Geo. Robertson & Co., 1890s)
photoengraving; 52.5 x 69.0 cm
Pictures Collection
nla.pic-an9025855-6

John Rapkin
Victoria, or, Port Phillip c.1851
(London; New York: John Tallis & Company, c.1851)
coloured map; 21.8 x 29.5 cm
Maps Collection
nla.map-t1235

80

8. Mineral exploration and geological surveys
The importance of mineral discoveries

European settlers acquiring land to graze livestock and for other agricultural pursuits increasingly sought out mineral resources for industry. Dutch expeditions had suggested the presence of minerals in Australia, but it was not until the establishment of a stable colony at Port Jackson that substantial deposits of ore could be exploited.

In 1791, black coal was discovered by escaped convicts near Nobbys Head, at the mouth of the Hunter River. In 1797, the first cargo of coal was shipped to Bengal and, in 1801, a convict mining settlement was opened at Coal River. Abandoned a year later, it was re-established in 1804 and renamed Newcastle.

Discoveries of coal-bearing strata in sedimentary basins at South Cape in Van Diemen's Land (1793), Wonthaggi in Victoria (1825), Ipswich in Queensland (1827), and elsewhere, were supported by the infant science of geology. Among the pioneers in the field were

the Reverend William Branwhite Clarke and Paul Edmund de Strzelecki, both of whom became more closely associated with the discovery of gold.

Scattered traces of metallic minerals were found in the early part of the nineteenth century, and lead was probably the first metal mined in Australia, in the Glen Osmond hills on the outskirts of Adelaide in 1841. A year later, copper mining began in the same area, at Kapunda. Copper was also discovered at Burra, in South Australia, in 1845. The young colony was quick to begin exporting agricultural products, but by 1850 exports of copper and lead from South Australia earned more than Australia's exports of wool and wheat.

The discoveries were soon overshadowed by a goldrush that trebled the immigrant population of Australia within 10 years. During 1849, many Australians migrated to the United States following

reports of rich gold discoveries in California. The New South Wales Government realised that if the wave of migration were to be reversed, it would have to provide incentives for Australians to find gold in their own country. Rewards offered for the discovery of 'payable' gold led to discoveries at Ophir, in New South Wales, in 1851. An exodus of settlers from other Australian colonies to Victoria's goldfields later that year created a need for better roads, improved coach services and construction of the first railway. The goldrush also prompted Victoria to adopt a protective tariff to foster industrial development. By 1860, gold exported through Melbourne amounted to five per cent of the revenue of the British Empire.

In the 1870s, Australia became an important producer of tin, and during the latter years of the nineteenth century, continued discoveries of lead, copper, tin, zinc and gold ore-bodies indicated the land's rich geological make-up.

Exploitation of silver, lead and zinc ore at Broken Hill from the 1880s was matched during the following decade by yet another goldrush, this time to Coolgardie and Kalgoorlie in Western Australia, and the first major iron ore deposits, which were discovered in South Australia's mid-north. Uranium was first identified at Radium Hill in South Australia's north-east in 1906, and the area was worked intermittently for the recovery of the mineral, mainly for medical purposes.

As early as the 1850s, government survey departments had begun to collate and interpret the country's geology. The formation of the Geological Survey of New South Wales in 1850, and a similar Victorian body a few years later, saw the adoption of standard techniques of field observation and the generalisation of findings. Gradually, it became possible to prepare a cartographic overview.

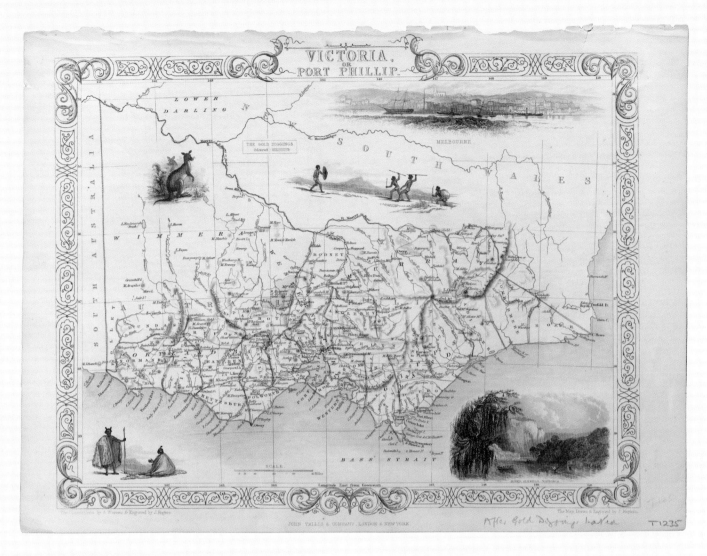

In 1873, Robert Brough Smyth (1830–1889) compiled a geological map of Australia, and *First Sketch of a Geological Map of Australia Including Tasmania* appeared in print two years later. William Clarke (1843–1903) then produced a more detailed geological map of New South Wales (1880). The map by Peter Drummond reflects the work of Charles Smith Wilkinson (1843–1891), who surveyed the Silver Mining Country, in western New South Wales, during the 1880s.

The 1931 national map compiled by Tannatt William Edgeworth David (1858–1934) stands as one of the most significant early contributions to Australian geology. David achieved a worldwide reputation for both himself and Australian geological science, and after World War I he began gathering details for a comprehensive account of the geology of Australia. David's large-scale *Geological Map of the Commonwealth of Australia* and a volume of *Explanatory Notes* were finished and published in 1932, and today the National Library of Australia holds an important collection of his mapping.

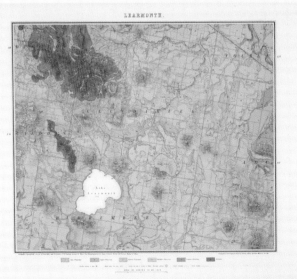

Department of Mines, Victoria
Learmonth
(Melbourne: Jas. Finnie Mining Department, 1882)
coloured map; 42.5 x 50.5 cm
Maps Collection
nla.map-rm2987

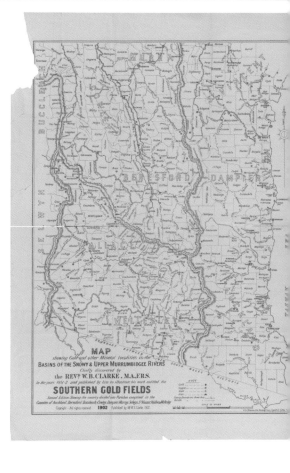

William Clarke's geological map of New South Wales, 1880

The Reverend William Branwhite Clarke (1798–1878), often described as the father of Australian geology, was the man who anticipated the discovery of gold near Bathurst and Ballarat.

Clarke is best known for his passionate interest in geology, zoology and meteorology. His 1880 map of the geology of New South Wales sums up an enormous amount of fieldwork and correspondence. In his time, he was one of the most highly educated scientists in Australia; he served as secretary of the Australian Museum from 1841 to 1845, and as a trustee and curator from 1853 to 1873.

Born in East Bergholt, Surrey, Clarke attended Dedham Grammar School and Jesus College, Cambridge, where he earned his Bachelor of Arts in 1821 and his Master of Arts in 1824, and where, to his good fortune, he heard the inspiring lectures of the Reverend Adam Sedgwick, the Woodwardian

Professor of Geology, who paved the way for fossil identification of the Devonian period of geological stratigraphy.

Ordained in 1821, Clarke took up an appointment as curate to Ramsholt, Suffolk, and during his spare time studied the geology of Suffolk and south-east Dorset, before consumptive illness forced him to seek the warmer climate of Australia.

After arriving in Sydney in May 1839, Clarke was appointed to the parish of Castle Hill and Dural, and as second headmaster of The King's School, Parramatta, but he resigned the latter position at the end of 1840. Four years later he was transferred to Campbelltown and, from 1846 to 1870, he served at St Thomas' Church, Willoughby.

Clarke became a frequent newspaper correspondent on topics such as a local earthquake, the Sabbath Bill, coal seams at Concord and Mount Keira, colonial education, a tornado at Parramatta, comets, books, water supply, artesian wells and Australian meteorology. He maintained a lengthy correspondence with Charles Darwin, who visited Sydney in 1836, especially after the famous naturalist had introduced him to the geological theories of Charles Lyell. By 1839, Clarke had established the stratigraphy of the Sydney Basin.

Clarke's published geological observations noted marble dykes in Argyle County and trilobite fossils at Burragood in the Hunter Valley (1846). As early as 1841, he had found specimens of detrital gold in the Hartley Valley. He theorised on the existence of

widespread gold deposits in granite country, and his discovery of gold traces in quartzite near Bathurst in 1845 caused Governor Gipps to ban public release of the news in case it caused the convicts to mutiny.

Clarke found tin ore at undisclosed locations during 1849, and his suggestion that a goldfield might exist near Ballarat anticipated the discovery of gold there in 1851. His studies of possible goldfields in the Tamworth and Armidale districts during 1854 also predicted the tin discoveries of the 1870s.

In 1856, Clarke visited his sister in Fingal, Tasmania, to recuperate from a mild stroke and, while there, he wrote several analyses of auriferous quartz. From 1860, he began recording details of the plant fossils in coal beds of the NSW Hunter Valley and the Queensland Maranoa district, raising questions concerning the geological age of NSW sedimentary formations. He shipped many fossil specimens to

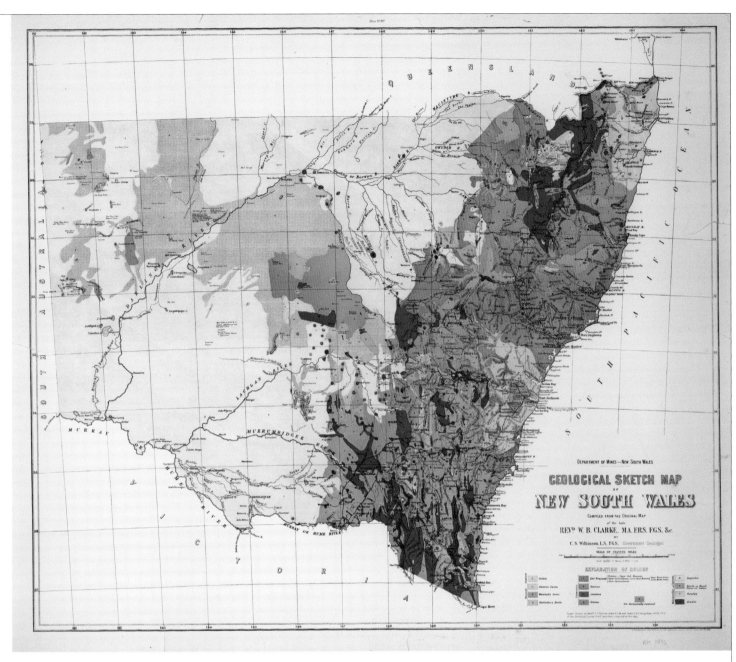

Department of Mines — New South Wales

GEOLOGICAL SKETCH MAP
OF
NEW SOUTH WALES

COMPILED FROM THE ORIGINAL MAP

of the Late

REVᴰ W. B. CLARKE, M.A. F.R.S. F.G.S. &c.

BY

C. S. Wilkinson, L.S. F.G.S. Government Geologist

SCALE OF STATUTE MILES

EXPLANATION BY COLOURS

Reverend Sedgwick in Cambridge, where today they form part of the Cambridge University collection.

Sedgwick had determined the Cambrian geological age and, from correspondence, Clarke became aware of Roderick Murchison's Silurian age and the Permian period, and he suggested that parts of New South Wales matched Silurian stratigraphy. In 1876, he was honoured as a fellow of the Royal Society and, a year later, he received the Murchison Medal of the London Geological Society.

Clarke's geological map of New South Wales, published posthumously at a scale of 1:2 027 520 (32 miles to one inch), is a tribute to Clarke by Charles Smith Wilkinson, the NSW Government Geologist. A distinctive feature is Clarke's application of an embryonic form of the geological time scale, including his recognition of limestone between rocks of Silurian and Devonian age, a distinction between Upper Carboniferous and Permian coal measures, and his naming of three Mesozoic sedimentary series (Hawkesbury sandstone, Wianamatta shales and the Clarence series). Clarke's extensive geological knowledge covered the eastern third of the colony, and provided a base for more detailed investigation by the NSW Geological Survey.

W.B. Clarke (1798–1878)
Geological Sketch Map of New South Wales
(Sydney: Surveyor General's Office, 1880)
coloured map; 55.9 x 66.1 cm
Maps Collection
nla.map-rm1992

Kiandra, New South Wales 1860
pen and pencil drawing;
20.5 x 27.5 cm
Pictures Collection
nla.pic-an6617949

John L. Buckland (1915–1989)
Silverton Tramway Locomotive 'A'
Class Number 21, Being Coaled by
Hand at Broken Hill, New South Wales,
September 1940
b&w photograph; 6.0 x 8.8 cm
Pictures Collection
nla.pic-vn3420582

Frank Hurley (1885–1962)
Looking North along Line
of Lode from B.H. South
[between 1910 and 1962]
glass negative
Pictures Collection
nla.pic-an23478488

84

Peter Drummond's map of the Silver Mining Country, Barrier Ranges, 1884

Following the lead of its Victorian counterpart, the Government of New South Wales set up a geological survey in 1873 and appointed Charles Smith Wilkinson of Victoria as its first geological surveyor. Wilkinson rode a horse from Melbourne to Sydney to take up his position, and within months of his arrival presented his first geological report—a survey of his route.

Seven years later, the discovery of a silver lode on the Umberumberka pastoral lease in the Barrier Ranges, in the far west of the colony, prompted a mining rush that in 1883 led Wilkinson to survey the town of Silverton (thought to have been named after the Colorado town of Silverton, the scene of a spectacular goldrush a few years earlier).

Wilkinson organised a survey of the metalliferous formation (shaded in pink on the map), described as Silurian mica-schists and clay slates, granite and

diorite, traversed by quartz reefs and lodes containing gold and ores of silver, lead, tin, bismuth, copper, manganese and iron. The unshaded country was reported as chiefly Devonian quartz pebble conglomerates, with extensive salt-bed plains of Cretaceous and Pleistocene formation.

The map, drafted in 1884 by Peter Drummond of the Department of Mines office in Sydney, was printed in the Government Printing Office by photolithography. Drummond copied cadastral details such as boundaries of pastoral leases, and he noted important topographic details such as lakes, hills, transport tracks, creeks, waterholes (with comments on depth and water quality), water 'tanks' and the location of sheep stations.

By 1884, camel trains led by 'Afghans'—actually Indians from Baluchistan and Sindh, now part of Pakistan—carried most freight to and from this dry district. Country west of the metalliferous formation

is described in Drummond's map as 'extensive open salt bush', while to the east 'saltbush plains' are noted. Portion of the route taken by the ill-fated Burke and Wills expedition of 1860 from Melbourne to the Gulf of Carpentaria is marked. Surface geological information identifies white sandstone, quartz reefs, quartzite dykes, copper lodes, tin lodes, bismuth lodes and the Red Jacket Gold Reefs north of Silverton. Near the town, Drummond named the Umberumberka, Thackaringa, Pinnacles and Rock Hole silver lodes, and the silver lode north of Mount Gipps.

The 1844 expedition of Charles Sturt was the first to identify the Barrier Ranges, and Sturt noted in his diary a 'broken hill' located in the most desolate country he had ever seen. In September 1883, Charles Rasp, a boundary rider on the Mount Gipps Station, pegged out 16 hectares of the great outcrop of ironstone as a mining lease in the mistaken belief that

it was a tin lode. The map shows the Broken Hill lode 24 kilometres east of Silverton, on the Alma lease, and describes it as 'Quartzite with massive Ironstone and Manganese'.

Rasp formed a syndicate of seven, including the station manager, George McCulloch, and applied for six more blocks of what eventually proved to be the world's largest silver-lead-zinc lode. On 10 August 1885, the syndicate floated the Broken Hill Proprietary Company (BHP) in Melbourne with 2000 shares at £20 each. During the Australian mineral boom of the late 1880s, the shares rose to £412, although many fortunes made by speculators evaporated during an economic depression a few years later. The mining city of Broken Hill that grew up nearby was for many years Australia's largest inland city and, by the 1980s, the Barrier Mines had yielded 201 million tonnes of galena (silver-lead-zinc ore).

DEPARTMENT OF MINES

MAP OF THE
SILVER MINING COUNTRY.
IN THE
Barrier Ranges ; Albert District.
NEW SOUTH WALES.

SOUTH AUSTRALIA

General Locality Map
SHOWING
The Routes of access to the Silver Mining Country

SCALE IN MILES

Queensland

South Australia

New South Wales

Victoria

NOTES.

C. S. WILKINSON, Geological Surveyor in Charge.

Scale of Miles.

left
Peter Drummond
**Map of the Silver Mining
Country in the Barrier Ranges,
Albert District, New South
Wales**
(Sydney: Government Printing
Office, 1884)
coloured map; 68.4 x 52.8 cm
Maps Collection
nla.map-f6

85

below
James Wooler
**Bullock Teams Carting Wool
from Mt. Gipps Station c.1908**
albumen photograph;
5.7 x 15.2 cm
Pictures Collection
nla.pic-an23378296

Map of the Hannan's Goldfield, West Australia
(London: Universal Publishing Company Limited, c.1898)
coloured map on 4 sheets mounted on linen; 96.4 x 289.0 cm
Maps Collection
nla.map-rm1328

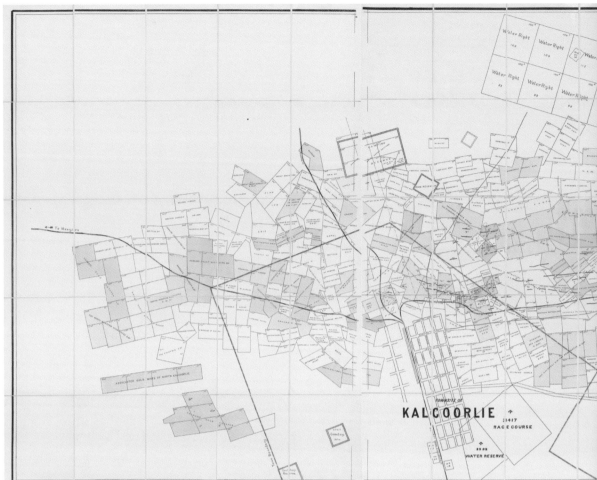

Map of the Hannan's Goldfield West Australia

The man who single-handedly saved the economy of Western Australia, Patrick 'Paddy' Hannan (1843–1925), immigrated to Australia from County Clare, Ireland, at the age of 21 with few skills and even fewer prospects.

On arrival in the colony of Victoria, Hannan travelled to Ballarat, where his uncle worked in the goldmines, before trying his luck as a prospector on the goldrushes in the Tuapeka district (New Zealand), Terama (New South Wales) and Teetulpa (South Australia). He was unsuccessful. In 1889, just as a severe economic depression began, he travelled to Western Australia as a pioneer prospector on the Coolgardie goldfield.

Four years later, at the age of 51, Hannan and two Irish mates, Tom Flanagan and Dan O'Shea, joined the rush to Mount Youle but, when a horse cast a shoe near Mount Charlotte, they were forced to stop.

It was a fortuitous delay. The men found traces of gold nearby and Hannan located 100 ounces in gold nuggets as evidence of a lode. His return to Coolgardie to apply for a reward claim triggered Australia's largest goldrush and focused international attention on 'Hannan's Find'. Virtually the entire town of Coolgardie (700 people) arrived at the site within three days. Hannan's discovery rescued the Western Australian economy.

Although he became an instant hero, Hannan made little profit from his find due to the nature and depth of the ironstone lode of what became known as the Golden Mile, one of the world's richest auriferous (gold-bearing) reefs. He continued to prospect until 1904, when the state government placed him on a lifetime pension.

The undated *Map of the Hannan's Goldfield West Australia*, compiled at 10 miles to the inch and published by the Universal Publishing Company Limited of Ludgate Circus, London, consists of three sheets showing mining leases (including acreage and identity number), lodes, shafts, stamper batteries, old workings, assay office, slime dams, brickyard, tramways, railway links (to Menzies, Kanowna and Coolgardie), telegraph line and pipeline.

Such information, products of the goldmining investment boom of 1897–1903, was probably intended to attract British capital, and dates the map at close to the turn of the century. An unusual feature is the map orientation, with north at the top left. The only topographic

features are Mount Gledden and Mount Ferrum.

Fifteen leases and their extensions bear the name of Hannan as a locality identity for goldmining companies registered in Perth. Others carry hopes of good luck, for example Golden Horseshoe, Croesus and Boulder Bonanza. Street layouts are shown for Great Boulder (now Boulder), a wage-workers' town on the Golden Mile, which was declared a townsite on 4 December 1896 and, six kilometres to the west, Kalgoorlie (named in 1895 after *galgurli*, the Maduwangka word for a local shrub).

Kalgoorlie is a regional service centre for an economy that until 1970 remained virtually dependent on gold extraction. Since 1980, the Golden Mile has been replaced

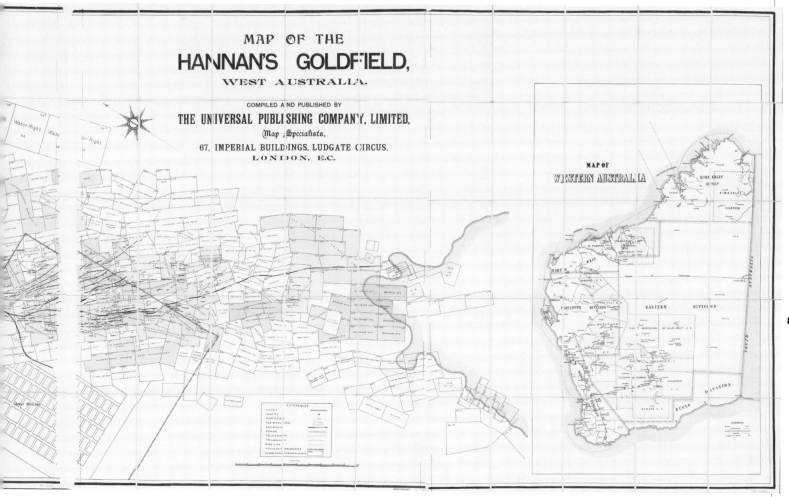

MAP OF THE
HANNAN'S GOLDFIELD,
WEST AUSTRALIA.

COMPILED AND PUBLISHED BY
THE UNIVERSAL PUBLISHING COMPANY, LIMITED,
(Map Specialists,
67, IMPERIAL BUILDINGS, LUDGATE CIRCUS,
LONDON, E.C.

MAP OF
WESTERN AUSTRALIA

by an open-cut mine called the Super Pit. The goldfield revealed persistent nearby gold lode discoveries long after the original find petered out. Since the late 1960s, the region has experienced a nickel boom.

Roy Millar (fl.1884–1900)
**'Happy Thought', Prospecting Party,
A.C. (?) Black, Leader, C.H. Stiles,
R.W. Johnston, R.A. Boyd, 1894**
albumen photograph; 14.6 x 20.2 cm
Pictures Collection
nla.pic-an23380332

T.W. Edgeworth David's geological map of Australia, 1931

Interest in the geology of Australia dates from 1791, just three years after European settlement, with Captain George Vancouver's description of Bald Head in Western Australia's King George Sound.

Subsequent discovery of coal in the Hunter River and Illawarra coastal districts was followed by various geological reports from inland explorers such as John Oxley, Allan Cunningham, Hamilton Hume and Thomas Mitchell.

The greatest impetus to systematic geological survey, however, came with the discovery of gold in 1851. Both the Victorian and NSW governments established survey teams, with the former producing several series of geological maps of the central goldfields. Departments of mines, or their equivalent, were established in all colonies and were soon conducting geological surveys. Chairs of geology were set up after the establishment of the

Sydney and Melbourne universities in the 1850s.

The first known attempt to map the geology of Australia, compiled by Joseph Beete Jukes in 1850, was limited by a shortage of contemporary knowledge. The 1873 map by Robert Brough Smyth ranks as the first serious map on the subject. By the turn of the century, further details had been issued under the auspices of the Victorian Mines Department, or by geologists such as John Gregory and Leo Cotton.

Meanwhile, one of Australia's eminent geologists, Tannatt William Edgeworth David (1858–1934), had immigrated to Australia from Wales in 1882 following his appointment as Assistant Geological Surveyor in the NSW Department of Mines. For nine years, David undertook surveys of the tin deposits of Vegetable Creek, Emmaville in New South Wales and the Hunter River Valley, where

he discovered the South Maitland coal measures.

In 1890, David became Professor of Geology and Physical Geography at the University of Sydney, a position he held until he resigned in 1924. Fieldwork proved essential to his active and extraordinary career, which covered several major disciplines within the geological sciences.

During 1897, David led an expedition to Funafuti, a coral atoll in the Ellice Islands (now Tuvalu), to test and prove Darwin's theory that coral atolls were built on a subsiding platform. To obtain evidence, he drilled a borehole to a depth of 1114 feet (340 metres). For this research and related studies, he was awarded the Bigsby Medal of the Geological Society of London. In 1900, he was elected to a fellowship of the Royal Society.

Inspired by a longstanding interest in glaciation, David accepted an invitation to join Ernest Shackleton's 1907 expedition to

Antarctica. As its oldest member, he led a team for the first ascent of Mount Erebus and, in the same year, set out with a former student, Douglas Mawson, and another team member to reach the South Magnetic Pole.

In 1920, David was knighted for wartime military services as a tunnel engineer with the Australian Imperial Forces and as chief geologist to the British Expeditionary Force.

As early as 1892, David had considered writing a textbook on the geology of Australia, accompanied by a detailed map, but it was not until 1915 that he signed a contract with London publisher Edward Arnold and Company. David began work on the book in 1922 but, due to various distractions and bouts of ill health, it remained incomplete when he died in 1934. William Rowan Browne, a former student, colleague and friend, published the book in 1950.

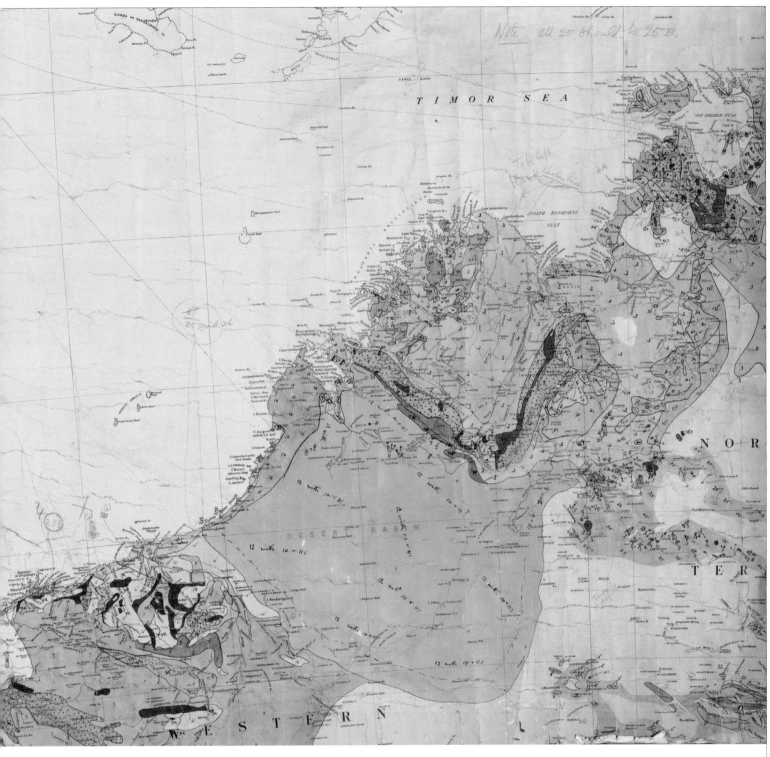

David's magnificent map, *Geo-logical Map of the Commonwealth*, with accompanying explanatory notes, appeared in March 1931 as four map sheets. He had begun the cartographic work in 1922 by plotting data onto a 1921 base map of Australia at a scale of 1:2 990 000. David compiled details from geological maps published by geological surveys of the states and the Commonwealth Government, and undertook further studies of his own. Efforts to publish the map in 1928 saw it sent to England for correction, but it was not returned until January 1929. After obtaining approval for publication from the Commonwealth Council for Scientific and Industrial Research, David continued to update the map during the remainder of that year.

Complex in detail and accompanied by large geological profiles, the map finally went to the printers in 1930. It lacked a geological legend, although some map elements can be identified from the profiles—granites are shown in red shading and Cretaceous sediments in green shading. An accompanying 177-page book of detailed explanatory notes, diagrams and tables appeared in time for the 1932 Australian and New Zealand Association for the Advancement of Science conference held in Sydney. David's map and notes brought him international acclaim.

S.T. Gill (1818–1880)
Surveyors
(Melbourne: Hamel & Ferguson, 1865)
chromolithograph print; 19.2 x 25.3 cm
Pictures Collection, nla.pic-an7150073

90

9. Land administration and management

Forms of land title

Before his departure for New South Wales, Governor Arthur Phillip received instructions that empowered him to establish the first British Colony in Australia and to grant land and to issue regulations. Land administration became paramount after free settlers began arriving in Australia, and specific regulations were introduced for the sale of 'Crown' land.

By 1820, much of the land within a radius of about 300 kilometres of Sydney was occupied by farmers and graziers. In 1826, the extent to which unauthorised occupation of land, or squatting, was occurring caused Governor Darling to specify limits outside which land could not be occupied. In 1829, the settled areas were extended to embrace the Nineteen Counties. The government would neither sell nor grant land outside this limit, nor allow permanent settlement there. Settlement was hard to police, and ran ahead of the limited means available to the survey office. By

1833, the government conceded that it could not remove squatters who had established unauthorised stock stations in the interior.

Despite the introduction of licences and fees, problems of unsurveyed land and boundaries remained and were the subject of negotiation between neighbours. Increasing conflict between squatters and gentry settlers required that land commissioners be appointed to determine boundaries and manage disputes. Many squatters held small landholdings, but some owned runs of between 200 000 acres (about 81 000 hectares) and 500 000 acres (202 000 hectares). Nearly the whole of what is now Victoria outside North Gippsland was held by less than a thousand identified owners.

Just as problematic were relations between squatters and local Aboriginal people. In 1835, the region south of the Murray River that had been explored by Mitchell

and others came under Crown law. When Geelong and Portland were officially opened to settlement, newcomers were attracted by the availability of fertile land that was occupied without regard to the entitlements of its Aboriginal owners. It was a pattern repeated on the Darling Downs and elsewhere, and 'border police' were installed to help control relations between settlers and Aboriginal people, impose authority and prepare for the rule of law. The cost of policing was funded by a levy on livestock.

Free settlers established the colonies of Western Australia and South Australia, and each colony devised its own land administrative system. At Swan River, regulations were issued to set out the specific terms by which land would be granted to intending free settlers. In a departure from the NSW county and parish system, both the Swan River and South Australian colonies applied the English unit of a hundred (about 100 square miles,

or 26 000 hectares), which provided some 30 acres of land (about 12 hectares) held without prejudicing the owner's rights to the common land nearby.

A more innovative measure was the Torrens Title System (named for its proponent Robert Richard Torrens), adopted by South Australia in 1856–1857. The original system of land title in New South Wales, based on British common law, had become cumbersome as settlement expanded. The Torrens Title was designed to obviate the necessity of searching the vendor's title through a series of documents. The new principle of title by registration, which was adopted in New South Wales and elsewhere from the 1860s, allowed for land to be identified by the portion or allotment number within its district, managed together with records of the dimensions of the land and its boundaries, the names of the registered proprietors, and

any legal interests that affected title.

During 1861, the Premier of New South Wales, John Robertson, attempted to break the monopoly of the squatter-pastoralists. He forced two Acts through the Parliament, and opened up free selection of Crown land by permitting any person to select up to 320 acres (about 130 hectares) on the conditions that they pay a deposit of one-quarter of the purchase price after survey and live on the land for three years. Robertson's intention—to give poorer purchasers access to land and to increase farming and agricultural development—proved only partially successful. Avoidance was possible, and conflicts between the squatters and the free-selectors ensued. At the same time, by enabling close settlement of pastoral lands still available for use by Aboriginal people, the Acts further limited the lands and economy of Australia's first occupants.

Although not a legal boundary, Goyder's rainfall line was used to limit South Australian settlement from the 1860s. Water availability and drought management were, and still are, key challenges throughout most of Australia. With little knowledge of the new country being opened up to the north and west, farmers needed reliable information. After a two-month survey in 1865, George Woodroffe Goyder, the South Australian Surveyor General, discouraged farmers from planting crops north of his line, declaring the land suitable only for light grazing. Although in good times many later ignored Goyder and headed north, the line has proven remarkably accurate, and entire towns and farms were abandoned when there was a return to longer-term average rainfall.

Three Australian territories were created subsequent to Federation. In 1825, the area occupied today by the Northern Territory was part of the colony of New South Wales. It was first settled by Europeans in 1824 at Fort Dundas, Port Essington. When the South Australian Government realised that there was an urgent requirement to identify additional arable land, it was annexed to that Colony. The port of Darwin was established in 1869, on the lands of the Larrakia Aboriginal people, and was originally known as Palmerston. The period from the mid-1860s to 1895 was a time of large-scale pastoral settlement and development in the Northern Territory. Immense runs were taken up, and hundreds and thousands of sheep, cattle and horses were overlanded to stock the new properties. On 1 January 1912, the Territory was separated from South Australia and became part of the Commonwealth of Australia. A year earlier, the Australian Capital Territory was suveyed. It was centred on the limestone plains and creeks south of Lake George, an area favoured for pasturing sheep. In 1911, an international competition to design the new national capital city of Australia was promoted. The winning entry was submitted by American architect Walter Burley Griffin and his partner and wife, Marion Mahony Griffin. Canberra was announced as the official name for the city in March 1913.

Other than legislation involving the recognition of Aboriginal land rights (referred to in Chapter 1), perhaps the most significant territorial legislation since the Australian colonial period relates to Antarctica. The Australian Antarctic Territory, the largest portion of Antarctica claimed by any nation, is inhabited by the staff of scientific research stations only, and is administered by the Australian Antarctic Division. The Antarctic Treaty, a unique agreement between nations, governs activities in Antarctica and its surrounding seas. Australia was one of 12 original parties to the Treaty, which came into force in 1961.

George Lacy (c.1816–1878)
Capture of Bushrangers at Night by Gold Police
c.1852
watercolour; 32.1 x 40.3 cm
Pictures Collection
nla.pic-an3103554

right
J.A.C. Willis
Part of the Police District of Binalong,
Co. of Harden–Lachlan Distt.,
Yass District Court
(Sydney: Surveyor General's Office, 1864)
coloured map mounted on linen;
58.2 x 100.5 cm
Maps Collection
nla.map-rm1799

J.A.C. Willis' Binalong Police District map, 1864

When the goldrushes of the 1850s increased the flow of people across the Limits of Settlement (the defined area of the colony in which Crown land could be purchased or granted), the colony of New South Wales began to experience significant social problems, the instability of large populations, labour shortages and new ethnic divisions.

Previously, virtually all control of law and order operated through the county courts of petty sessions within the Settled Districts. After the goldrushes, a policy of free selection under the *Crown Lands Alienation Act 1861* gave incoming selectors the right to occupy land for agricultural purposes (16 to 128 hectares), before survey and for an allotted period of three years before full payment.

This lithograph map of the Binalong Police District, compiled at a scale of 1:126 720 by J.A.C. Willis at the Surveyor General's Office in Sydney, is typical of

many important efforts to provide geographical and cadastral information relevant to the work of police officers, clerks of petty sessions, magistrates and local government land agents responsible for Crown land sales.

During the 1820s, squatters were known to have moved across the Limits of Settlement west of Yass decades before the town of Binalong na Barwang (a name taken from a Ngunnawal resident, Bennelong of Barwang) was surveyed on Bungalala Creek. Examples of early squatting properties identified on the map by predominantly Aboriginal nomenclature include the Cunningar and Beggan Beggan runs (both registered to John Macansh, who brought in merino rams valued at £130 each during 1858), Bookham (T. Drummond), Bogolong (A. Armour), Mahkoolma (M. Armour), Mylora (J.J. Garry), Coppabella (J. Lehane) and Cootamundry (J. Hurley). Squatting runs adjacent to the

Murrumbidgee River included Goodradigbee (J. Swift), Childowla (F. Carroll), Burrandaroo (P. Hyles) and Wadgegalong (J. Pring).

In May 1858, Sydney authorities redefined the Binalong Police District west of the Yass Police District, transferring the northern portion to a newly created Boorowa Police District centred on Boorowa courthouse. At the same time, Binalong police duties were extended westward to take in the new villages of Jugiong and Cootamundry, where additional selections were taken up.

Early in 1860, the Yass courthouse rose to quarterly district status, with judge and jury as the court of reference for both Binalong and Boorowa petty sessions. After anti-Chinese riots at the Lambing Flat gold-diggings required a military detachment complete with artillery (1860–1861), a third subordinate police court opened north of Binalong at Young. Red edging on the map shows the limits within

which the court 'behelden at Yass shall have jurisdiction'.

By 1864, the major police activity concentrated on bushrangers such as Scottish-born Frank Christie (aka Gardiner), who 'stuck up' mail coaches along the Main Southern Road and robbed the unwary on roads to Boorowa and Young. John Joseph Garry of Mylora Station was incensed when the Ben Hall gang stole his two champion racehorses and ruined them by hard riding to escape police troopers. A mounted patrol operated from Yass under the able supervision of Sub-Inspector Brennan, but it was the

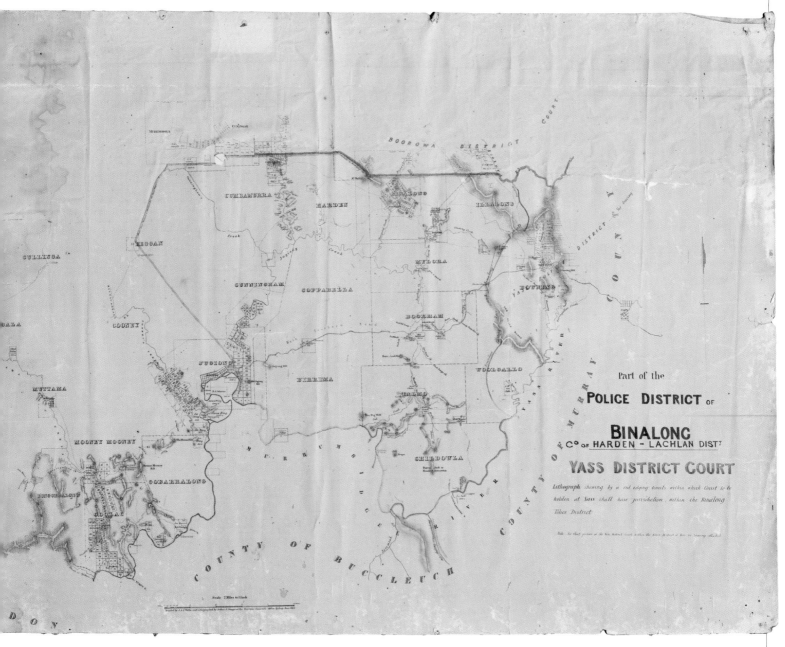

Binalong police contingent of four constables, led by Senior Constable Hales, that achieved fame by shooting Canadian-born 'Flash' Johnny Gilbert on the Boorowa Road in May 1865.

Elements of nineteenth-century social life within the Binalong Police District and adjacent areas have been preserved through the poetry of Andrew Barton 'Banjo' Paterson (1864–1941), who rode to Binalong School from his father's property, Illalong. For this reason alone, the map provides an essential historical reference to identify the location of the

Bogolong Races (where Pardon won 'the Cup' on a light saddle actually borrowed from Paterson's mount).

Bogolong (now Bookham) had two pubs—according to Paterson, one to catch 'the coves coming from Yass' and the other to catch travellers from Jugiong. Parts of the author's poem 'The Bush Christening' are set in the village of Binalong, 'The Wargeilah Handicap' refers to Conroy's Gap, and 'The Mylora Elopement' takes a run near Illalong as its reference but changes the names of the heroine and hero. Paterson's novel,

The Old Station, makes frequent reference to Kuryong, and 'The Shearer's Colt' recaptures boyhood memories from Illalong. The Willis map helps locate the setting of these ballads.

right
McFarlane & Erskine
Gold Escort Attacked by Bushrangers
(Edinburgh: McGready, Thomson & Niver, 1870s)
coloured lithograph; 25.0 x 16.3 cm
Pictures Collection
nla.pic-an8420450

Malby & Sons
Sydney Bay, Norfolk Island, to Which Place a Portion of the Pitcairn Islanders are in Course of Removal c.1885
hand-coloured lithograph;
11.9 x 21.5 cm
Pictures Collection
nla.pic-an9060932

right
Thomas Kennedy
Plan of Norfolk Island c.1860
manuscript map
mounted on linen;
254.0 x 298.5cm
Maps Collection
nla.map-rm642

94

Thomas Kennedy's survey of Norfolk Island, 1860

Volcanic Norfolk Island, rising from the sea along the Norfolk Ridge between New Zealand and New Caledonia, was the first discovery made by James Cook on his second voyage to the Pacific in 1774.

Like the Australian mainland, Norfolk Island's subsequent European settlement began with a penal colony after Philip Gidley King landed on the island on 6 March 1788. Attempts to establish industries from the native flax and pine failed, and more convicts were sent to establish a farm to supply food to the colony of Sydney. Pests and climate destroyed initial attempts, but the situation improved after additional supplies and more convicts were sent from the mainland. By 1792, the population of the island had grown to more than 1000 (the first child was born in 1789). Over the next 15 years, however, successive additions of convicts and the fluctuating success of the grain harvests led to gradual withdrawal of the population from 1808 to

1814, leaving a small population of pigs, goats and dogs.

Ten years later, the British Government decided to reopen Norfolk Island as a penal colony to take the worst criminals from New South Wales and Van Diemen's Land. The second penal settlement, established on 6 June 1825, lasted until 1856. Earlier buildings, abandoned after the end of the first settlement, were restored and new buildings were erected as the island received successive shipments of convicts. Settlement was largely confined to Kingston and outposts such as Longridge agricultural station.

Over the years, the colony saw several riots and escapes. But matters came to a head under the administration of Major Joseph Childs, whose reintroduction of the harsh penal code led to a revolt in 1846. In the same year, the British Government signalled its intention to abandon the settlement, but no action was taken until 1852,

when Bishop Robert Wilson from Van Diemen's Land reported on the shocking conditions of the convicts and recommended that the penal colony be closed.

At the same time, a recommendation was made to relocate to Norfolk the settlers of Pitcairn Island, who had outgrown the resources on their own island. By June 1855, all but five of Norfolk Island's prisoners had left the island and arrived at Port Arthur in Van Diemen's Land. A year later, the last convicts were removed and the colony abandoned. In June 1856, following an Act of the British Parliament in July 1855 and an Order in Council on 24 June 1856, which separated Norfolk Island from Van Diemen's Land and created a distinct and separate settlement, the Pitcairners arrived on the island.

Captain Henry Denham, of the British Navy ship HMS *Herald*, arrived on Norfolk Island in 1855 to conduct an Admiralty survey of the

island to determine the allotment of land to the Pitcairn families. A detailed survey was finally conducted by Second Corporal Thomas Kennedy and Sapper George Jamieson in 1858 and 1859, resulting in the magnificent map shown here. A free grant of 20 hectares was offered to the head of each family; and, for some years, a similar arrangement continued for the Pitcairners' descendants on marriage. Later issues of the reduced printed cadastral map taken from the Kennedy survey show the successive take-up of land over the next 40 years and the inevitable subdivisions that followed.

Nepean Id, Norfolk Island
1911–1915
b&w sepia-toned photograph;
8.7 x 13.6cm
Pictures Collection
nla.pic-an23815413

Klaus Hueneke (b.1944)
Old Currango on the Currangorambla Plain in 1978
b&w photograph; 16.1 x 24.1 cm
Pictures Collection
nla.pic-vn3092669

right
**Plan of Snow Leases Lots Numbered
61 to [69] Inclusive, Parishes of
Murray, Cooleman, Long Plain,
Nattung, Yarrongobilly, The Peaks
and Peppercorn, Counties of Cowley
and Buccleuch**
(Sydney: New South Wales
Department of Lands, 1892)
map; 118.4 x 80.2 cm
Maps Collection
nla.map-rm3690

96

High country snow lease map, 1892

Less than 50 years after the landing of the First Fleet, stockmen reached the Kiandra district in the Snowy Mountains of New South Wales—some as early as 1834.

It was not until the goldrush of the 1850s and a severe drought in 1855, however, that a regular pattern of transhumance (grazing cattle in the high country during summer) was established. In 1865, W. Davis Wright, the manager of William Bradley's northern runs, commented on his idea of driving cattle and sheep into the mountains: 'My idea was quite untried at the time although now it is one of the commonplace incidents of every station'.

Local graziers such as the Litchfield family, which held extensive acreage around Cooma, managed their properties and economic returns solely on their ability to move older wethers into the high country during summer for fattening. The practice took pressure off the home pastures,

allowing the family to use them for their more valuable stock.

Government legislation dealing with the use of land for this purpose did not appear until 1889, following an amendment to the NSW *Crown Land Act 1889*. One of the oldest surviving snow lease maps of the period was the *Plan of Snow Leases Lots Numbered 61 to 69 Inclusive, Parishes of Murray, Cooleman, Long Plain, Nattung, Yarrongobilly, The Peaks and Peppercorn, Counties of Cowley and Buccleuch*. This map, published in 1892, clearly indicates the large tracts of land required by the graziers for summer grazing, even though at the time most of the leases had not been taken up. Demand was low due to the costs of survey, rent, improvements and the limited lease of seven years.

Following the initial lease grants, efforts for a more uniform and manageable system were made during the years before the amending Act of 1917, which

extended the leases to 14 years. In the meantime, alternative tenancies were also offered, ranging from improvement leases of a few thousand acres to scrub leases at tens of thousands of acres. As a result, well-placed Western Division graziers acquired a complex network of licences after they took advantage of the agreements to obtain vast tracts of land for their own purposes, to the exclusion of smaller, local graziers.

Whether it was the improvement in the lease arrangements or a combination of drought and competition for more land, demand for snow leases increased during the 1920s. With the increase came a regular pattern of renewal, particularly from Monaro graziers, which was reflected in the parish maps. Permissive occupancies or the occupation or use of Crown land leases flanked the high country, generally to the west and south of the snow leases.

In about 1944, concern began to emerge over the impact of stock movement and grazing practices, such as control burning (still practised today on the Victorian side). The proclamation of the *Kosciusko State Park Act* in 1944, along with the Lands Department's controls in the same year, saw the beginning of the total exclusion of graziers from the area.

Initial concern, and the subsequent enactment of the *State Park Act* in 1944, was aimed at maintaining and protecting the quality of the water-catchment potential of the high country rather than promoting pure conservation values. Controlled use of the park for pastoral purposes was still permitted. A NSW Cabinet meeting in 1957 on the issue of terminating snow leases in country above 4500 feet (1371 metres), which had been promoted by the Catchment Areas Protection Board established in 1955, recommended termination of the leases.

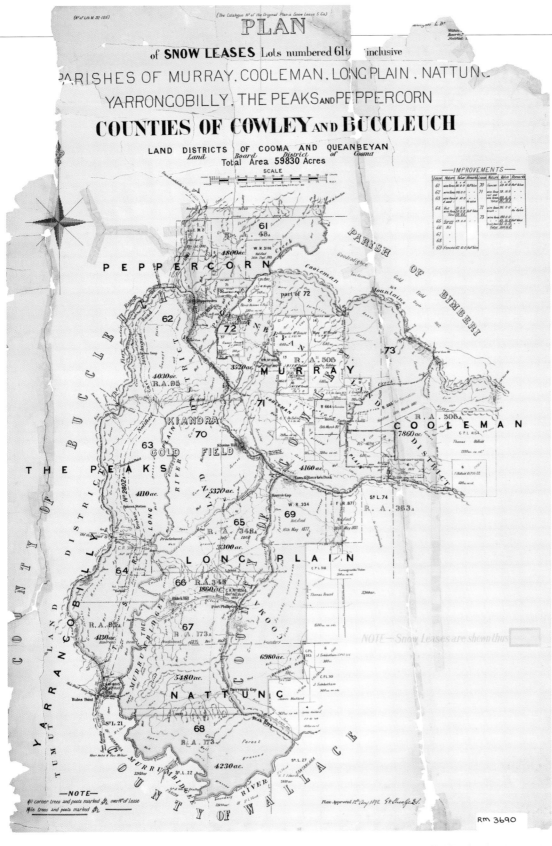

PLAN
of **SNOW LEASES** Lots numbered 61 to inclusive
PARISHES OF MURRAY, COOLEMAN, LONG PLAIN, NATTUNG
YARRONGOBILLY, THE PEAKS AND PEPPERCORN
COUNTIES OF COWLEY AND BUCCLEUCH
LAND DISTRICTS OF COOMA AND QUEANBEYAN
Total Area 59830 Acres

Rm 3690

In 1968, the NSW Premier, Robert William Askin, announced an investigation into controlled grazing and longer-term leases within certain areas of the park. The subsequent Edgar Report recommended the total abolition of grazing in the national park. By the end of May 1969, the government had accepted every recommendation of the report and all grazing ceased within the park.

Frank Hurley (1885–1962)
Eucumbene Dam & Lake 1950s
plastic negative; 11.2 x 15.5 cm
Pictures Collection
nla.pic-an23816887

Model of the Snowy Mountains Hydro-Electric Development, 1949

Laurie John Failes (1899–1976)
Site of Guthega Dam Project [between 1954 and 1965]
slide
Pictures Collection
nla.pic-an20118662-2

The incidence of droughts as a regular occurrence in the life of rural Australia became apparent soon after the arrival of the First Fleet in 1788. Ways of overcoming their devastating impact were identified early in the nineteenth century.

In 1845, Polish explorer Paul Edmund de Strzelecki (1797-1873) announced that irrigation could be used to improve agriculture, pinpointing the central lakes of Tasmania and the rivers of New South Wales and Gippsland as likely water sources. By the end of the century, a succession of individuals and royal commissions in both New South Wales and Victoria had identified the snow-fed Murrumbidgee River or the Murray River, or both river systems, as suitable for diversion.

Following Federation, the choice of the Monaro region as a suitable site for the capital of Australia was influenced largely by its proximity to the Snowy River as a source

of hydro-electricity and dependable water supplies. The River Murray Agreement (1915) brought together Commonwealth, NSW, Victorian and South Australian interests in water supply from that river. The River Murray Commission was formed two years later to monitor water use.

Continuing droughts and a growing demand for reliable electricity led to the establishment of the Snowy River Investigation Committee, set up by the Premier of New South Wales, William John McKell, in 1943. The committee's subsequent report provided a technically and economically practicable scheme. A report by Trygve Olsen, a Norwegian engineer with the Victorian State Electricity Commission, led to the

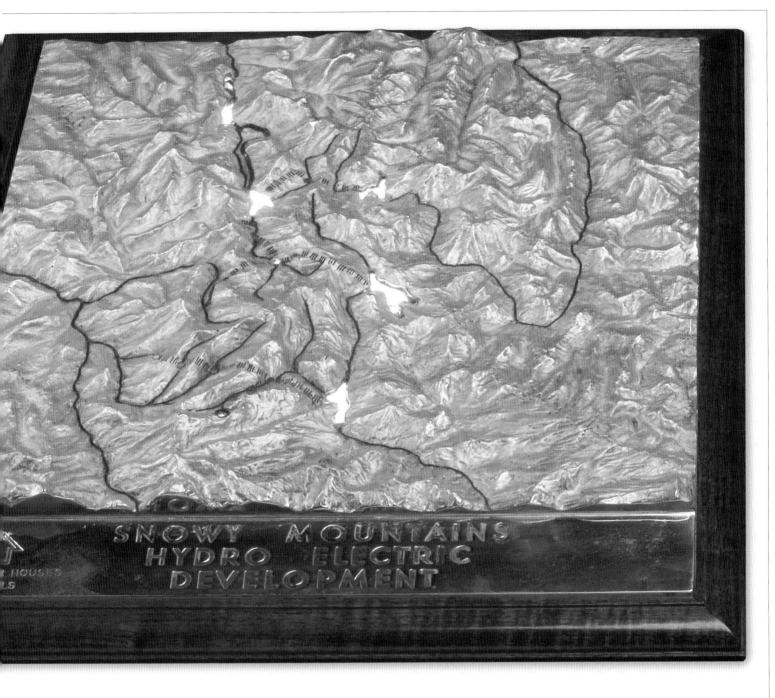

principle of developing water-powered electricity stations to be used during peak-load periods—the basis of the future Snowy Mountains Hydro-Electric Scheme.

The two reports formed the foundation of a ministerial conference in June 1946, which was followed by further investigations and reports through to June 1949. On 7 July 1949, Commonwealth legislation was enacted to establish the Snowy Mountains Hydro-Electric Authority. The scheme was officially launched in mid-October

1949. By providing an environment in which many cultures and nationalities could work and live together successfully, the scheme formed the nucleus of Australia's diverse multicultural society.

This presentation model was presented to McKell after he was appointed Governor-General of Australia in March 1947, and it acknowledged his work and commitment to the scheme since 1941. The model shows the initial plan for the scheme, although it lacks the three amendments

made over the next 10 years that would improve the scheme and increase its capacity through the enlargement of the Eucumbene reservoir and the inclusion of reverse-flow tunnels.

Snowy Mountains Hydro-electric Authority
Snowy Mountains Hydro-Electric Development 1949
coloured silver-plated relief model mounted in wooden case; 33.0 x 28.4 cm
Maps Collection
nla.map-remo1

Laurie John Failes (1899–1976)
Munyang Power Station, Infra-red Treatment of Pipes [between 1954 and 1965]
Pictures Collection
nla.pic-an20118662-4

Felicity Jenkins
**Leader of the Helicopter Impacts Program,
Melissa Giesse Removes an Artificial Egg
from Beneath an Adelie Penguin
[between 1997 and 1998]**
gelatin silver photograph; 20.0 x 25.0 cm
Pictures Collection
nla.pic-an14144994-16

Felicity Jenkins
**'The Chapel' Old Mawson Station
[between 1997 and 1998]**
gelatin silver photograph; 20.0 x 25.0 cm
Pictures Collection
nla.pic-an14144994-40

Felicity Jenkins
**Carpenters Equipment Kept for Recreational
Use [between 1997 and 1998]**
gelatin silver photograph; 20.0 x 25.0 cm
Pictures Collection
nla.pic-an14144994-41

Felicity Jenkins
**Traverse Vans Left on the Plateau behind
Mawson Station [between 1997 and 1998]**
colour digital image; 12.5 cm
Pictures Collection
nla.pic-an20037022-40

Charles Wilkes' charts of the Antarctic continent, 1844–1874

On his second voyage to the Pacific, after crossing the Antarctic Circle and observing icefloes, Captain James Cook established that yet another unknown landmass existed, separate from and further south of the Australian continent.

Reports of the existence of penguins opened up a flurry of sealing, and later whaling, by commercial operators in Britain and America. By the 1830s, several subantarctic islands, including Macquarie and Heard, had been discovered.

During the following decade, major expeditions to Antarctica were launched to determine the nature and extent of the land. One of the most remarkable, if not contentious, was that of the United States Exploring Expedition, commanded by Lieutenant Charles Wilkes from 1839 to 1843, with six small ships and a crew of 490 personnel and scientists.

Wilkes' initial foray into Antarctica, in February 1839, was hampered by bad weather but nevertheless provided enough incentive to return later in the year. With one ship lost and another ordered home, the expedition left Australia for Antarctica in December 1839 and made landfall on 23 January 1840, when one of the vessels, the *Peacock*, struck an iceberg. By early 1841, the crew had surveyed 1500 miles (2414 kilometres) of the Antarctic coastline between 160°E and 100°E, now known as Wilkes Land, in the Australian Antarctic Territory.

Wilkes' *Chart of the Antarctic Continent Shewing the Icy Barrier Attached to It* sums up a forgotten achievement of the expedition, which not only determined a significant length of the coastline but also established that a continental landmass lay beyond. The published charts of the expedition were the first to use the term 'Antarctic Continent'.

Wilkes' claims of discovery of the Antarctic continent were disputed by British explorer James Clark Ross, who reported that he had sailed over the position of Wilkes' continent without locating any of the features observed. Perhaps because of Ross' comments and a shift of interest by the Americans in Antarctica to the area known as West or Lesser Antarctica, Wilkes' observations and chart of what is now the Australian Antarctic Territory were largely discredited.

On its return to America, the expedition was faced with a disinterested public, an unfriendly Congress and a tarnished reputation resulting from a series of court martials that occupied naval officers. Despite the setbacks, Wilkes was placed in charge of the collections acquired during the voyage, and he took responsibility for the publication of 19 volumes of reports and charts which were eventually published between 1844 and 1874. Wilkes' claims

of discovery of the Antarctic continent remained in dispute.

During the 1950s, however, honour was restored. In 1958–1959 the Australian National Antarctic Research Expedition, led by Phillip Law, carried out an aerial survey between Horn Bluff and Cape Freshfield, and reconnaissance in the Oates Land and George V Land sections. Law was following up on groundbreaking exploratory work undertaken by the US navy's Operation Highjump aerial reconnaissance survey in 1947.

Grappling with poor weather conditions, Law managed to obtain sufficient aerial photographic coverage of the coastline between Cape Horn and Cape Freshfield (1958) and Oates Land (1959) so that, when added to the photographs taken during Operation Highjump, the expedition's photographs allowed comparison with Mawson's and Wilkes' observations. The photographs were passed to

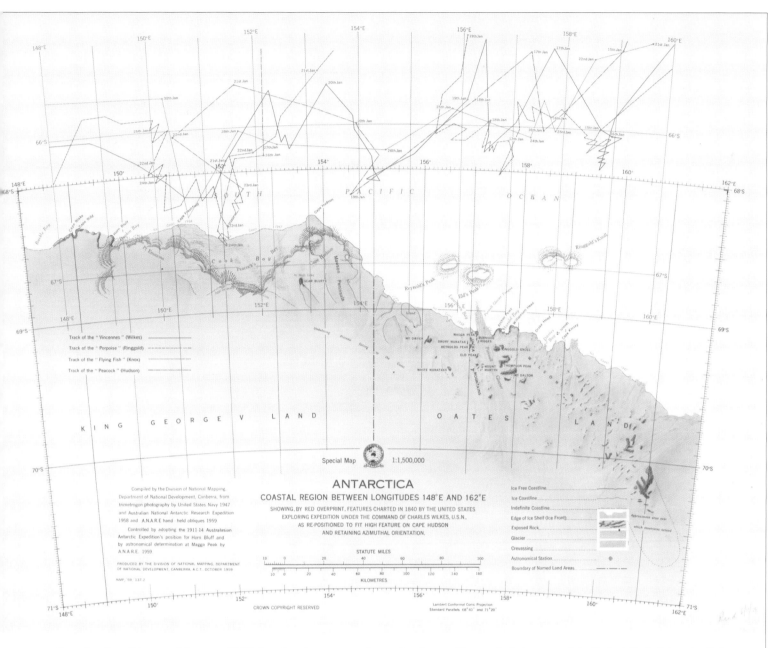

The following map labels are visible on the chart:

Track of the " Vincennes " (Wilkes)
Track of the " Porpoise " (Ringgold)
Track of the " Flying Fish " (Knox)
Track of the " Peacock " (Hudson)

Special Map   1:1,500,000

ANTARCTICA
COASTAL REGION BETWEEN LONGITUDES 148°E AND 162°E

SHOWING, BY RED OVERPRINT, FEATURES CHARTED IN 1840 BY THE UNITED STATES
EXPLORING EXPEDITION UNDER THE COMMAND OF CHARLES WILKES, U.S.N.,
AS RE-POSITIONED TO FIT HIGH FEATURE ON CAPE HUDSON
AND RETAINING AZIMUTHAL ORIENTATION.

Compiled by the Division of National Mapping,
Department of National Development, Canberra, from
trimetrogon photography by United States Navy 1947
and Australian National Antarctic Research Expedition
1958 and A.N.A.R.E hand - held obliques 1959

Controlled by adopting the 1911-14 Australasian
Antarctic Expedition's position for Horn Bluff and
by astronomical determination at Magga Peak by
A.N.A.R.E. 1959

PRODUCED BY THE DIVISION OF NATIONAL MAPPING, DEPARTMENT
OF NATIONAL DEVELOPMENT, CANBERRA, A.C.T. OCTOBER 1959

NMP. 59. 137.2

STATUTE MILES

KILOMETRES

Ice Free Coastline
Ice Coastline
Indefinite Coastline
Edge of Ice Shelf (Ice Front)
Exposed Rock
Glacier
Crevassing
Astronomical Station
Boundary of Named Land Areas

CROWN COPYRIGHT RESERVED

Lambert Conformal Conic Projection
Standard Parallels 68°40' and 71°20'

Bruce Lambert, Director of the Division of National Mapping and a member of the Australian National Antarctic Research Expeditions Planning Committee. Converting Wilkes' chart to the scale of Mawson's provisional chart, and superimposing one over the other, Lambert noted several points of alignment, notably Wilkes' Point Emmons with Mawson's Cape Wild–Horn Bluff–Cape Freshfield features, and Peacock Bay with Cook Bay.

After analysing the differences between Wilkes' original chart (sent to Ross) and results obtained by both Douglas Mawson and Phillip Law, Lambert suggested that:

> Consistent difference in latitude and the under-estimated distances from the ship to the Reynolds and Eld Peak and to Ringgold Knoll are both thought to be due to abnormal atmospheric refraction existing at the time of observation.

In *South by Northwest*, G. Allen Mawer suggests that adjustments to Wilkes' fair drawing, supplied to Ross before publication of the chart, more than likely account for the discrepancies between the initial and published version of Wilkes' chart.

Lambert and Law took their new chart to the Antarctic Symposium in Buenos Aires in 1959, before the Antarctic Treaty was signed. Vindication of Wilkes was finally accepted by the Unites States, where the news made the front page of the *New York Times*.

Mawer attempts, in part, to review both Lambert and Wilkes by analysing Wilkes' charted and published landfall coordinate readings and what Wilkes may have actually observed—land or refraction (cloud). Only future analysis using satellite imagery and more accurate instruments is likely to end the controversy.

Antarctica Coastal Region between Longitudes and Latitudes 148° E and 162° E
(showing, by red overprint, features charted in 1840 by the United States exploring expedition under the command of Captain Wilkes, USN …)
[Lambert's chart superimposing Wilkes' charts 1844–1874 to the scale of Mawson's provisional chart]
Geoscience Australia

background
R.T. Forsyth
The Aussies Estate, Willoughby (detail)
(Sydney: William Brooks & Co. Ltd, 1918)
map; 85.6 x 53.7 cm
Maps Collection; nla.map-lfsp3170

Hugh Duff & Co.
Abbotsford Estate, Parramatta River: Directly opposite Searl's Monument (details)
(Sydney: Batson & Co. Ltd, 1907)
coloured map; 34.0 x 47.8 cm folded in booklet
Maps Collection; nla.map-lfsp11

right
E.J.H. Knapp
108 Allotments the Property of T. Barker Esquire: to be Sold by Auction by Mr Blackman
(Sydney: Bakers Lithogy.
Hibernian Printing Office, 1842)
hand-coloured map; 44.1 x 60.1 cm
Maps Collection; nla.map-f873

right, below
R.B. Bate (Firm)
Label on Box of Surveying Instruments Used by Sir Thomas Mitchell during His Three Expeditions 1831–1846
Pictures Collection
nla.pic-an6393476

102

10. Urban planning

Town planning ideas

The timing of the first British settlements has left a critical and enduring legacy for town and urban planning in Australia.

The establishment of planned and orderly town centres related more to the immediate concerns of the British Government and to European ideas and institutions than to any specific understanding of the Australian landscape. The first penal settlements were established during the Enlightenment, when towns were centres for trade and defence, and a civilising influence. By the time Adelaide and Melbourne were founded, planning doctrines were more utilitarian, with the result that the complexion of both cities differed from that of earlier settlements.

The earliest colonial towns were laid out on a grid developed by the abolitionist Granville Sharp in Sierra Leone, where a society he had founded was trying to resettle American slaves. The principles outlined by Sharp were adopted by Governor Ralph Darling and put into practice by Surveyor General Thomas Mitchell. Streets were to be 66 feet (about 20 metres) wide, with main streets 80 feet (24 metres) wide, and land allotments were to be of equal size, with a balance between public and private land. However, in a dispute with Mitchell, Darling took advice from his brother-in-law Edward Dumaresq to adopt the wider streets of colonial India for many rural towns such as Braidwood.

By the time Robert Hoddle surveyed Melbourne in 1837, greater attention was being paid to symmetry, balance and regularity, and squares were devoted to open space or public buildings. As settlement grew along coastal and inland regions, towns were designed as key centres for local administration. Towns were surveyed and positioned according to the lie of the land, with roads and other likely transport options marked. Sites were set aside for a courthouse and gaol, for churches and schools, and for public use.

Compared with the relatively orderly development of townships, the rapid growth of Sydney and Melbourne, particularly during the goldrush years, created other pressing demands.

Problems involving health and congestion, safe and reliable water supplies, and the disposal of sewage confounded legislators for many years. The need to undertake (at great expense) the supply of public services led eventually to the formation of government-sponsored capital works. But, until the 1880s and 1890s, suburbs in the major cities were subdivided by individual developers, with little government intervention. The larger cities became crowded and poorly serviced centres, where infant mortality and other adverse health markers became the norm. By the middle of the nineteenth century, urban and sanitary reform in Sydney and elsewhere had become a matter of urgency, while on the fringes of cities a healthier lifestyle was promised, and the growth of train and light rail saw the beginnings of a network of public transport.

By the turn of the century, the steady growth of cities was accompanied by the construction of large public buildings, including libraries and art galleries. City residents began to question the way their environment was expanding, and in 1901 the Melbourne Congress of Engineers, Architects and Surveyors hosted the first Australian conference on post-colonial town planning. The conference considered not only the building of a federal capital but also the importance of aesthetic elements relating to the location of public buildings, 'picturesque features', and a scheme for architectural adornment. New commuter suburbs were envisaged that expressed a move away from the traditional gridiron patterns.

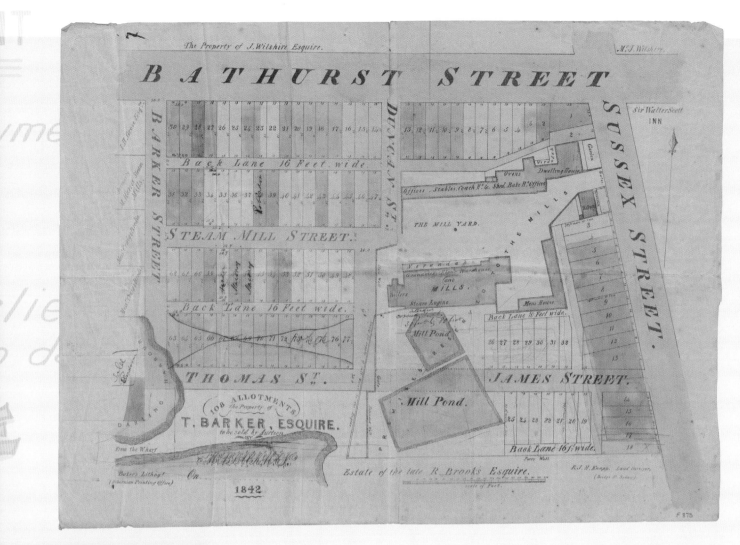

During the early years of the twentieth century, some architects and planners began to see the improved aesthetics of the city as an integral element of town planning reform. The development of the federal capital preoccupied the minds of planners for most of the first two decades of the new century, with the 137 plans submitted for the design competition providing a kaleidoscopic overview of contemporary town planning.

Walter Burley Griffin's winning design was distinctive for the way in which its geometry sensitively related to the natural terrain of the Molonglo River Valley. In his design for Canberra, Griffin was influenced by L'Enfant's plan for Washington and the principles of the 'City Beautiful' and 'Garden City' movements seen at the Chicago World's Fair. These designs integrated architecture, landscape, water features and grand processional ways.

In the same decade as the federal capital competition, town planning associations were established in each state, and large-scale urban expansion after World War I provided fresh fields for an expanded ideal of the 'garden suburb' during the interwar years. However, although boulevard parks and agricultural belts were favoured in several cities, for the most part the ideal proved to be a more useful tool with which to sell land. The period after World War II was distinguished by a 'long boom' of prosperity and full employment, a rise in living standards, a greatly expanded manufacturing industry, and an explosion in domestic consumer spending. Major public works, such as the enormous Commonwealth-funded Snowy Mountains Hydro-Electric Scheme, contributed to a rapid population increase in the 1950s and early 1960s, with almost 60 per cent of the growth of the major cities coming from immigration.

State planning institutes and planning courses were established in universities, and legislative and administrative frameworks for metropolitan strategies to address urban growth were introduced. Government policies and services supported large-scale urban housing developments, and by the end of the 1960s owner occupation had reached almost 70 per cent of all households.

'Suburban sprawl' characterised most Australian cities in the late twentieth century, although a counter-emphasis on higher-density residential development has been favoured in the urban policies of some State and local governments. Even so, expansion into the rural–urban fringe of Australian cities poses continuing problems at the intersection of environmental protection and resource management.

right
John Helder Wedge
(1793–1872)
**Map of Port Phillip from the
Survey of Mr. Wedge
and Others**
(Sydney: R. Clint, 1836)
map; 31.0 x 37.1 cm
Maps Collection
nla.map-rm3595

Robert Russell (1808–1900)
**Deputy Collector of Customs and Surveyor's
Camp, on Arrival at Port Phillip, December 1836**
watercolour; 20.0 x 26.8 cm
Pictures Collection
nla.pic-an2969814

John Helder Wedge (1793–1872)
Near Port Phillip Bay c.1883
lithograph; 7.9 x 10.6 cm
Pictures Collection
nla.pic-an8737384

104

John Helder Wedge's map of Port Phillip, 1836

Constructed from field notes made by surveyor John Helder Wedge (1793–1872) between 1835 and 1836, this is the first published map to show European settlement in the vicinity of present-day Melbourne.

Born in Cambridge, England, John Wedge and his brother Edward arrived in Launceston in 1824. John found work as an assistant surveyor and, for the next decade, surveyed near Scamander (1825), St Helens, Iron House Point (1829) and St Paul's Plains (now South Esk Valley), where in 1833 he marked out the towns of Fingal and Avoca.

In 1834, John Batman, one of the first Europeans to settle in the Melbourne area, appointed Wedge as Surveyor General of the Port Phillip Association. Wedge arrived at Port Phillip on 7 August 1835 to survey about 600 000 acres (242 811 hectares) of pastoral land, 'purchased' two months earlier by treaty from the local Aboriginal people. Wedge, however, believed

Batman's choice of settlement at Indented Head was too exposed to the wind and lacked sufficient fresh water. Within three days, he recommended an alternative site by the Yarra Yarra River that had good water above a reef that checked the tides and provided a natural basin suited to shipping. The site also appealed to John Pascoe Fawkner, a Launceston businessman who landed his party from the *Enterprise* on 29 August and set up camp.

Although this rare map, acquired by the National Library of Australia in December 2001, focuses on the Port Phillip district as a survey made on foot, Wedge also surveyed the coastal lands from Indented Head to Port Fairy for sheep pastures. He related well to the Indigenous people and mapped many local names from his field book, such as 'Weariby Yallock' (now Werribee River), 'Kondak Baarwon' (now Barwon River), 'Yowham Hills', 'Lake Modiwarra' (now Lake Modewarre), Geelong,

'Corayio' (now Corio) and 'Anaki-yoo-wam'.

His field book includes a glossary of Aboriginal words, along with a sketch of Aboriginal women collecting shellfish, depictions of the terrain and a drawing of William Buckley, an escaped convict who lived for 32 years among Aboriginal people near Geelong. Regrettably, Wedge's harmonious relations were seriously upset in July 1836 when Aboriginal men speared squatter Charles Franks and a shepherd in retaliation for their animosity and cruelty. The entire European community attended the men's funeral service and organised several reprisal attacks.

South of Mount Dromedary, the words 'Open Plains rich pasture' mark the pastoral purpose of Wedge's survey, with sheep properties allocated by lot to the 17 members of the Port Phillip Association, and 12 000 acres (4856 hectares) shown to be set

aside for a 'Mr Mann'. Wedge drew allotment 13 and, by November 1836, his nephew, Charles, had arrived with 400 sheep. But neither Lieutenant-Governor Arthur of Van Diemen's Land nor Governor Bourke in Sydney accepted the validity of the Association's treaty and all property boundaries lapsed. Wedge surveyed the route from 'the Settlement' to 'Barrabull' (now Barrabool) Hill and marked the position of Buckley's farm and the Aboriginal camps of 'Bunia Wullee' and 'Bunia Yoke'. Important map references taken from Flinders' coastal survey are Arthurs Seat, the 'strong Tide ripplings' near Point Nepean and Station Peak (now Mount Vilumnata).

The unique feature of this copy of Wedge's survey is a handwritten notation, made by the Headlam family, early leaders of the Church of England in Melbourne, to show the specific location of post-1836 dwellings (each marked by a cross). The dwellings include homes built by John and Henry Batman,

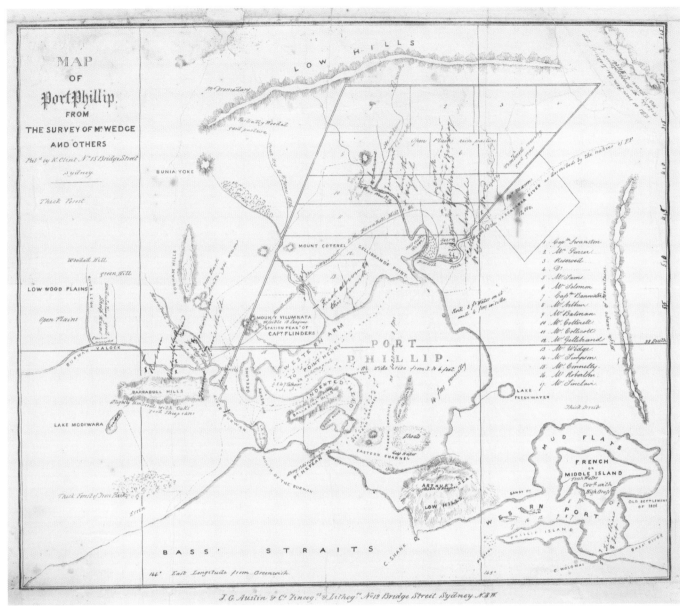

Captain William Lonsdale (the first police magistrate of Port Phillip), Anthony Cottrell (formerly Chief Constable in Launceston and then land auctioneer in Melbourne Town) and Joseph Gellibrand, the Association lawyer. The Headlam comments include the location of homes established by non-Association residents, especially in the Werribee Valley and west of Geelong. A township, surveyed as a grid plan by Robert Hoddle in 1837, was named by Governor Bourke in honour of Viscount Melbourne, Prime Minister of Great Britain from 1835 to 1841.

Following a sojourn in England, Wedge returned to Tasmania, where he served as a politician from 1855 to 1868.

Robert Russell (1808–1900)
**Melbourne from the Falls,
June 30, 1837**
watercolour; 29.7 x 43.0 cm
Pictures Collection
nla.pic-an2969818

106

William Light's survey of Adelaide, 1840

Published in London in 1840, with additional handwritten notation in 1841, this map is a record of the survey of Adelaide completed in 1837 by South Australia's first Surveyor General, Colonel William Light (1786–1839).

Light, the son of the superintendent of the East India Company at Georgetown, spent his first six years in Penang, where he had been born. Educated in England, he entered the navy in 1799 as a 'volunteer boy' but was discharged as a midshipman two years later. He escaped in 1804 from brief internment in France and in 1808, at the age of 22, joined the 4th Dragoons. Promoted to lieutenant, he served with distinction during the Peninsular War, acquiring mapping and field survey skills that placed him on the personal staff of General Wellesley (later the Duke of Wellington). He purchased his captaincy in 1814, but resigned from army service seven years later with the rank of brevet major.

Light's legal success against the East India Company for wrongful alienation of his father's property won him compensation of £20 000, a fortune that allowed him to marry and travel widely in Europe (including cruises on the Mediterranean aboard his 43-ton yacht, *Gulnare*). He later served as recruitment officer for the fledgling Egyptian navy and as first lieutenant on the paddle-steamer the *Nile*, delivered from England in 1834. The *Nile* was captained by Captain John Hindmarsh RN (1785–1860), the new commander of the Egyptian navy and later the first Governor of South Australia.

In 1835, Light was appointed Surveyor General of South Australia and, in May the following year, he arrived in the new colony to select a site for settlement.

Light found a small safe estuarine anchorage at Port Adelaide, but insufficient staff and instruments seriously handicapped his survey. In June 1838, pressure from

speculators impatient to increase the pace of land sales led the South Australian Colonisation Commissioners to insist on running surveys in place of slower, accurate trigonometrical surveys. Light and most of his staff resigned in frustration. Governor Hindmarsh had also antagonised Light, the Resident Commissioner in Adelaide, James Hurtle Fisher, and the colony's Secretary, Robert Gouger, by pushing for the entire settlement to be moved to the coast near the Murray estuary.

The colony of 5000 became paralysed, and in July 1838 Hindmarsh was recalled to London. He was replaced immediately by Lieutenant Colonel George Gawler (1795–1869), who offered the Surveyor General post to Captain Charles Sturt (1795–1869), the Murray River explorer whose report had impressed the commissioners in London. The

Colonial Office, however, had already appointed Edward Charles Frome (1802–1890) to the post and so Sturt instead took up office as Assistant Commissioner for Lands.

Gawler spent all of his private means to relieve Adelaide of acute food shortages, but the British Government dishonoured his London drafts for £270 000. In May 1841, he was replaced by Captain George Grey (1812–1898), a hostile critic of Gawler, Gouger and Sturt.

Light's highly original city plan, a square mile of streets, was surrounded by parkland, with the Governor's residence placed on the banks of the Torrens River— named after the Chairman of the Commissioners, Robert Torrens.

Light's 1841 map of Adelaide, published by John Gleddon, the South Australian Agent in London, shows that 1042 land allotments

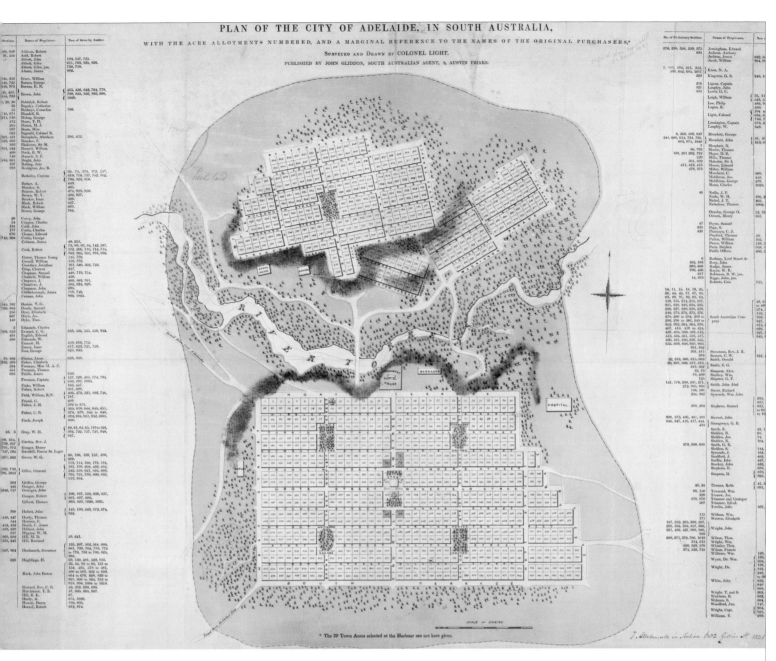

PLAN OF THE CITY OF ADELAIDE, IN SOUTH AUSTRALIA,

WITH THE ACRE ALLOTMENTS NUMBERED, AND A MARGINAL REFERENCE TO THE NAMES OF THE ORIGINAL PURCHASERS.

SURVEYED AND DRAWN BY COLONEL LIGHT.

PUBLISHED BY JOHN GLIDDON, SOUTH AUSTRALIAN AGENT, 5, AUSTIN FRIARS.

* The 29 Town Acres selected at the Harbour are not here given.

had been purchased, and the names of the original purchasers are added in the margins. The list identifies the largest landowners: John Barton Hack, 64 allotments; John Whyte, 32; Osmond Gilles, 25; Samuel Stephens, 25; Governor Hindmarsh, 23; and John Morphett, 18. The South Australian Company retained 157 allotments. The only roads out of Adelaide connected with Port Adelaide and Holdfast Bay, the freshwater site at Glenelg where Light advised Hindmarsh to land the main body of settlers.

Streets and squares were formally named on 23 May 1837. Many street names record early landholders (Angas, Brown, Finniss, Gillies, Gouger, Gover, Morphett, Sturt and Wright), with the names of the colony's leaders reserved for terraces or small parks (Strangways Terrace, Roberts Place, Mann Terrace, Kingston Terrace, Hindmarsh Square, Light Square, Hurtle Square and Whitmore Square).

Other places take their names from influential English supporters (for example, Charles Hindley MP; Lefevre; Edward Stanley-Smith, the Secretary of State for War and the Colonies; and Charles Rundle) or members of the House of Lords (Wakefield and Halifax). It was

Lord Wakefield who first proposed that revenue from the sale of Crown lands at a 'sufficient price' be used to finance colonisation. King William Street and Victoria Square honour royalty.

Distant View of the Landing Place and Iron Stores at Port Adelaide, South Australia
(London: J.C. Hailes, c.1838)
hand-coloured lithograph; 20.1 x 35.1 cm
Pictures Collection
nla.pic-an7830533

right
R.W. Stuart (1843–1914)
**Kangaroo Hunt
near Braidwood,
New South Wales 1870s**
oil on canvas; 46.5 x 68.5 cm
Pictures Collection
nla.pic-an2256919

far right
Trisha Dixon (b.1953)
**Bedervale Homestead,
Braidwood, New South Wales,
October 1999**
colour slide; 35 mm
Pictures Collection
nla.pic-an23125124

J. Roche Ardill's plan of Braidwood, 1859

This plan of Braidwood, drawn by Irish-born John Roche Ardill, is the second plan of the town on Gillamatong Creek (now Monkittee Creek), New South Wales, which was first surveyed by James Larmer according to Governor Darling's town planning principles and gazetted on 24 April 1839.

The town's name and site were taken from Braidwood Farm (2560 acres or 1036 hectares), which belonged to Dr Thomas Braidwood Wilson RN (1792–1843). A humane Scottish naval surgeon superintendent who made nine voyages between England and Australia from 1814 to 1831, Wilson took up his land grant in 1833 and, with the help of assigned convicts, dammed the creek and began breeding sheep. He is credited with bringing the first hive of European bees to Australia in 1831.

Wilson built residences to house 141 convicts on Braidwood Farm and, in his role as a justice of the peace, also built a courthouse and lockup. Land sales of half-acre lots during 1840 brought in free settlers and quickly lifted the local population to 1100 by the following year, although nearly half the residents were convicts. Wilson's neighbour, Captain John Coghill, commanded the convict ship *Mangles* during four voyages to Australia and established Bedervale Station (about 6000 acres or 2428 hectares) on land purchased in 1826. Designed by Sydney architect John Verge for £16, by 1842 Bedervale homestead, off Monkittee Street, was completed in Regency style in sandstone with convict labour, and is today an impressive National Trust building. By this time, Coghill had become director of the Bank of Australia.

During the 1840s, drought was followed by a severe rural depression and collapse of the wool industry. Coghill purchased Braidwood Farm after Wilson's death, and in 1853 his son-in-law, Robert Maddrell, inherited Bedervale and expanded the estate to 33 000 acres (13 354 hectares). Since then, single ownership of all rural land on three sides of Braidwood has effectively contained expansion of the town.

The discovery of gold in the region in 1851 attracted a rush of 15 000 prospectors. Before long, Braidwood began to expand; additional hotels and stores were built (some very temporary), a hospital was established and the first chapel constructed. Large tent camps also appeared near diggings at Jembaicumbene and Mongarlowe.

Ardill's plan shows the prosperity of Braidwood in June 1859, when the town was the sixth largest in New South Wales. Although the early lure of gold had slowed, the Braidwood–Goulburn gold escort remained important and Braidwood continued to attract investment in many fine buildings, as can be seen in Ardill's sketches on the map's margins. The oldest public house, The Doncaster Inn (1841), still stands. On Mackellar Street, the main merchants (Hendricks and Jacob) built the Victoria Store containing the post office and a dispensary, as well as the granite Albert Buildings as two storefronts. Facing Market Place Reserve, at the top of the hill (a trading area established by Wilson), were the impressive two-storey Commercial Hotel and Larmer's Beehive Store (1848). All the buildings listed in this paragraph may still be found, each with heritage classification.

Ardill also captured the appearance of the four churches, Henry Farmer's House of Content (inn), Thomas Draper's Emerald Isle (inn), Wallis' auction rooms, the Oriental Bank, Larmer's Joint Stock Bank building, the *Observer* office, Larmer's Royal Hotel and the Britannia brewery. Several fine homes, such as James Larmer's Willow Cottage, S. Walker's two-

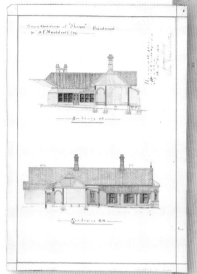

above
**Plan of Additions at 'Mona' Braidwood
for H. F. Maddrell Esq. 1901**
pen, ink & watercolour drawings;
54.4 x 37.8 cm
Pictures Collection
nla.pic-vn3415331

storey villa, and William Darke's
cottage row, still stand.

Ardill's plan outlines the floor area
of all buildings, shaded according
to whether they were built of
stone, brick or wood, or erected as
calico tents. The police paddock
and barracks for six mounted
troopers are shown, as well as
the courthouse, the school and
a teacher's residence. There are
reserves for a church and school
estate west of the town, a water
supply, a road, public recreation
areas, a livestock pound and
a cemetery (Roman Catholic,
Anglican and Presbyterian). The
120-foot (36-metre) width of
Wallace Street follows Governor
Darling's experience in colonial
India, with each street grid marked
as one square mile, a feature of
Georgian town planning (a design
opposed by Thomas Mitchell as
being 'too breezy'). The western
town boundary was surveyed
at a time when poor surveying
equipment did not allow it to be
pegged parallel to Wallace Street.

Street names pay tribute to the
first flock owners and magistrates
(Wilson, Coghill and Duncan
Mackellar, who sold Strathallan
to Coghill in 1836), a folk hero
(Wallace, of Scottish fame),
politicians (Lascelles, Cowper and
Ryrie), and geographical location
(Monkittee, Araluen and Clyde).

above
J. Roche Ardill
Plan of Braidwood
(Sydney : Allan & Wigley, 1859)
coloured map; 88.2 x 42.7 cm
Maps Collection
nla.map-tsc1

Hugh Duff & Co.
Broughton Estate, Municipality of Lane Cove,
Longueville
(Sydney: William Brooks & Co. Ltd, 1909)
coloured map; 84.8 x 51.4 cm
Maps Collection
nla.map-lfsp1384

NSW real estate sales plans, 1860–1940

The Australian dream of home ownership is not a recent phenomenon—its origins can be traced back to the 1860s.

Testament to the dream is a relatively unknown collection of about 14 000 real estate and land developer plans of land sales in Sydney and NSW regional centres from the 1860s to the 1940s.

Gathered by Sir John Ferguson and now held in the National Library, the plans are reproduced on poor-quality paper or newsprint. Often brightly coloured and with photographs or drawings of buildings or the land to be developed, they reflect the ambitions of land developers during the latter part of the nineteenth century. While most show the actual or an estimate of land prices for individual blocks, many have been annotated to reveal the realised price.

Sydney experienced its greatest period of continuous growth during the 1870s and 1880s. Several concurrent factors influenced the development. In the first instance, effective financial control of the pastoral industry was transferred to urban interests from the end of the 1860s. Land speculators, including banks, previously restricted to rural areas, saw an opportunity to invest in town land.

At the same time, the pastoral boom excluded all but the wealthy from farm ownership, leading to an alternative dream—the suburban block. Farm improvements achieved through technological developments reduced the demand for rural labour, and forced many to find urban employment.

During the 1870s and 1880s colonial governments, particularly those of the eastern states, sponsored the expansion of the rail networks across the country, together with better communication systems, including the telegraph. Unemployment in Britain also led to increased migration to Australia.

During the period, Sydney experienced an average growth of 3.6 per cent a year, which grew to 5.5 per cent between 1881 and 1891. The development of the tram during the latter part of the decade allowed suburban expansion and growth of the inner city. Railway services encouraged settlement along routes to the western suburbs such as Ashfield, Burwood and Summer Hill. Manufacturing industry followed the railways, particularly towards Parramatta, which also had the advantage of river craft to aid the transport of goods and materials. As a result, Sydney became a 'paradise for speculators in the early 1880s'.

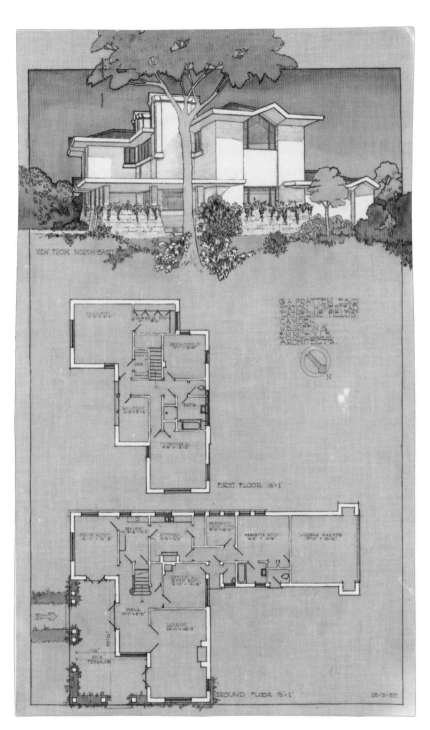

VIEW FROM NORTH-EAST

FIRST FLOOR 16'-1

GROUND FLOOR 16'-1

left
Walter Burley Griffin (1876–1937)
Perspective View and Plan of Station Homestead, for G.A. Pratten Esq., Catherine Fields, Camden, 1937
b&w photographic reproduction of perspective architectural drawing; 14.4 x 8.6 cm
Pictures Collection
nla.pic-vn3603884a-s136

below
H.J. Graham (1858–1929)
Lane Cove River, Sydney c.1884
wash drawing; 10.8 x 15.7 cm
Pictures Collection
nla.pic-an6441331

The 1890s ushered in Australia's worst depression of the nineteenth century. Banks such as Excelsior, which had flourished with the advent of the suburban land boom, were forced to close their doors or restructure with limited company operations.

There was considerable loss of business confidence, social disruption and evaporation of capital, which brought an end to the property boom for most of the decade. Attempts to develop community centres at Pitt Town, Bega and Wilberforce proved unsuccessful. The depression led to a general fall in property values, and the 'Federation drought' shook the economy of New South Wales. Meanwhile, a falling birth rate and a stop to immigration increased the number of empty houses.

By 1905, the advent of the car and an electricity supply, together with improved manufacturing output, heralded an increase in the demand for housing. Property values began to rise, with the greatest gains in the northern and eastern suburbs. More land was opened up as exclusive estates, such as the area from Centennial Park to Vaucluse, and the extension of the railway and tram services to the north encouraged the growth of suburbs such as Mosman and Lane Cove. The practice of issuing covenants ensured that the value of the houses would be in proportion to the value of the land (which was not the case in the working-class suburbs).

In 1914, the NSW State Savings Bank introduced a home loan scheme to those breadwinners earning below £400 a year and who did not already own a house. The new craze of surfing stimulated the land market along Sydney's ocean beachfront. The cycles of immigration, a rise in the birth rate and a general increase in prosperity, along with improvements to living standards, continued to stimulate the land boom as the population pushed towards the suburbs.

The Depression years, particularly 1931–1934, brought the second decline to Sydney's land boom; many left the city for the country or went overseas to seek work. As with the 1905 revival, however, manufacturing led the way and the city began to recover after 1935.

**Cycloramic View of Canberra Capital
Site, View Looking From Camp Hill**
(Sydney: John Sands, c.1911)
Pictures Collection
nla.pic-an7746421-2
nla.pic-an7746421-4
nla.pic-an7746421-5

Federal capital site map, 1909

During the decade before Federation in 1901, the depth of commercial rivalry between Sydney and Melbourne forced the colonies of New South Wales and Victoria to agree, in 1888, that a separate seat of government should be created well beyond any existing capital city and its commercial influence.

Potential sites for the federal government included places as far apart as Dubbo, Armidale, Bathurst, Goulburn and Cooma in New South Wales; Mildura and Ballarat in Victoria; and Mount Gambier, Eugowra, Naracoorte and Kingston in South Australia. Early in 1899, a meeting of colonial premiers in Melbourne accepted that NSW voters needed encouragement to favour federation (a majority 'yes' vote was only narrowly achieved a month later). To gain this support, the premiers recommended that the site should be in New South Wales, provided that it was at least 100 miles (161 kilometres) from Sydney.

The NSW Government commissioned Alexander Oliver, President of the NSW Land Appeal Court, to head an inquiry to study sites nominated by local interests. Worried by extreme drought, Oliver noted that no inspected site possessed adequate rainfall to support a city of 40 000 people. Taking into account the value of the Snowy River surplus overflow, Oliver recommended the southern Monaro district. He rejected timid adhesion to a proposed territory of 100 square miles, and enlarged the site map 10 times to fit river catchment boundaries. His first preference was to locate the future seat of government near Bombala, on a proposed railway to Sydney and Melbourne and with access to a possible naval base at Twofold Bay, a harbour second only to Port Jackson.

Oliver planted the idea of a central ornamental lake and wrote that the water feature should influence the location of the building site, with topographic depressions converted into artificial lakes as emergency water storage. He added that the mountainous background, snow-clad in winter, would relieve the monotony of large flat landscapes found elsewhere in Australia.

In 1903, as a result of political indecision and promotion of further alternative sites, the Commonwealth Minister for Home Affairs, Sir John Forrest, a surveyor, and his Inspector General of Works, Lieutenant Colonel Percy Owen, met with NSW District Surveyor, Charles Scrivener. The three men agreed that Buckley's Crossing at Dalgety in southern New South Wales formed the best site, and they proposed a three-mile lake on the Snowy River as its central feature.

Both houses of parliament favoured Dalgety, with access to the port of Eden. The site was gazetted in April 1904, but was shelved following objections from the NSW Government on the grounds that a new federal port at Twofold Bay might eventually outrank Port Jackson. A federal ballot of 11 sites concluded that the Yass–Canberra district should be chosen, and a new *Seat of Government Act* passed on 14 December 1908 identified the choice.

Prime Minister Andrew Fisher specifically requested that Scrivener should lead a Commonwealth team to mark out a territorial water catchment and determine a city site. Scrivener's report of 22 May 1909 rejected much of the Yass district as too dry or too windy, and instead focused southwards on the Cotter, Molonglo and Queanbeyan catchments as a proposed boomerang-shaped federal territory of 2630 square kilometres.

Scrivener identified four possible city sites, which were reduced to two after Charles Caswell, a NSW engineer, completed plans for water and sewerage provisions (the National Library holds the

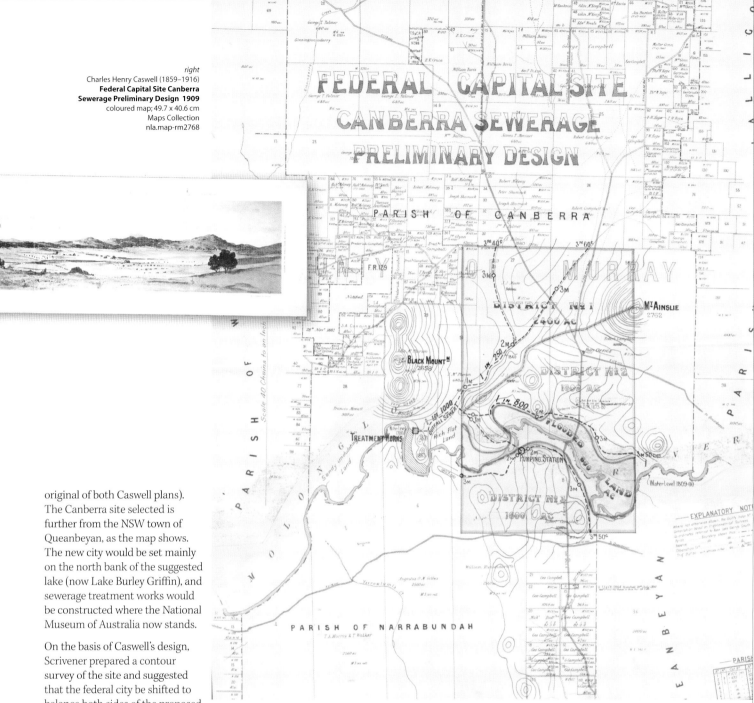

right
Charles Henry Caswell (1859–1916)
**Federal Capital Site Canberra
Sewerage Preliminary Design 1909**
coloured map; 49.7 x 40.6 cm
Maps Collection
nla.map-rm2768

original of both Caswell plans). The Canberra site selected is further from the NSW town of Queanbeyan, as the map shows. The new city would be set mainly on the north bank of the suggested lake (now Lake Burley Griffin), and sewerage treatment works would be constructed where the National Museum of Australia now stands.

On the basis of Caswell's design, Scrivener prepared a contour survey of the site and suggested that the federal city be shifted to balance both sides of the proposed lake, with Parliament House to be on a southern hill. Scrivener's topographic map accompanied the site recommendation presented to Parliament on 19 June 1909 but, aware that parliamentarians had rejected Canberra as a nomination only six months earlier (before Yass–Canberra was selected), it avoided reference to the name.

The absence of names led to much public speculation and attracted suggestions such as Federalia,

Boomerang City, Eucalypta, Kookemuroo, Gonebroke, Swindleville and Syd-Mel-Ad-Per-Bris-Ho. Caswell later recalled a wager with Scrivener who, convinced that politicians would never agree to the name 'Canberra', offered Caswell his horse as a wager. It is known that Scrivener subsequently took to riding a motorcycle.

left
William James Mildenhall
(1891–1962)
**Main Trunk Sewer
Under Construction,
Yarralumla c.1920s**
b&w photograph
Pictures Collection
nla.pic-an11030057-389

Richard Clough (b.1921)
Design, Construction and Landscaping of Lake Burley Griffin and Adjacent National Areas of Canberra. Walter Burley Griffin. Perspective. View from the Summit of Mt. Ainslie
35mm colour slide;
Pictures Collection
nla.pic-an14324452-20

114

J.T.H. Goodwin's manuscript map of Canberra, 1916

Early planning for the 'seat of government' of Australia followed a long and tortuous process, from debate over the idea of a federal capital during the latter part of the nineteenth century and selection of a site, to a controversial international design competition in 1912 that awarded first prize to American Walter Burley Griffin (1876–1937).

The *Commonwealth of Australia Constitution Act 1900* required that the federal capital be in the state of New South Wales, not less than 100 miles (160 kilometres) from Sydney.

There was also an element of an aesthetic landscape in the city's setting. Recommended by Charles Scrivener in 1909, the Canberra site was an 'amphitheatre of picturesque hills with an outlook towards the north and north-east, well sheltered from both southerly and westerly winds'.

A copy of Scrivener's topographic survey of the seat of the

government territory was included in the set of base plans issued in 1911 to contestants participating in the international federal city design competition. The winning design, by architects Walter Burley Griffin and his wife, Marion, of Chicago, incorporated landscape elements of the US 'City Beautiful' and English 'Garden City' ideals. It is likely, however, that the topographic orientation and organic themes also appealed to the Federal Capital Designs Board.

Walter Burley Griffin, who was appointed Federal Capital Director of Design and Construction in 1913, ran into numerous management problems, which were not helped by his several design changes and an alternative Commonwealth Board of Works plan. Griffin's 1918 'final plan' achieved consensus and was gazetted in 1925 after formation in 1921 of the Federal Capital Advisory Committee. In its final report for 1926, the committee noted:

The decision to proceed on the lines of the Board's plan was subsequently reviewed, and Mr Griffin's plan was substituted for it …

The Committee noted the various stages of the development of this design, as indicated in the Schematic Plan (scale 400 feet to an inch) presented to the Minister for Home Affairs in 1915—the larger Contour Plan (scale 200 feet to an inch) which was approved and signed by the Minister for Home Affairs on the 3rd November, 1916, and the plan of the City and Environs (scale 800 feet to an inch) bearing the date of the 2nd January, 1918.

At the Committee's suggestion the Minister approved and arranged for the reproduction of these plans by lithograph in order that the originals might be placed in safe custody for retention as valuable documents.

All but the largest scale map—known as the Goodwin manuscript map, named after the

Commonwealth Surveyor General and member of the Federal Capital Advisory Committee, Colonel John Thomas Hill Goodwin—were reissued as printed lithographs.

Printed on six sheets, the hand-drawn map measures more than three metres by four metres. Its scale allows detail as small as the assignment of allotments within each section, along with roads and the limit of the 1891 flood line. The Griffin concept of a suburban railway, shown here, was largely abandoned.

116

11. Military mapping
Naval hydrographic surveys and army field mapping

European settlement of the Australian continent towards the end of the eighteenth century created not only a penal colony but also a significant military and strategic centre. Australia's earliest military surveys and maps were of the continent's coastline, for all British naval officers of the eighteenth century were trained in surveying and mapping techniques.

Lieutenant George Raper and Captain John Hunter, both of whom sailed aboard HMS *Sirius* in the First Fleet, provided the first maps of the coastline and detailed hydrographic surveys of Port Jackson. Over the next 20 years, other naval officers, notably Matthew Flinders and Philip Parker King, were to chart the coastline in more detail and establish the base on which coastal surveying continues.

British ships charted in Australian waters until 1920, when the Royal Australian Navy assumed responsibility, building a significant record of maritime charting and safe passage in Australian waters, and paving the way for the beginnings of Australian coastal shipping.

Due to cost constraints in the 1930s, hydrographic surveying was virtually abandoned, and from 1939 to 1941 the survey branch of the Navy was dispersed. Following World War II, the Australian Government endorsed the Navy's responsibility for hydrographic surveying and charting, and instituted a 25-year program.

Throughout the 1960s and 1970s, developments in mineral exploration and exports encouraged more deep-draught ships to visit Australian ports. These vessels required renewed emphasis on the quality and accuracy of surveys. The introduction of the Laser Airborne Depth Sounder in 1993 has had a considerable impact on the detail, quality and rate of coverage, with more than 100 000 square kilometres of ocean now surveyed.

The first land-based mapping was undertaken by surveyors with British military backgrounds who brought considerable experience and ingenuity to the Australian colonies. Men such as John Oxley, Thomas Mitchell, William Light and others surveyed the lands, providing settlers with reliable boundaries.

In the nineteenth century, colonial survey departments were concerned almost exclusively with producing maps of property registration, and little topographic mapping was done. Topographic surveys became a basic tool in planning infrastructure and resource exploitation. After Federation, the Commonwealth began to produce topographic maps, but progress was slow. The establishment in 1910 of the Survey Section of the Royal Australian Engineers saw a coordinated program, and in 1911 a military-mapping conference proposed topographic mapping of Australia at one inch to one mile (1:63 360).

In 1914, the Survey Section established a five-mile baseline and carried out the first triangulation, comprising 1840 square miles at Sunbury, north-west of Melbourne. From 1918 onwards, four sheets, on average, of one inch to the mile topographic maps were produced annually using the plane-table survey method.

Aerial photography (provided by the Royal Australian Air Force) was first introduced in the 1920s to supplement the ground trigonometrical survey, and by the mid-1930s aerial photographs replaced plane-tabling as the basis for map production.

In 1935, the newly established Commonwealth Survey Committee proposed a national mapping scheme serving both defence and civilian purposes. Australia had recently adopted the transverse Mercator projection and applied

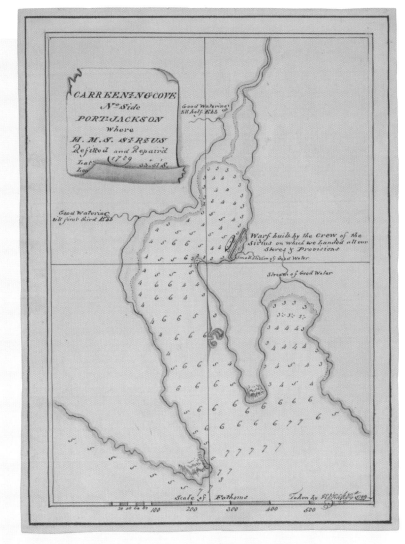

George Raper (1769–1797)
**Carreening Cove No. Side Port Jackson where
H.M.S. *Sirius* Refitted and Repair'd 1789**
coloured manuscript map; 20.3 x 14.4 cm
Maps Collection
nla.map-rm3459

the British system for its national grid. Further improvements were made in photogrammetry techniques, giving greater resolution and allowing for more accurate map-building. By 1939, triangulation connecting bases from Queensland to South Australia had been carried out.

During World War II, most resources had been transferred to overseas requirements though, with arrival of the war in the Pacific, an emergency mapping program over much of Australia was undertaken. In January 1945, the National Mapping Council replaced the Commonwealth Survey Committee. The Royal Australian Survey Corps undertook a series of projects, including the first topographic mapping for the Snowy Mountains Hydro-Electric Scheme. Subsequently, the Corps focused on the topographic mapping of Australia at 1:250 000, replacing the technique of fair drawing with scribing with use of tellurometers (for measuring

distances in microwaves), theodolites and helicopters.

Throughout the 1950s and 1960s, the Survey Corps was involved in developing its military skills to Australia's north. Joint mapping activities with the Americans followed the ANZUS Treaty in 1952, and a New Guinea Survey Unit was raised in 1954. During the 1950s, many aspects of military mapping changed, and in 1956 metric scales were adopted in line with standardisation agreements.

In 1966, a survey unit was sent to Vietnam to undertake surveys of the bases and maps for patrols. Four years later, a cooperative topographic mapping venture with the Indonesian and Papua New Guinea governments began to produce maps at 1:250 000 to the denser 1:50 000 scale. In 1982, the 1:100 000 Australian topographic mapping program, which had begun in the early 1970s, was completed (covering approximately 50 per cent of the Australian

mainland). The Survey Corps launched an ambitious 1:50 000 Australian topographic program, and published aeronautical charts for the Royal Australian Air Force (Joint Operation Graphics—Air).

During the 1970s, the Survey Corps also began employing digital mapping systems. The installation in 1976 of Automap 1 brought greater utilisation of geographical information in digital form. Automap 2 added capabilities in presenting geographical information and, by the mid-1980s, geographical products included not only maps but also data in various formats for use in command and control systems, weapons systems and terrain modelling.

After a series of government reviews, the National Mapping Council was disbanded in 1986. In the 1990s, Survey Corps mapping staff were transferred to a new government organisation, the

Army Topographic Support Establishment. The 1:50 000 topographic program was refocused on northern Australia.

Concurrent advances in data collection methods—notably, digital imagery collected by satellites, airborne platforms, unmanned aerial vehicles and other methods—has revolutionised topographic mapping. Rather than being just a picture of a surface feature, imagery also has the characteristic of identifying the location of imaged features. In this sense, imagery is a geospatial (mapped) as well as photographic information source.

Since 2000, responsibility for the collection, processing, dissemination and archiving of geospatial imagery used by the Australian Defence Force and other government agencies has been invested in the Defence Imagery and Geospatial Organisation (DIGO).

Charles Louis Gabriel (1857–1927)
The Seventh Light Horse, Gundagai, World War 1
glass negative
Pictures Collection; nla.pic-an8526479-245

W.L. Vernon,
Map of District
North of the Hunter River
(Sydney: W.A. Gullick,
Government Printer, 1907)
map on linen; 44.0 x 74.5 cm
Maps Collection
nla.map-f909

Australian Light Horse map of north of the Hunter River, 1907

Printed as a lithograph at a scale of one inch to one mile, this map is a rare example of cartography used to train volunteer mounted troops long before World War I.

The map was produced in 1907 by the NSW Government Printer to show a portion of the Paterson Valley where it joins the Hunter River. It was 'specially prepared for April manoeuvres' of the 2nd Brigade of the Australian Light Horse near the NSW towns of West Maitland, Morpeth, Raymond Terrace and Seaham. It is primarily a location map, containing very few topographic features.

All officers and a quarter of the ordinary ranks were drawn from the Commonwealth Militia Forces, but most of the troops at the time required the fundamentals of military drill. The Brigade's three regiments were the Hunter River Lancers, the Northern River Lancers and the New England Light Horse, each comprising about 500 men, some of whom

later served in Palestine during World War I.

Australia's history of mounted militia dates from 1846, following a reduction of the NSW Garrison to help fight the Maori Wars. After the withdrawal of British troops, the colony was expected to raise its own volunteers, but Crown funds became available only after the outbreak of the Crimean War in 1854.

In 1863, a resurgence of volunteer enlistment supported the Mounted Rifle detachment (New South Wales), the Royal Volunteer Cavalry Regiment (later renamed the Prince of Wales Light Horse Hussars in honour of the marriage of Edward), an amalgamation of the Castlemaine Dragoons, the Kyneton Mounted Rifles and the Victorian Yeomanry Cavalry, two troops of Mounted Rifles (Queensland), four troops of the Adelaide Mounted Rifles and a troop each in Perth and Launceston.

Patriotism abroad led to the formation of a contingent sent to the Sudan in 1885, and in 1889 the Australian colonies offered troops for the war in South Africa. Following the British declaration of the Boer War on 11 October 1899, Australia committed 838 officers, 15 327 troopers and 16 314 horses to the conflict. The war demonstrated a considerable difference between Australian-bred horses and English army horses. 'Walers' exported from New South Wales after the late 1850s as remounts for British troops in India appear to have been developed from a variety of stock, thanks mainly to the interest of Irish–Australians west of Yass in tough, wiry stockhorses, immortalised by 'Banjo' Paterson for their stamina and the skills of their riders (Paterson's father and uncle initiated such exports).

To Australian eyes, the great round-hipped English cavalry chargers and hunters looked lumbering and underbred, and

yet they could carry much heavier saddles and equipment at an average pace of 13 kilometres per hour all day. At £40 per head, they were more expensive than the weedier but faster Australian mounts, which cost £12 and were less susceptible to illness or starvation.

By 1905, all colonial militia had been restructured into eight Light Horse brigades totalling 18 regiments. Mounted troops formed two categories. Horsemen

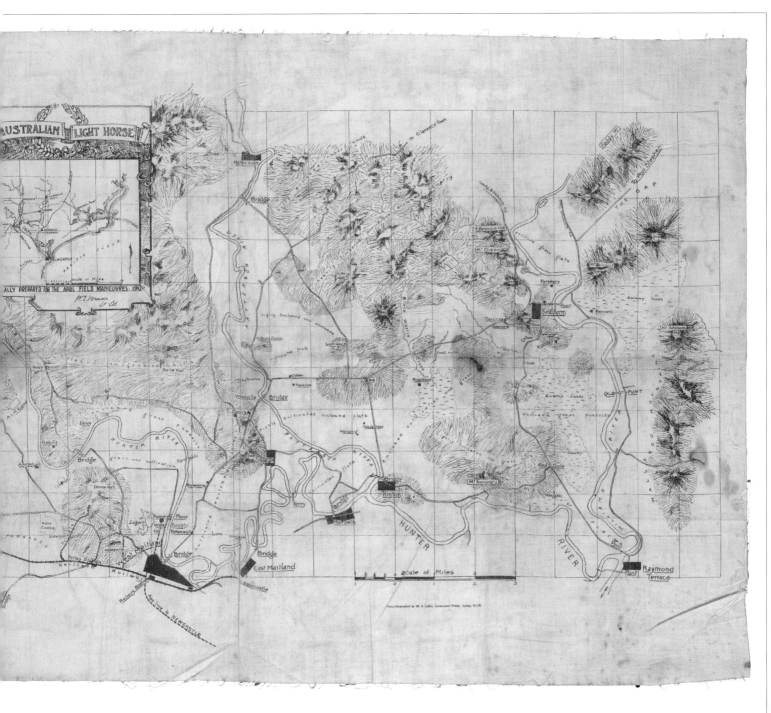

(for example, the Light Horse) were trained to fight on foot, whereas Mounted Infantry were described in the Mounted Service Manual as 'soldiers temporarily provided with increased powers of locomotion'. The first Defence Bill of 1908 prompted Lord Kitchener to advise that Australian forces be increased to 80 000, with the compulsory training of Citizen Forces extended from age 20 to 25. The Mounted Service Manual of 1910 stated that 'each troop should be composed of men raised in the same locality', on the grounds that 'men will naturally fight better and with more confidence among those whom they know and trust rather than among strangers'. Heavy casualties of troops from single districts during the Gallipoli campaign led to reconsideration of this advice.

When Britain declared war against Germany in 1914, Prime Minister Andrew Fisher pledged Australia's support 'to the last man and the last shilling'. As many as 16 Light Horse regiments saw action during World War I and were considered 'the national arm of Australian defence'.

In some instances, the wives of Light Horse officers followed their husbands to serve as nurses in field hospitals. Following the retreat from Gallipoli, a number of Light Horse actions in Palestine included the battle of Romani, action at Magdhaba and the successful heroic charge of 800 horsemen against artillery and entrenched machine guns at Beersheba. Australia contributed 160 000 horses to the war. Due to quarantine restrictions, however, none returned.

**Sgt Jack Cullen with Plane Table
at Wonthaggi, c.1921**
Courtesy R. Morris and *Mapmakers of
Fortuna: A History of the Army Survey
Regiment* by Valerie Lovejoy (Bendigo,
Vic.: Ex-Fortuna Survey Association
Incorporated, 2003)

right
Anglesea (Sheet 5)
Royal Australian Survey Corps Plane
Table Surveys Special Collection
Maps Collection
nla.cat-vn1493014

120

Plane-table surveys, 1910–1936

Before Federation in 1901, topographic mapping in Australia was uncommon. The colonial governments attended primarily to cadastral mapping of surveyed property boundaries, so that land allocation could keep up with the rapid push for pastoral land and new settlements.

Following the formation of the Australian Intelligence Corps in 1909, Colonel William Throsby Bridges, with the assistance of Lieutenant Colonel Charles Frederick Close of the British Geographical Section, General Staff (War Office), devised a program of providing tactical maps as detailed recordings of landforms around each state capital.

Under the plan, the scale of the maps was set at one mile to the inch (1:63 360), with sheet coverage of half a degree longitude by a quarter of a degree latitude. Colonel Close also recommended that contoured sheets drawn by

the plane-table method should be compiled, based on triangulation without field books or compilation sketches.

The plane-table consisted of a perfectly flat rectangular board, which could be rotated, attached to a waist-high tripod and set so that the tripod was stable and the board surface lay in a horizontal plane. A paper sheet containing the plot of the survey control points for the area to be mapped was then attached to the board. Once the table was levelled, work commenced with the aid of a sighting vane or alidade, a clinometer for measuring angles and a compass needle. With the additional aid of an aneroid barometer to measure height distances and some mathematical competency, it was then possible to compile a map in the field. Such surveys were best compiled in open and rolling country devoid of heavy vegetation or limited by very flat country. Without assistance from other tools, plane-table

surveys persisted in Australia until 1926, with the introduction of aerial photography extending use of the method until 1936.

By March 1910, the Survey Section of the Royal Australian Engineers had begun recruiting draftsmen, among them John J. Raisbeck, who rose to the rank of Lieutenant Colonel and worked in map drawing and general cartography until his retirement in 1943. Over the following years, the plane-table method was used to compile a number of tactical or manoeuvre maps in Victoria, Tasmania and South Australia. It was during this period that Raisbeck produced the first of the surveys that formed the basis of the new military one-mile topographic map sheets, the Cowes sheet, which covered Victoria's Westernport Bay from Cranbourne to Phillip Island. Compiled by Raisbeck, the design of the sheet became the standard for the next 30 years. Today, the National Library holds a collection of 195 plane-table surveys,

representing 32 map sheets dating from 1910 to 1936.

Surveys also began in Tasmania, the Newcastle area and the federal capital territory, but work was impeded by the absence of triangulation surveys until 1914. On 3 July 1915, a notice appeared in the Commonwealth *Gazette* announcing that the Survey Section was to become the Survey Corps, a separate part of the Royal Australian Engineers. The outbreak of World War I effectively halted any further surveying until 1920.

Three military survey sections in the field—one in each of the eastern states of Queensland, New South Wales and Victoria— concentrated on mapping the coastal areas, particularly around each capital city. In 1924, the acquisition of a larger-capacity process camera for map reproductions up to 36 inches by 26 inches (91.5 centimetres by 66 centimetres) allowed the

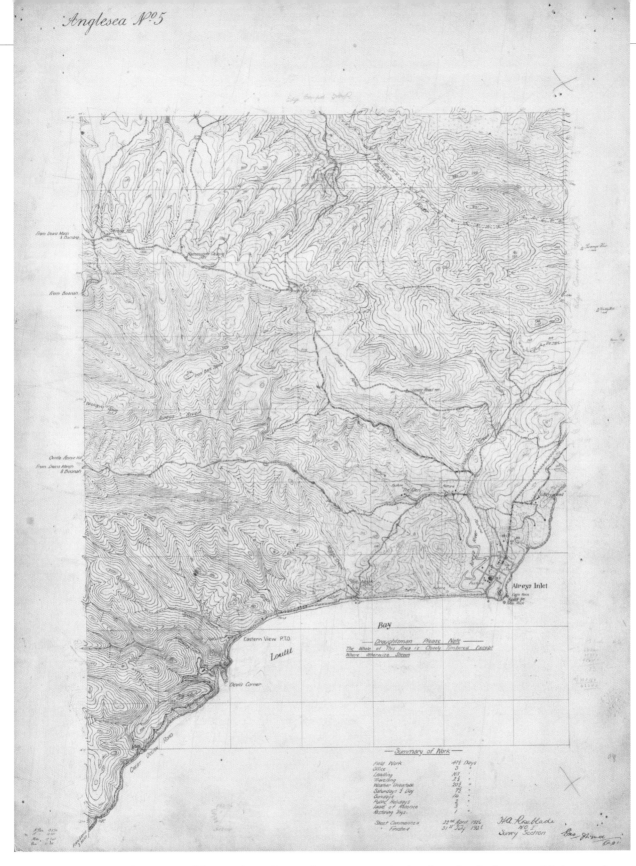

production of the one-mile topographic sheet in one piece. In the same year, plane-table field sheets were compiled at a scale of two inches to the mile (1:31 680) to improve detail. The introduction of the use of zinc plates under the sheets in 1928 considerably improved the stability of the table during the compilation phase.

In 1926, aerial photography was introduced to assist in topographic surveying, but the outbreak of World War II revealed that more than 90 per cent of Australia was not covered by military topographic maps. A vastly expanded Survey Corps drew on aerial photography as the primary source for an emergency mapping program.

left
Wolfgang Sievers (1913–2007)
**Geologists Examining Aerial Survey Photographs
in Mt. Isa, Queensland 1979**
coloured photograph; 25.1 x 20.1 cm
Pictures Collection
nla.pic-an22920062

right, above
**Two Aeroplanes on the Airfield, an Ex-Dutch
Lockheed 12 on the Left, and a C-54 Douglas DC-4 on
the Right, RAAF Base Fairbairn, Canberra, ACT, 1944**
gelatin silver photograph; 7.9 x 11.4 cm
Pictures Collection
nla.pic-an23529650

right
Royal Australian Air Force
Sydney Survey 1928
b&w remote sensing image;
19.0 x 24.0 cm
Maps Collection
MAP Aerial Photo Collection

Australian aerial photographs, 1919–1994

The earliest known Australian aerial photograph in the National Library of Australia's collection was taken from a dirigible over Sydney in 1919. The main collection of aerial photographs, however, began in 1928, with flights over Sydney and over Christmas Island in the Indian Ocean.

The impetus for a systematic aerial survey program of the nation came from a Royal Australian Air Force officer, Flight Lieutenant Gerald Packer, who trained in aerial survey with the Royal Air Force in Britain during 1926. Among the techniques Packer learned was the Arundel Method, which produced plots from aerial photographs. By laying out overlapping aerial photographs in strips, or flight runs, and then photographing the layout, the distortions caused by aircraft tilt and terrain could be rectified by graphical means.

On his return to Australia, Packer taught pilots the method and became the Royal Australian Air Force chief adviser on aerial survey matters. Aerial surveying began in 1929 over the Moss Vale–Kiama area, and a similar revision survey was conducted in the following year over the western suburbs of Melbourne. In 1930, the technique was adopted for topographic survey and the Albury sheet became the first map compiled from both plane-tabling and aerial photographs. The technique not only saved time and money, but also revealed problems with the existing trigonometrical surveys of New South Wales and Victoria in determining the precise position of control points within map boundaries.

Measures to resolve the problems included the adoption of Alexander Clarke's calculation of the size and shape of the Earth, published in 1858 ('figure of the Earth'), as the mathematical base for plotting all geodetic

coordinates. Difficulties with print quality led to Royal Australian Air Force consultation with the Royal Australian Engineers Survey Section on the direction and length of the photographic flight runs before aerial work began. In 1936, production of the one-mile topographic series, derived totally from aerial survey, began with publication of the Sale (Victoria) 1:63 360 topographic sheet.

Aerial photography for mapping purposes was also extended to external territories. In 1962, the Topographic Squadron of the Survey Regiment flew to Papua New Guinea to carry out a mapping program and establish geodetic control over the territory. New equipment, including the radar air profile recorder and the Aerodist distance measuring kit, enabled more accurate profiling of mountainous terrain, essential in determining heights from the photographs and in plotting contours.

The aircraft-mounted Aerodist, a form of tellurometer (an instrument that measures distances using microwaves), constantly transmitted microwaves to two ground stations simultaneously, allowing distances between them to be accurately determined. From 1972 to 1974, a new operation—Operation Skai Piksa—carried out a systematic survey over the country, resulting in the publication in 1980 of the first metric national topographic map series, the Papua New Guinea 1:100 000 topographic survey. From 1989 to 1994, further fieldwork and aerial surveys were conducted to produce 1:50 000 topographic survey maps along the PNG and Irian Jaya border.

Over the next decade, the Royal Australian Air Force conducted aerial surveys on behalf of the Indonesian Government over Sumatra and western New Guinea (Irian Jaya), the Moluccas and island groups south of Singapore,

and in the South China Sea. Aero-triangulation of the aerial photography was carried out by the Australian Army Survey Regiment, and returned to the Indonesian army for plotting and publication of maps of the areas.

right
Arthur G. Foster
Aerial View of Sydney
[between 1920 and 1945]
b&w glass negative; 16.5 x 21.5 cm
Pictures Collection
nla.pic-vn3105664

far right
Harold Cazneaux (1878–1953)
Wheat Silos, Darling Harbour 1920s
b&w photograph; 30.4 x 39.7 cm
Pictures Collection
nla.pic-an2383859

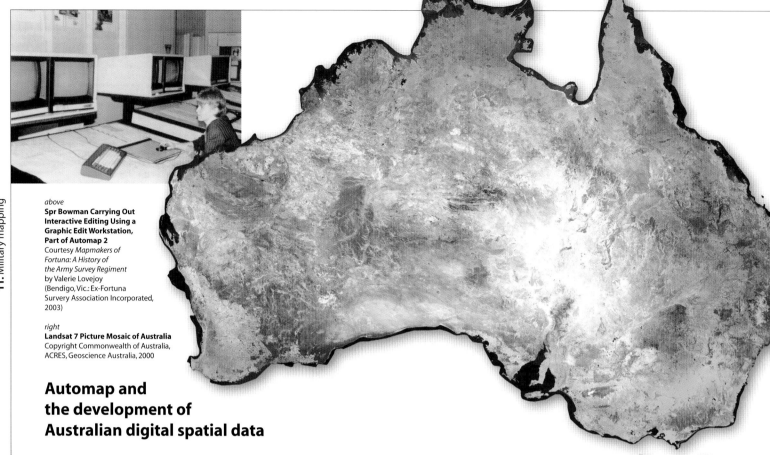

Automap and
the development of
Australian digital spatial data

When it acquired Automap 1 in 1976, the Australian Army Survey Regiment became the first cartographic agency in Australia to take advantage of new computing technology for mapping.

Conceived as a three-phase project to introduce digital mapping techniques to the Survey Corps, the Automap program was an integrated mapping system comprising photogrammetric equipment, visual display units and computing interfacing plotters.

The most significant aspect of Automap 1 was its flexibility and speed of operations; it allowed a draughtsman to scribe a map sheet in a few hours with a blind digitiser (that is, no screen), compared to five weeks by hand. The importance of the system lay not in the number of sheets produced but in the skills and experience it provided for the Corps to proceed to the next step. The system initiated automated cartography in Australia and encouraged future

development by government and commercial agencies in Australia and overseas.

Between 1976 and 1981, when Automap 2 was introduced, further refinements and developments were made, including changes to training methods. The distinction between cartographer and surveyor slowly began to disappear, while new trades that combined both skills and embraced the new technology, such as the cartographic technician, emerged. Other trades involved in the production of maps, lithography and photography were also replaced.

The contract for Automap 2, awarded to a US firm, Intergraph Corporation, resulted in the expansion of the capabilities of the first system in data capture, computing power and data handling, specifically for the 1:50 000 topographic mapping project. Interactive graphics as a production tool were introduced

and the system became almost totally digital—data could be processed and manipulated within the Corps network by inter-computer communication. The system, installed by August 1983, allowed the presentation of geographical information products in map-sheet form and terrain models, along with other products for use in command and control systems, and weapons systems.

Production rates had been stipulated as part of the contract for Automap 2 but, by 1985, acceptance testing found that two of the three subsystems did not perform satisfactorily, resulting in only 30 per cent of the required output. Intergraph Corporation was unable to develop the software required, leading to a significant downturn in army mapping output: in 1985–1986 the section produced 153 new maps, compared with 303 the previous year. In-house Army Survey Corps software development finally resolved the problems, leading to a significant

increase in the production of new maps from 1987.

While the Survey Corps was developing Automap systems, other agencies, notably the Australian Hydrographic Service, the Division of National Mapping and several state land departments, were also applying digital cartography. In the private sector, developments in digital data management handling were also gathering momentum. During the 1980s, software was developed that allowed query and analysis of geospatial data. Geospatial Information Systems offered the ability to manipulate data from a variety of sources, to analyse it and to visualise the results. Today, much geospatial data collected for military purposes involves remote sensing equipment, and is the responsibility of the Defence Imagery and Geospatial Organisation (DIGO), which provides maps, charts and digital

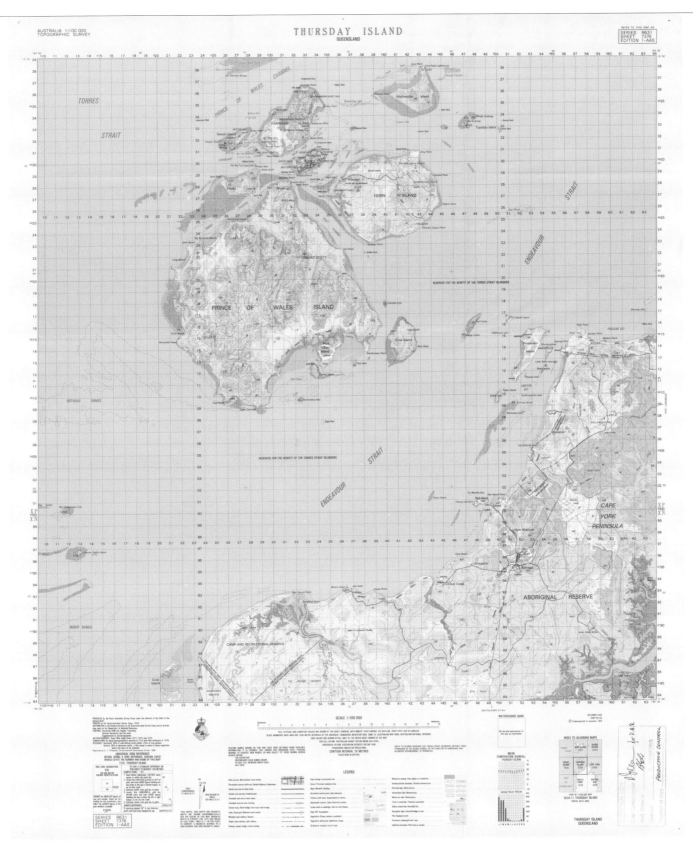

THURSDAY ISLAND
QUEENSLAND

topographic support to the Australian Defence Force. Remote sensing and imagery analysis are growing disciplines which use some of the most sophisticated science and technology available. DIGO performs complex analysis of imagery collected by a range of sensory equipment and facilities, and visualisation products in support of military, Department of Defence and wider government customers.

Australia. Division of National Mapping
Thursday Island
(Canberra: Division of National Mapping, 1978)
MAP G8960 s100
Geoscience Australia

12. Overland transport
Overcoming the tyranny of distance

above
G. E. Peacock (b.1806)
First Australian Railway, July 3rd 1850
(Sydney: J. Allan, c.1850)
hand-coloured lithograph; 34.1 x 50.0 cm
Pictures Collection
nla.pic-an9897183

left
Thomas Foster Chuck (d.1898)
River Murray, Echuca, Victoria
[between 1870 and 1879]
albumen photograph; 22.1 x 29.0 cm
Pictures Collection
nla.pic-an23378338

For three-quarters of a century after settlement, Australia's colonies relied on muscle—human and animal—to power their overland transport needs.

Early British settlers followed tracks laid down over centuries by local Aboriginal people. There are numerous examples of Aboriginal guides leading explorers along traditional pathways or chains of water sources. In some cases, major vehicular thoroughfares followed Aboriginal tracks that once served as trading routes between grasslands, hunting grounds or bountiful fishing areas.

Thanks to a shortage of pack animals in early colonial New South Wales, and to contemporary notions of punishment, convicts were sometimes required to haul considerable loads. At the time there were few carriages, or even roads, so horses did little harness work.

Roadworks were a priority of Governor Lachlan Macquarie,

who set the tone by going about town in a splendid carriage drawn by four horses. As roads were developed and settlement spread around Sydney, coaches and harness horses were imported. Bullocks were better suited for heavy haulage on the poor roads, so heavier breeds of horses, such as Clydesdales and Shires, came later.

The bullock team was essential for the frontier or anywhere beyond the reach of formed roads; early explorers were inclined to use donkeys, mules and horses as pack and draught animals. Where roads existed, draught horses began to replace bullocks from as early as the 1830s, and by the 1850s more manoeuvrable 'pony wagons' were being fitted with springs. The introduction of the light American Conestoga wagon in the 1880s particularly suited hawkers and drovers. At the other end of the scale, the giant flat-top wagon, which carried loads of up to 32 tons, was especially effective for

long-distance bullock transport of wool and wheat.

An alternative to road haulage was the paddle-steamer. The first service was introduced in 1831 to ease the burden of transporting passengers and freight between Sydney and the Hunter River region. Paddle-steamers began to appear along the Murray and Darling rivers during the 1850s. They opened up the western districts of New South Wales, and so the volume of trade between coast and inland increased enormously. Paddle-steamers towed barges carrying supplies to pastoralists upriver, to the Victorian gold-diggings and to newly established towns, and returned laden with wool. As the volume and value of river transport grew, the building of the steamers became a major enterprise, and the development of port towns such as Echuca and Wagga Wagga provided a stimulus to agriculture and other industries.

Among the gold-seekers in Victoria were a number of Americans who had worked for Wells Fargo and Adams Express Co. in the United States. Coach services were in operation in the Australian colonies as early as the 1820s, and by the 1830s coaches were being built in Sydney. In construction, they followed English design, with metal-bound wheels and steel springs. In 1853, Americans Freeman Cobb, John Peck, James Swanton and John Lamber imported several American coaches, which were more suited to Australian conditions than the vehicles of English design. They commenced services from Melbourne to Sandridge (Port Melbourne) in 1854, and later to the goldfields. Cobb & Co.'s coaches were virtually the only rapid means of transport to and from the mining areas, and the company soon returned a steady profit. Although there were soon competitors, the Cobb & Co. service expanded into New South

Wales and Queensland in the following decades. Particularly in back country not covered by rail, coach services were partly instrumental in opening up these areas for settlement by establishing reliable communication between them and the centres of supply.

From the time it first appeared in Australia in the 1850s, the railway made the biggest impact on early overland transport. By the late 1870s, Australia's railway system had approached maturity: in New South Wales and Victoria, a few lines became extensive networks; similar growth took place in South Australia and Queensland; and even the sparsely populated colonies of Tasmania and Western Australia opened their first lines. The annual growth in goods tonnage in New South Wales increased for a decade from 1878, and passenger traffic quadrupled to 14 881 604 in 1888.

The railway boom was part of a wider upturn in the Australian colonies. It was the era of Melbourne's land boom and the heyday of European colonial expansion. Rail proved a good investment. British capital flooded into Australia, where almost all railways were built by colonial governments, with capital raised in London in the form of government-guaranteed bonds.

While the boom affected all Australian colonies, there were considerable differences between railway systems, including rail gauges, across the land. The 1890s depression, the worst of the 19th century, dramatically halted the spread of roads and railways. An international financial crisis, together with falling wool prices, dampened the entire economy. The railway system appeared to have reached its logical limits. With the exception of Western Australia, which was experiencing a boom around Kalgoorlie, many railways built during the late 1880s held dubious financial prospects.

For the years after Federation, Australia's capital cities grew rapidly. The processes of urbanisation, and suburbanisation, required more accessible forms of transport. While rail and tramways were embraced during the twentieth century, competition emerged from the roads. From the 1920s, motor buses began to compete with tramcars and rail, but it was the private motor car that later typified Australian transport (in 1919, only about five per cent of all motor vehicles were used for pleasure).

Against this background, motor vehicle registration, as we know it today, was introduced in each state to provide for the construction and maintenance of an effective road system. At first the system was aimed solely at providing roads for trade, commerce and development—the widespread use of motor vehicles was not envisaged—but circumstances would soon change. In 1914, about 37 000 vehicles were registered

nationally, with the number rising to 571 000 in 1930.

The late 1930s in Australia was a period of renewed industrialisation and investment, including the building of major new road infrastructure. In turn, use of the private motor vehicle and improved highways, together with overseas transport connections, had a marked effect on the Australian economy. The establishment of airlines, such as the Queensland and Northern Territory Aerial Services Ltd (Qantas) in 1920, brought considerable pressure to bear on intercity rail and coastal shipping. Meanwhile, steam trains gave way to diesels on the railways, and gauge standardisation allowed more efficient transportation of goods across the country.

Murray–Darling river pilot charts

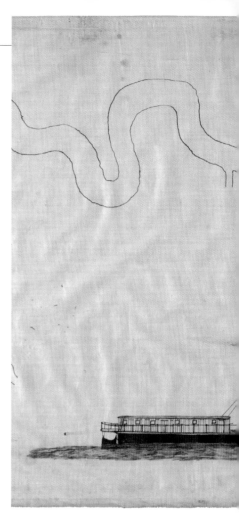

Rising at opposite ends of the Great Dividing Range, the Murray–Darling river system has provided a lifeline to the large pastoral properties and numerous settlements of western New South Wales, Victoria and South Australia.

During the latter part of the nineteenth century, the system also served as the conduit for a unique transport system—the paddle-steamers, or riverboats, that shipped large supplies of goods and services to and from scattered communities.

Both rivers had been reached by 1830, but it was not until 1853 that the first steamer appeared on the Murray River. In the same year, a race between the paddle-steamer *Mary Ann*, captained by William Randell, and the paddle-steamer *Lady Augusta*, skippered by Francis Cadell, announced the arrival of the riverboats.

Over the next seven years, both Randell and Cadell extensively explored the Murray and Darling rivers, noting in particular their snags, twists and billabongs. By 1860, 17 steamers were plying the Murray and, three years later, the town of Echuca was established. Nearly 10 000 kilometres of the tributaries of the Murray, particularly the Murrumbidgee and Edwards rivers, were opened up and explored.

The advent of the steamers, and the resulting regular supply of goods and services and transport of produce, helped to open up the country, and land along the river was quickly taken up. The future of large pastoral properties and towns such as Albury was assured.

Transport by paddle-steamer reached its peak between 1870 and 1879, with terminal ports established at Albury and Goolwa on the Murray, Walgett on the Darling, and Wagga Wagga on the Murrumbidgee. Steamers were also able to ply 40 miles (64 kilometres) up the Wakool, 140 miles (224 kilometres) up the Edwards and reach Nagambie on the Goulburn River.

In 1855, the Victorian and NSW governments introduced customs duties for goods landed at Albury and Wodonga from South Australia. These were dropped a few years later, however, when the cost of collection was found to be greater than the receipts. Meanwhile, import and export levies on almost every item transported along the river were collected until Federation in 1901, leading to the establishment of customs houses at Albury, Goolwa, Corowa, Wodonga and Wahgunyah.

The extension of the railways to the Murray River at Echuca saw the beginning of the end of the riverboats for transporting goods. Initially, the railways worked in conjunction with the river ports but, as the railways were extended, the river trade slowly died. By 1881, it had substantially disappeared, although boats were still plying the Darling River into the early 1920s. (Passenger or tourist steamers still operate on the Murray River, which is navigable for 1986 kilometres.)

Essential to the safe navigation of the rivers was the development of the river pilot charts, usually compiled by riverboat captains.

From the nine charts held in the National Library of Australia's collection, it appears that the charts were made on continuous lengths of calico or drafting linen, about 46 centimetres wide, with some measuring up to 50 metres in length. Changes in the river course, particularly the Darling, due to floodwaters and the regular occurrence of snags were the main reasons for the charts. Some historians believe they were also compiled on commission to provide a competitive edge over rivals, and as a requirement for mariners' certification.

The charts were mounted on rollers, which were hung in sockets

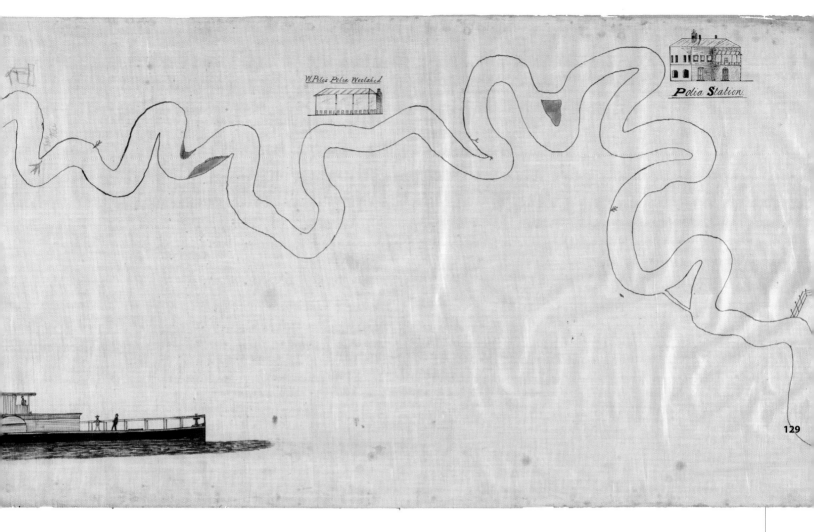

placed about 23 centimetres apart, usually within a glass-fronted box, and wound left to right as the steamer traversed its course. Night viewing of the charts was aided by a hurricane lamp, or similar light source, placed beneath the chart.

The very nature of the charts in the National Library's collection suggests that they were compiled while navigating the river, with corrections made at a later date. Most charts note not only the course of the river and hazards but also tree snags and shoals, marked with crosses and stippling. The artistic skill of the chartist was reflected in the decorative inclusion of buildings and other landmarks along the riverbank.

Seven of the charts in the Library's collection were compiled by members of the Budarick family, although none of the charts is signed. The Budarick Brothers, registered as a company at Murray Bridge, plied the rivers from 1912 to 1922. Their surviving charts

in the collection relate to the Darling River, with six forming a sequence covering the river from Para Station, about 50 kilometres upstream from Wentworth, to near Nelyambo Homestead, about 80 kilometres north-east of Wilcannia. Numerous dated annotations on four of the charts suggest they were used by Captain Wilson Horace Budarick when he travelled the river in the PS *Murrabit* in 1917.

Today, 102 river pilot charts are held by the state libraries of South Australia, Victoria and New South Wales, and by the National Library and museums. Centres such as Echuca hold a significant number of charts, covering not only the Murray and Darling rivers but also less frequently traversed rivers, such as the Murrumbidgee and Edwards rivers.

Arthur Laycock (1881–1960)
The River Steamer Jandra, c.1911
glass negative; 8.2 x 10.7 cm
Pictures Collection
nla.pic-an24527191

below
George French Angas (1822–1886)
Sketches From the Artist's Travels Along the Murray River 1877
pen and ink drawing; 34.0 x 24.0 cm
Pictures Collection
nla.pic-an2872149

Cobb and Co. Coach Near Longreach,
Queensland, c.1916
b&w negative; 12.5 x 10.0 cm
Pictures Collection
nla.pic-an22851635

right
Map of New South Wales Railways
(Sydney: Department of Lands, 1905)
coloured lithograph; 30.6 x 35.5 cm
Maps Collection
nla.map-rm2353

130

NSW railways and coach routes, 1905

John L. Buckland
**The Newcastle Express Coming off the
Hawkesbury River Bridge, New South Wales,
c.1930**
b&w photograph; 20.2 x 15.1 cm
Pictures Collection
nla.pic-an24768250

Archibald James Campbell (1853–1929)
**Stage Coach on the Road to Tweed River, New
South Wales [between 1870 and 1929]**
sepia-toned photograph; 15.0 x 10.0 cm
Pictures Collection
nla.pic-an24751354

British railway mania of the 1840s, part of a global revolution in overland transport, had a profound influence on the Australian colonies.

The British private railway enterprise lacked coordination, so in 1848 the Colonial Secretary, Lord Grey, recommended that the Australian colonies adopt a uniform gauge, in line with the British *Gauge of Railways Act* of 1846.

The legislatures of New South Wales and the South Australian Land Company had already recognised the need for a uniform gauge, with the sensible argument that the British standard gauge of 4 feet 8½ inches (1435 millimetres) should be adopted on the grounds that all railway equipment, locomotives and rolling stock would be imported.

Following his appointment as Chief Engineer to the Sydney Railway Company (formed in October 1849), Francis Webb Shields, an Irishman, recommended that the Irish gauge of 5 feet 3 inches (1600 millimetres) would be better suited to the vast spaces of Australia. The board adopted his advice and the governments of Victoria and South Australia followed suit.

Shields resigned, to be replaced by James Wallace, a Scottish engineer committed to the Stephenson British standard gauge. NSW railway plans were reassessed, but the other two colonies had already invested in broad gauge locomotives and rolling stock. When Queensland and Western Australia entered the railway era (in 1883 and 1871 respectively), budgetary constraints forced them to adopt a narrow gauge track (1066 millimetres). The result was that in Australia, like India, railway building followed three gauges, even into the twentieth century. Tasmania began with a broad gauge but in 1876 opened its second track and later lines as a narrow gauge.

Because of financial difficulties, all assets of the Sydney Railway Company were taken over in 1855 and it became the first government-owned steam railway in the Empire, operating from then on as the NSW Government Railways (NSWGR).

The first section of the Southern Railway, from Sydney to Goulburn, reached Granville to serve Parramatta and the Rosehill racecourse. It then stopped at Campbelltown until 1860 before track work began again. In February 1881, the line reached Albury on the southern border,

a distance of 621 kilometres. For the first time, overland passengers between Sydney and Melbourne could reach their destination faster than by coastal ship (initially, two days by rail instead of a minimum of six by sea). Two years later, the opening of a bridge over the Murray River allowed Victorian trains to reach the Albury platform, but passengers were obliged to

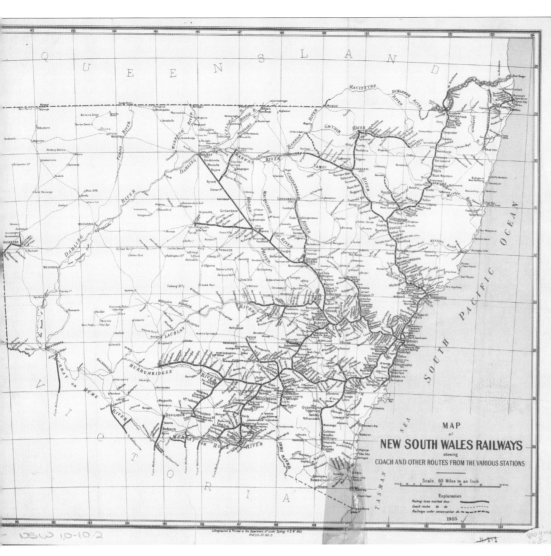

MAP
of
NEW SOUTH WALES RAILWAYS
showing
COACH AND OTHER ROUTES FROM THE VARIOUS STATIONS

Scale, 60 Miles to an Inch

Explanation

1905

change trains because of the differing gauges.

Meanwhile, in 1857, the private Hunter River Railway Company had built the first section (27 kilometres) of the Great Northern Railway from Newcastle to East Maitland, although a much older Australian Agricultural Company tramway carried coal from the mines by gravity to the port.

John Whitton, an Englishman, arrived in Sydney in 1857 as chief engineer responsible for all NSWGR construction for the next 40 years. The Great Western Railway quickly extended to Penrith, but a labour shortage required the hiring of 2000 Scots as emigrant labourers. Whitton was confronted by the eastern and western escarpments of the Blue Mountains, but crossed each by a zigzag track on a one-in-50 grade

involving two reverses, with several enormous sandstone viaducts.

No one suggested that major population centres should determine the routes. The NSWGR track stopped at Bourke (809 kilometres from Sydney), on the banks of the Darling River, in 1885 to load cattle, and the Great Northern Railway arrived at the Queensland border three years later, with a transition at Wallangarra to a narrow gauge track to Brisbane. A year later, Newcastle and Sydney were linked following the opening of a new bridge spanning the Hawkesbury River, a massive engineering achievement requiring 50-metre piers to be sunk into a 30-metre mud base.

This 1905 lithograph (above) of NSW railways and coach routes identifies the extending tentacles of the nineteenth-century

transport system, with a number of branch lines and a new Lismore-to-Murwillumbah track (via Byron Bay) determined by local vote-buying, the influence of wealthy graziers and an emerging north coast butter and cheese industry.

The four westward lines to Bourke, the Cobar copper mines, Condobolin and Hay reflect government uncertainty about the best link to Adelaide through semi-arid to arid country, especially as the map also shows a narrow gauge track to take silver-lead-zinc ores from Silverton and Willyama (Broken Hill) to a smelter opened in 1889 at Port Pirie. Meanwhile, a broad gauge track from Melbourne to Deniliquin had tapped the lucrative wool, livestock and grain trade of the Riverina.

In terms of capital investment, track distance, passenger usage and freight tonnage moved, the

NSWGR system was the largest in Australia. In 1900, the total route distance of NSW railways was 4523 kilometres, but by 1920, when motorised vehicles began to challenge railway efficiency, it had grown to 8115 kilometres.

The coach routes shown on the map were also funded by government contracts, first awarded along the Southern Road to Albury and the Western Road to Orange during the late 1850s to support passenger movement and the delivery of mail (including bank promissory notes). As the railway system expanded, however, the number of coach services began to decline.

Charles Kingsford Smith's Pacific flight, 1928

Seven pencil-annotated and occasionally ink-stained marine navigation charts in the National Library of Australia's collection bear witness to one of the world's greatest aeronautical feats—the 1928 crossing of the Southern Pacific Ocean by Charles Kingsford Smith and a crew of three.

Charming but reckless, Charles Edward Kingsford Smith (1897–1935) had his passion for noise and power satisfied when, after serving at Gallipoli, he was posted in March 1917 to No. 8 Reserve Squadron at Netheravon, Wiltshire, to begin flying lessons with the Royal Flying Corps (RFC). By July, 'Smithy', as he came to be known, had flown his first combat mission over France and been severely injured in the left leg over German lines.

Returning to duty in August 1918, Kingsford Smith was posted as a training instructor to No. 204 Training Depot Station at Eastchurch, where he developed a passion for stunt flying and aerial poaching. Following the Armistice in November 1918, Smithy and fellow Australian RFC pilot Cyril Maddocks set up a small business offering barnstorming flights. The venture subsequently failed, however, and on his way back to Australia via America in 1921, Smithy hatched the idea of a pioneering flight across the Pacific, from the United States to Australia.

In 1922, Kingsford Smith began working for a new airline, Western Australian Airways, and for two years he flew supplies between Carnarvon and Derby. Retrenched in 1924, he bought a garage and petrol station in Carnarvon along with a three-ton truck and began to ship wool from the Gascoyne district to Carnarvon.

Later, he formed a small company, Interstate Flying Services, and set up office in Pitt Street, Sydney. In 1927, Charles Ulm joined him as business manager. To gain sponsorship for the first flight across the Pacific, the two men entered a competition to break the round-Australia record. They were successful and straightaway announced that they were going to the United States to enter a trans-Pacific race.

On arriving in California, the men found that the single-engine plane provided was unsuited to the distance. Australian polar explorer Captain Hubert Wilkins came to the rescue and offered an alternative craft, a Fokker FVII/3M monoplane.

Continuous wrangles over finances for the trip led to a blow-out in the budget, and the NSW Government withdrew its backing and ordered the men to sell the aircraft. The team was rescued at the last minute by a wealthy director of the California Bank, Allan Hancock, who was interested in the commercial possibilities of an air route across the Pacific. Hancock offered to fund the flight and advance money for living expenses.

Two Americans were recruited, navigator Harry Lyon and wireless operator Jim Warner, with Ulm appointed co-commander. Although the aircraft, christened the *Southern Cross*, boasted the latest radio transmitters and compasses, communication between the crew consisted of short notes clamped to the end of a long broomstick. On 31 May 1928, the *Southern Cross* took off from Oakland Airport, California.

The most difficult part of the journey was the leg between Hawaii and Suva, the longest leg

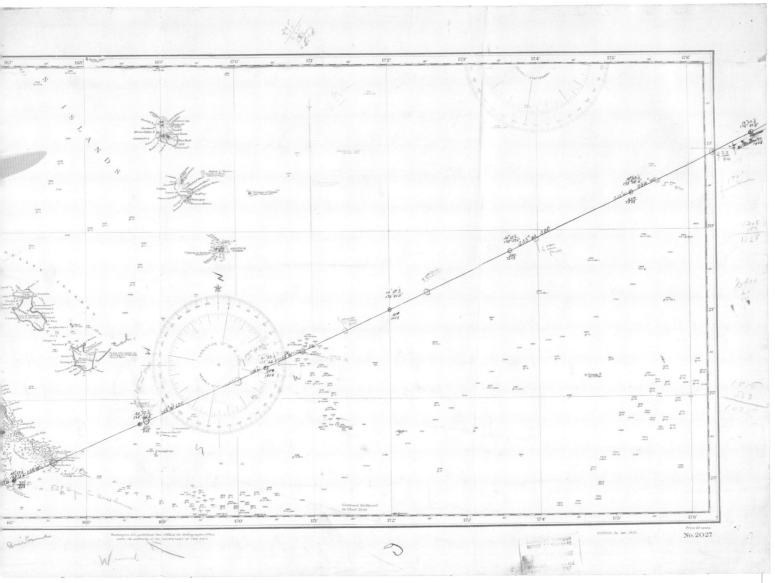

of the flight without any land to confirm dead reckoning and celestial navigation. The crew were also without radio bearings from either shore or ship after the transmitters broke down during a severe tropical storm. Constant detours from their course during the night played havoc with Lyon's navigation.

Kingsford Smith flew the 3150 miles (5000 kilometres) from Hawaii in 34 hours and 30 minutes. When they landed, the men had just 85 US gallons (320 litres) of fuel left from a load of 1300 gallons.

The *Southern Cross* made landfall over Australia at Ballina, New South Wales, and landed at Eagle Farm, Brisbane, on 9 June. The 7200-mile (11 600 kilometres) flight had taken eight-and-a-half days

in a flying time of 83 hours and 50 minutes. Smithy became an international hero and was later honoured with a knighthood.

Tragically, Smithy and Ulm were to die in similar circumstances just a few years later. On 4 December 1934, Ulm and two companions, in the twin-engine Airspeed *Stella Australis,* disappeared between San Francisco and Hawaii on the first leg of a trans-Pacific flight to Australia. Less than a year later, Kingsford Smith and Tommy Pethybridge, in the *Lady Southern Cross*, disappeared off the Malay Peninsula while attempting to break the London to Australia speed record.

Of the nine charts used during the successful flight, seven have survived. Six cover all of the flight

except the last leg into Brisbane and the area covered by 3°S to 12°S.

Six charts were retained by Lyon and were found among his possessions after he died. After they were presented by his cousin, William (Bill) Hunt, to the Australian Government in 1979, they were kept by the Federal Airports Authority in Brisbane, until the Authority's public relations officer, Ken Williams, donated them to the National Library in 1988 on his retirement.

Of the three charts retained by Kingsford Smith, only one has survived—a large-scale chart of Fiji. It was subsequently donated to the National Library by his son, Charles Arthur 'Chuck' Kingsford Smith.

above
The Southern Cross on its Arrival in Sydney from the Flight Across the Pacific, 10 June 1928
b&w photograph; 30.9 x 38.6 cm
Pictures Collection
nla.pic-an24664462

**Panoramic View of Manly Beach,
NSW c.1900**
b&w photograph; 25.6 x 101.1 cm
Pictures Collection
nla.pic-vn3418835

Fancy Dress Football Carnival 1888
albumen photograph;
14.5 x 19.9 cm
Pictures Collection
nla.pic-an21318808

Excursion map of Sydney and surrounds, 1887

This rare lithograph (opposite), produced to coincide with the jubilee year of Queen Victoria's reign, reveals Sydney's railway, tramway, harbour ferry, horse-drawn bus and coach routes, and the city's surroundings towards the end of the nineteenth century.

Compiled by Poole and Noble, of 250 George Street, Sydney, and published by 'the Proprietors of The Tourist Bureau' of 6 Bridge Street, it is accompanied by a concise guide to the highlights of Victorian-era Sydney, along with details such as fares and guides to the hiring of a hansom cab and payment of boatmen's fees. In 1887, Sydney's population is estimated to have been more than 300 000.

At a scale of one inch to the mile (1:63 360), the map coverage extends to 20 miles (32 kilometres) from the General Post Office and shows the Parramatta River and Port Jackson constraining the city's expansion northward. The Pacific Ocean and Port Hacking forced

suburban growth westward to Burwood ('a large and fashionable railway suburb'). To the south, an extension to the steam tramway track from Rockdale Station to Sans Souci and Sandringham is reported as under construction. Trams from Bridge Street serve Leichhardt, Enmore, Banks Meadow (now Banksmeadow) and Bondi, passing through the most populous suburbs.

The Sydney Tramway and Omnibus Company operated three-quarters of the tram and bus fleet. All omnibuses started from Miller's Point, west of the Quay, and the guide advised passengers to place the exact fare of threepence in the box provided. Country and local steam-train services arrived at the four platforms at Redfern Station (now Central Station).

Shopping excursions into the city centred on The Block on George Street, between King and Hunter streets. With its shops, cafes, bookstores, banks, arcades, flower

barrows, newspaper boys and busy traffic, The Block was 'the promenade of Sydney'.

A map number gives the locations of the emporiums of David Jones, Farmer and Company (Victoria House) and Hordern Brothers (Pitt Street). Tourists were encouraged to visit the top of Victoria House—at seven storeys, Sydney's tallest building—to take advantage of the magnificent views of the Pacific Ocean, Botany Bay, the Blue Mountains and Hornsby heights. Recommended hotels are also mapped.

During the 1880s, Sydney was a major market centre. Souvenir hunters were expected to buy Australian furs ('Opossum' skin, bear, kangaroo and rock wallaby), but to be wary of dyed black furs. Fruit and vegetable markets west of The Block were rated as rundown.

Fennelly's ran a horse bazaar at least three times a week from yards between Pitt and Castlereagh

Streets. Wares for Market Street were carted or carried by Chinese labourers four blocks uphill, from Market Wharf near the Darling Harbour swinging bridge. The guide describes Darling Harbour as 'the great centre of shipping business', with a railway goods depot on the western shore, a sawmill to the south, and wharves and storage buildings on the eastern shore. Coastal steamers left there for the Clarence and Richmond rivers and Newcastle.

Sightseeing attractions marked on the map include the Sydney Town Hall, Parliament House on Macquarie Street, the Australian Museum, the National Gallery of Art ('a very ugly plain building'), Bray's Museum of Curios, the Observatory (open only on Mondays, from 3 pm to 5 pm), the university uphill from Victoria Park, and the Domain—the 'principal park of the city' and popular for Sunday afternoon debates after church services had concluded.

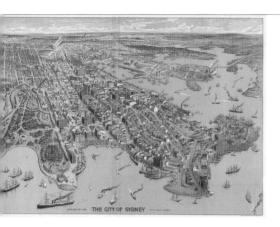

THE CITY OF SYDNEY

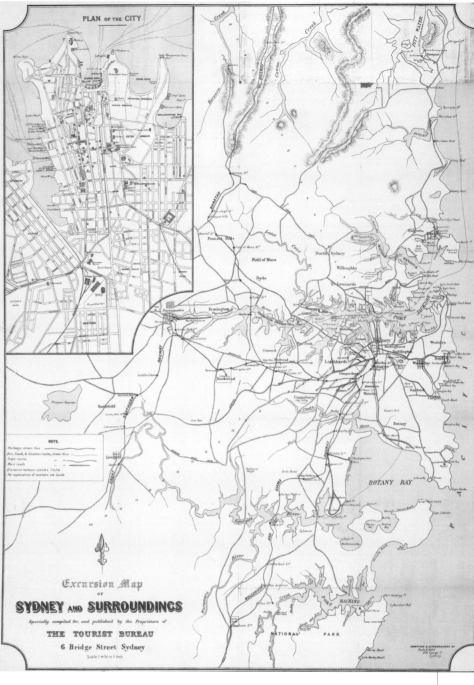

right
**Excursion Map of Sydney and
Surroundings**
(Sydney: Tourist Bureau, 1887)
coloured lithograph; 96.2 x 70.3 cm
Maps Collection
nla.map-rm1794

top
M.S. Hill
The City of Sydney
(New York; Sydney: Saml. Crump Label
Co., c.1888)
chromolithograph; 51.0 x 75.5 cm
Pictures Collection
nla.pic-an8337483

A stroll along the harbour foreshore from the Domain might take in Farm Cove (anchorage of Her Majesty's fleet) and the Biloela Docks (now Cockatoo Island), but walkers were discouraged from visiting the less savoury Woolloomooloo and its fish market.

The Exhibition Building, in Prince Alfred Park, housed displays, bazaars, balls, concerts and, during winter, 'a first class Skating Rink'. Summer swimming facilities included 10 open-air bathhouses and Wigzell Turkish Baths in Oxford Street (haircutting extra).

More adventurous tourists might take a cab, tram or bus to the recreation grounds of Moore Park, which included a zoological garden, the Agricultural Society Grounds (annual Show during May, and trotting races) and Association Grounds. Or they might take a tram to Bondi Beach Aquarium ('general surroundings somewhat bleak'), to The Gap or to the hard

white sand at Lady Robinson's Beach on Botany Bay. Shooting grounds at Canterbury Park and Botany were also recommended.

Harbour steamers from Circular Quay offered a day's outing to Manly (1500 inhabitants), with its public baths, aquarium and beaches. Day excursions on the *Grande* to Middle Harbour departed from a floating jetty three times a day, another steamer sailed beyond the Heads to Broken Bay, and ferries from the Quay served various harbourside bays. A regular ferry from No. 3 jetty provided quick transport to Double Bay (sixpence single, ninepence return) but passengers to Darlinghurst or Paddington were advised to take the bus from Macquarie Place (fare threepence). The orchards

and orangeries of Lane Cove River were accessible by boat to Fig Tree Wharf, and a steamer on Botany Bay connected Tom Ugly's Point with Ruby Point, Doll's Point and Banks Meadow.

Boat transport to Parramatta (8500 residents), described as 'one of the prettiest steamer trips', stopped at Balmain, Gladesville (site of the principal Lunatic Asylum of the colony) and Hunter's Hill, before passing the Champion Sculling Course.

Rosehill punters arrived by train via Granville Station or special ferry from Darling Harbour. 'Irish Town'

(now Bankstown) held races at Canterbury and country folk might take the train to the Homebush livestock sales or Belmore 'Paddy's' Market.

North of the Harbour, transport services were undeveloped. Black's of Manly ran a daily coach service to the Narrabeen Lakes (two shillings each way) and Newport (four shillings single, six shillings return). Meanwhile, lengthy coach routes to Gordon from Milson's Point and from Parramatta to Pennant Hills revealed the need for a harbour bridge to the north shore.

References

Note: all websites were consulted in July 2007 and the addresses below were correct at time of printing.

Introduction

Barber, P. (ed.), *The Map Book*. London: Weidenfield and Nicolson, 2001.

Barber, P. and Board, C., *Tales from the Map Room: Fact and Fiction about Maps and their Makers*. London: BBC Books, 1993.

Harley, J.B. and Woodward, D. (eds), *The History of Cartography*. Chicago: University of Chicago Press, 1987.

Monmonier, M., *Mapping it Out: Expository Cartography for the Humanities and Social Sciences*. Chicago: University of Chicago Press, 1993.

National Library of Australia, Service Charter, November 2006: www.nla.gov.au/charter.

National Library of Australia, Collection Development Policy, Chapter 8: Maps, November 2006: www.nla.gov.au/policy/cdp/chapter_8.html.

Schilder, G., *Australia Unveiled*. Amsterdam: Theatrum Orbis Terrarum Ltd, 1976.

Thrower, N.J.W., *Maps and Civilization: Cartography in Culture and Society*. Chicago: University of Chicago Press, 1996.

Turchi, P., *Maps of the Imagination: The Writer as Cartographer*. San Antonio, Texas: Trinity University Press, 2004.

Wood, D. with Fels, J., *The Power of Maps*. New York: Guildford Press, 1992.

1   Aboriginal Australia

Berndt, R.M. and Berndt, C.H., *The World of the First Australians*. Sydney: Ure Smith, 1981.

Grolier Society of Australia, 'Australian Aborigines', in *The Australian Encyclopaedia*, 4th edn. Sydney: Grolier Society of Australia, 1983.

http://www.crystalinks.com/aboriginals.html

Mapping the landscape

Sutton, P., 'Icons of Country: Topographic Representations in Classical Aboriginal Traditions', in Woodward, D. and Lewis, M. (eds), *The*
History of Cartography, Volume 2.3: Cartography in the Traditional African, American, Arctic, Australian, and Pacific Societies. Chicago: Chicago University Press, 1998.

Sutton, P., 'Aboriginal Maps and Plans', in Woodward, D. and Lewis, M. (eds), *The History of Cartography, Volume 2.3: Cartography in the Traditional African, American, Arctic, Australian, and Pacific Societies*. Chicago: Chicago University Press, 1998.

Taylor, J., 'Mapping Techniques and the Reconstruction of Aspects of Traditional Aboriginal Culture', *Australian Institute of Aboriginal Studies Newsletter*, no. 5, 1976.

von Sturmer, J., 'Maps and Mapping', in Barwick, D., Mace, M. and Stannage, T. (eds), *Handbook for Aboriginal and Islander History*. Canberra: Aboriginal History, 1979.

The Daisy Bates Special Map Collection

Bates, D., *The Native Tribes of Western Australia*. (Edited by I. White). Canberra: National Library of Australia, 1985.

Bates, D., *My Natives and I* [incorporating *The Passing of the Aborigines: A Lifetime Spent among the Natives of Australia*]. Perth, WA: Hesperian Press, 2004.

Jones, P., 'Naming the Dead Heart: Hillier's Map and Reuther's Gazetteer of 2,468 Placenames in North-eastern South Australia', in Hercus, L., Hodges, F. and Simpson, J. (eds), *The Land is a Map: Placenames of Indigenous Origin in Australia*, Canberra: Pandanus Books, 2002.

National Library of Australia, *Papers of Daisy Bates: Ms 365* [Finding aid]. Canberra: National Library of Australia, 2002.

Norman Tindale's *Aboriginal Tribes of Australia*, 1940

Birdsell, J.B., 'A Preliminary Report on the Trihybrid Origin of the Australian Aborigines', *American Journal of Anthropology*, vol. 28, 1941.
Horton, D.R. (ed.), *The Encyclopaedia of Aboriginal Australia: Aboriginal and Torres Strait Islander History, Society and Culture*. Canberra: Aboriginal Studies Press, 1994.

http://dia.wa.gov.au/Heritage/FamilyHistory/

http://samuseum.sa.gov.au/tindale/boundaries.htm

http://www.anu.edu.au/linguistics/nash/aust/nbt/

http://www.sydneyline.com/Pygmies%20Extinction.htm

Nash, D., *Norman B. Tindale, 1900–1993*. Canberra: Australian National University Press, 1999.

Parry-Okeden, W.E., 'Report on the North Queensland Aborigines and the Native Police', *Votes and Proceedings of the Legislative Assembly*, Brisbane, 1897.

Spencer, W.B., *Native Tribes of the Northern Territory of Australia*. London: Macmillan, 1914.

Tindale, N.B., 'Ethnological Notes from Arnhem Land and from Tasmania', *Transactions of the Royal Society of Australia*, vol. 52, 1928.

Tindale, N.B., 'Distribution of Australian Aboriginal Tribes: A Field Survey', *Transactions of the Royal Society of Australia*, vol. 64, 1940.

Tindale, N.B., *Aboriginal Tribes of Australia*. Berkeley, Los Angeles and London: University of California, 1972 (reprinted by Australian National University Press, Canberra, 1974).

Tindale, N.B., *Aboriginal Tribes of Australia: Geographic II Spelling Versions of 4 Sheet Map*. Canberra: Australian Institute of Aboriginal Studies, 1975.

Tindale, N.B. and Birdsell, J.B., 'Result of the Harvard–Adelaide Universities Anthropological Expedition 1938–1939: Tasmanoid Tribes in North Queensland', *Records of the South Australian Museum*, vol. 7, 1941–1943.

The Mabo maps and native title

http://austlii.law.uts.edu.au/au/cases/cth/high_ct/175clr1.html/MAB
http://rodhagen.customer.netspace.net.au/nativetitle.html

http://www.biographybase.com/biography/Mabo_Eddie.html

2   European theories of *Terra Australis Nondum Cognita*

The heritage of an ancient Greek theory

Berggren, J.L. and Jones, A., *Ptolemy's Geography: An Annotated Translation of the Theoretical Chapters*. Princeton: Princeton University, 2000.

http://historic-cities.huji.ac.il/mapmakers/schedel.html

http://www-groups.dcs.st-and.ac.uk/~history/Mathematicians/Ptolemy.html

http://www.ibiblia.org/expo/vatican.exhibit/exhibit/d-mathematics/Ptolemy-geo.html

Hartmann Schedel's *Secunda Etas Mundi*, 1493

http://www.lib.umd.edu/RARE/Exhibits/Worldview.html

http://www.newadvent.org/cathen/13525a.htm

http://www.philographikon.com/schedel.html

Wilford, J.N., *The Mapmakers: The Story of the Great Pioneers in Cartography from Antiquity to the Space Age*. Pimlico, London: Random House, 2002.

Johann Honter's *Astronomia,* 1545

http://www.hungarian-history.hu/lib/transy/transy07.htm

http://en.wikipedia.org/wiki/Johannes_honter

Abraham Ortelius' world map, 1570

Monmonier, M., *Rhumb Lines and Map Wars: A Social History of the Mercator Projection*. Chicago and London: University of Chicago, 2004.

http://en.wikipedia.org/wiki/Abraham_Ortelius

http://memory.loc.gov/ammem/gmdhtml/gnrlort.html

http://www.newadvent.org/cathen/11328b.htm

van den Broecke, M.P.R., et al. (eds), *Abraham Ortelius and the First Atlas: Essays Commemorating the Quadricentennial of his Death 1598–1998*. Utrecht: HES Publishers, 1998.

Benito Arias Montano's world map, 1572

http://en.wikipedia.org/wiki/Benito_Arias_Montano

Rekers, B., *Benito Arias Montano (1527–1598)*. London: Studies of the Warburg Institute, 1972.

Shalev, Z., 'Sacred Geography, Antiquarianism and Visual Erudition: Benito Arias Montano and the Maps in the Antwerp Polyglot Bible', *Imago Mundi*, vol. 55, 2003.

3   Recorded European knowledge of the South Land

European arrival in Asia and the South Pacific

Badger, G., *The Explorers of the Pacific*. Kenthurst: Kangaroo Press, 1996.

Shalev, Z., 'Sacred Geography, Antiquarianism and Visual Erudition: Benito Arias Montano and the Maps in the Antwerp Polyglot Bible', *Imago Mundi*, vol. 55, 2003.

Collingridge, G., *The First Discovery of Australia and New Guinea*. Sydney and London: Pan Books, 1982.

Estensen, M., *Terra Australis Incognita: The Spanish Quest for the Mysterious Great South Land*. Crows Nest: Allen and Unwin, 2006.

Price, A.G., *The Western Invasions of the Pacific and Its Continents: A Study of Moving Frontiers and Changing Landscapes 1513–1958*. Oxford: Clarendon Press, 1963.

Spate, O.H.K., *The Spanish Lake*. Canberra: Australian National University Press, 1979.

Spate, O.H.K., *Monopolists and Freebooters*. Canberra: Australian National University Press, 1983.

Spate, O.H.K., *Paradise Found and Lost*. Sydney: Australian National University Press, 1988.

Ferdinand Verbiest's *Kunyu Wanguo Quantu*, 1674

http://www.faculty.fairfield.edu/jmac/sj/scientists/verbiest.htm

http://www.newadvent.org/cathen/15346a.htm

Menzies, G., *1421: The Year China Discovered the World*. London: Bantam Press, 2002.

Ptak, Roderick, 'Maritime Southeast Asia in the World Map of Ferdinand Verbiest and its Korean Version', *Journal of the South Seas Society*, vol. 56, 2002 (republished in Macau Ricci Institute [ed.], *Religion and Culture: Past Approaches, Present Globalization, Future Challenges*. Macau: Macau Ricci Institute, 2004).

Smith, R.J., *Chinese Maps*. Hong Kong: Oxford University Press, 1996.

Walravens, H., 'Father Verbiest's Chinese World Map (1674)', *Imago Mundi*, vol. 43, 1991.

Yee, C.D.K., 'Traditional Chinese Cartography and the Myth of Westernization', *History of Cartography*, vol. 2, book 2: 'Cartography in the Traditional East and Southeast Asian Societies'. Chicago: University of Chicago Press, 1994.

Cornelis Danckert's record of Tasman's 1642–1644 voyages to Australia

Anderson, G., *The Merchant of the Zeehan: Isaac Gilsemans and the Voyages of Abel Tasman*. Wellington: Te Papa Press, 2001.

Caudell, A.B., *The Discovery of Tasmania (24 November 1642): Extracts from the Journal of Abel Janszoon Tasman*. Hobart: Government Printer, 1985.

Duyker, E. (ed.), *The Discovery of Tasmania: Journal Extracts from the Expeditions of Abel Janszoon Tasman and Marc-Joseph Marion Dufresne*

1642 and 1772. Hobart: St David's Park Publishers, 1992.

Keunig, J., 'Cornelis Danckerts and his "Niew Aerdsch Pleyu"', *Imago Mundi*, vol. 12, 1955.

http://www.muffley.net/pacific/dutch/tasman.htm

Melchisédech Thévenot's chart of New Holland, 1663

http://en.wikipedia.org/wiki/Melchisedech_Thevenot

http://www.janswannerdam.net/pals.htm.

William Dampier's survey of Shark Bay, 1699

http://www.muffley.net/pacific/dampier/dampier.htm

Norris, G. (ed.), *William Dampier: Buccaneer Explorer*. London: The Folio Society, 1994.

Pinkerton, J., *Early Australian Voyages: Pelsaert, Tasman, Dampier*. Melbourne: Cassell and Co., 1886.

Gerard van Keulen's manuscript charts of New Holland, circa 1700

Eisler, W. and Smith, B., *Terra Australis: The Furthest Shore*. Sydney: Art Gallery of New South Wales, 1988.

http://www.voc.iinet.net.au/vlamingh.html

Kenny, J., *Before the First Fleet: Europeans in Australia 1606–1777*. Kenthurst: Kangaroo Press, 1995.

Koeman, C., *Collections of Maps and Atlases in the Netherlands: Their History and Present State*. Leiden: E.J. Brill, 1961.

Schilder, G., *The Southland Explored: The Voyage by Willem Hesselsz. de Vlamingh in 1696–97*. Alphen aan den Rijn, Netherlands: Uitgeverij, 1984.

4   Theories of the east coast of New Holland

The struggle for maritime supremacy

Boxer, C.R., *The Dutch Seaborne Empire, 1600–1800*. London: Hutchinson, 1965.

Israel, J., *The Dutch Republic: Its Rise, Greatness and Fall, 1477–1806*. Oxford: Oxford University Press, 1995.

Padfield, P., *Maritime Supremacy and the Opening of the Western Mind: Naval Campaigns that Shaped the Modern World, 1588–1782*. London: John Murray, 1999.

Pedley, M.S., *The Commerce of Cartography: Making and Marketing Maps in Eighteenth Century France and England*. Chicago and London: University of Chicago, 2005.

Jean-Baptiste Nolin's world map, 1700

Brown, H., *Scientific Organization in Seventeenth Century France (1600–1680)*. New York: Russell & Russell, 1934 (reissued 1967).

Eisler, W. and Smith, B., *Terra Australis: The Furthest Shore*. Sydney: Map Gallery of New South Wales, 1988.

Konvitz, J., *Cartography in France (1660–1848): Science, Engineering and Statecraft*. Chicago: University of Chicago Press, 1987.

O'Connor, M., 'Jean-Baptiste Nolin's Rare 1700 Wall Map', *Gateways*, no. 56, 2002.

Shirley, R.W., *The Mapping of the World: Early Printed Maps, 1472–1700*, 3rd edn. London: East World Press, 2001.

Richard Cushee's new terrestrial globe of the world, 1731

http://www.nmm.ac.uk/collections/search/listResults.cfm?name=Pocket20%globe&sortby=year&category=Globes

O'Connor, M., 'Map Collection: British Depiction of East Coast of Australia (Cushee Globes, 1731)', *Gateways*, no. 74, 2005.

Thomas Bowles' world map, 1740

http://www.georgeglazer.com/prints/portraits/hysingcarol.html

http://www.lclark.edu/~jhart/printsellers/printsellers.html

Didier Robert de Vaugondy's chart of Australasia, 1756

Konvitz, J., *Cartography in France (1660–1848): Science, Engineering and Statecraft.* Chicago: University of Chicago Press, 1987.

Pedley, M.S., 'The Map Trade in Paris, 1650–1825', *Imago Mundi*, vol. 33, 1981.

Pedley, M.S., *Bel et Utile: The Work of the Robert de Vaugondy Family of Mapmakers.* Tring, Herts.: Map Collector Publications, 1992.

Shirley, R.W., *The Mapping of the World: Early Printed Maps, 1472–1700.* London: Holland Press, 1993.

5 European coastal surveys of Australia

British and French hydrographic surveys 1770–1850

Badger, G., *The Explorers of the Pacific.* Kenthurst: Kangaroo Press, 1996.

Kenny, J., *Before the First Fleet: Europeans in Australia, 1606–1777.* Kenthurst: Kangaroo Press, 1995.

McLynn, F., *1759: The Year Britain Became Master of the World.* London: Jonathan Cape, 2004.

Moorehead, A., *The Fatal Impact: The Invasion of the South Pacific, 1767–1840,* 2nd edn. London: Hamish Hamilton, 1987.

Smith, B., *European Vision and the South Pacific 1768–1850.* London: Oxford University Press, 1960.

James Cook's chart of the east coast of New Holland, 1770

Aughton, P., *Endeavour: The Story of Captain Cook's First Great Epic Voyage.* London: Cassell & Co., 2002.

Edwards, P. (ed.), *James Cook, The Journals: Prepared from the Original Manuscript by J.C. Beaglehole.* London: Penguin Books, 2003.

Hough, R., *Captain James Cook: A Biography.* London: Hodder & Stoughton, 1994.

http://en.wikipedia.org/wiki/James_Cook

http://www.muffley.net/pacific/cook/cook1.htm

http://www.queensland.co.uk/james.html

Rienits, R. and Rienits, T., *The Voyages of Captain Cook.* London: Paul Hamlyn, 1968.

Skelton, R.A., 'James Cook as a Hydrographer', *The Mariner's Mirror*, November, 1954.

Thomas, N., *The Extraordinary Voyages of Captain James Cook.* New York: Walker & Co., 2003.

Williams, G. (ed.), *Cook's Voyages 1768–1779.* London: The Folio Society, 1997.

Matthew Flinders' chart of *Terra Australis,* 1814

Badger, G., *The Explorers of the Pacific.* Kenthurst: Kangaroo Press, 1996.

Brosse, J., *Great Voyages of Exploration: The Golden Age of Discovery in the Pacific.* Lane Cove: Doubleday Australia, 1983.

Brunton, P. (ed.), *Matthew Flinders: Personal Letters from an Extraordinary Life.* Sydney: Hordern House, 2002.

Colwell, M., *The Voyages of Matthew Flinders.* Dee Why West: Paul Hamlyn, 1970.

Fornasiero, J., Monteath, P. and West-Sooby, J., *Encountering Terra Australis: The Australian Voyages of Nicolas Baudin and Matthew Flinders.* Kent Town: Wakefield Press, 2004.

Hill, E., *My Love Must Wait: The Story of Matthew Flinders.* Sydney: Angus & Robertson, 1952.

http://www.sl.nsw.gov.au/flinders/

Ingleton, C., *Matthew Flinders: Navigator and Chartmaker.* Guildford: Genesis Publications, 1988.

Taft, K., *The Navigators: Flinders vs. Baudin: The Race between Matthew Flinders and Nicolas Baudin to Discover the Fabled passage through the Middle of Australia.* Potts Point, NSW: Duffy & Snellgrove, 2002.

Louis-Henri de Freycinet's chart of the Derwent River, 1802

http://www.abc.net.au/navigators/captains/baudin.htm

http://www.ambafrance-au.org/article.php3?id_article=475

Brosse, J., *Great Voyages of Exploration: The Golden Age of Discovery in the Pacific.* Lane Cove: Doubleday Australia, 1983.

Horner, F.B., *French Reconnaissance in Australia, 1801–1803.* Carlton, Vic.: Melbourne University Press, 1987.

Hunt, S. and Carter, P., *Terre Napoleon: Australia through French Eyes, 1800–1804.* Sydney: Historic Houses Trust of New South Wales in association with Hordern House, 1999.

O'Connor, M., 'Recent Acquisitions for the Map and Pictures Collections from Christie's Auctions', *Gateways*, no. 61, 2003.

Plomley, N.J.B., *The Baudin Expedition and the Tasmanian Aborigines.* Hobart: Blubber Head Press, 1983.

Taft, K., *The Navigators: Flinders vs. Baudin: The Race between Matthew Flinders and Nicolas Baudin to Discover the Fabled Passage through the Middle of Australia.* Potts Point, NSW: Duffy & Snellgrove, 2002.

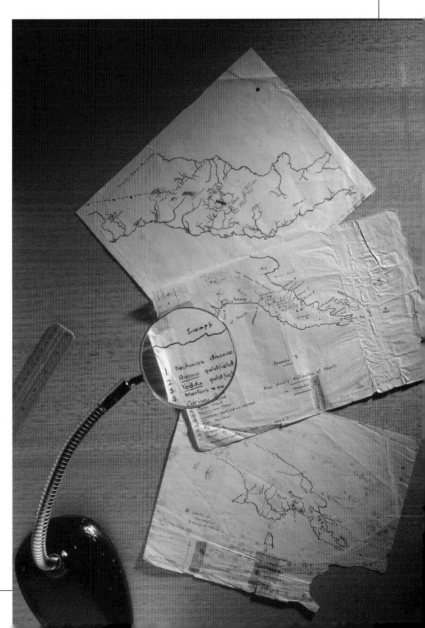

Daisy Bates (1859–1951)
Selection of maps showing Western Australian
Aboriginal tribal group associations
Maps Collection

Owen Stanley's chart of the Torres Strait, 1885

Badger, G., *The Explorers of the Pacific*. Kenthurst: Kangaroo Press, 1988.

Barrow, J., *Mutiny of the Bounty*. Oxford: Oxford University Press, 1980.

Brosse, J., *Great Voyages of Exploration*. Lane Cove: Doubleday Australia, 1983.

Hakluyt, R., *The Principal Navigations Voyages Traffiques & Discoveries of the English Nation, Made by Sea or Overland, to the Farthest Distant Quaerters of the Earth, at Any Time within the Compas of the 1600 Yeeres*, vol. 11, Hakluyt Society edition. Sydney: Angus & Robertson, 1904.

Hilder, B., *The Voyage of Torres*. St Lucia, Brisbane: University of Queensland Press, 1980.

http://www.navicharts.net/prod_britishcharts.htm

http://www.worldbook.com/features/explorers/htm/newworld_spanish_other.html

Lubbock, A., *Owen Stanley RN, 1811–1850, Captain of the* Rattlesnake. London and Melbourne: Heinemann, 1968.

MacGillivray, J., *Voyage of HMS* Rattlesnake *Commanded by the Late Captain Owen Stanley During the Years 1846–1850, including Discoveries and Seaways in New Guinea, the Louisiade Archipelago, etc.*, 2 vols. London: TD & W. Boone, 1852. Reprinted Adelaide: Libraries Board of South Australia, 1967.

6 British colonial settlement and port mapping
The importance of colonial seaports

Bach, J.P.S., *A Maritime History of Australia*. Sydney: Pan Books, 1982 (revised).

Francis Fowkes' survey map of Sydney Cove, 1789

Cobley, J., *Sydney Cove 1788*. London: Hodder & Stoughton, 1962.

Collins, D., *An Account of the English Colony in New South Wales*. Adelaide:

Libraries Board of South Australia, 1798.

Hirst, J.B., *Convict Society and Its Enemies*. Sydney: Allen & Unwin, 1983.

http://members.tripod.com/~midgley/convictlist.html

http://nla.gov.au/nla.map-nk276

http://users.bigpond.net.au/convicts/

http://www.oldbaileyonline.org/html~sessions/T17861213.html

Tench, W., *Sydney's First Four Years*. Sydney: Angus & Robertson, 1961.

Weidenhofer, M., *The Convict Years: Transportation and the Penal System, 1788–1868*. Melbourne: Lansdowne, 1973.

George Raper's chart of Port Jackson, 1791

Hindwood, K.A., 'George Raper: An Artist of the First Fleet', *Journal and Proceedings of the Royal Australian Historical Society*, vol. 50, 1964.

http://www.nla.gov.au/exhibitions/georgeraper/

http://www.teachersfirst.com/summer/autoframe.htm

Olsen, P., *Feathers and Brush: Three Centuries of Australian Bird Art*. Melbourne: CSIRO Publishing, 2001.

John Lort Stokes' hydrographic chart of approaches to the Swan River, 1841

Cygnet, *The Story of HMS* Challenger *(1826–1835): The Ship in Which Captain Fremantle Took Possession of Western Australia for the British Crown in 1829*. Perth: Swan River Press, 1938?

Hordern, M., *Mariners are Warned! John Lort Stokes and HMS* Beagle *in Australia, 1837–1843*. Melbourne: Melbourne University Press, 2002.

Stokes, J.L., *Discoveries in Australia*, 2 vols. London, T. & W. Boone, 1846 (reprinted 2004).

7 Overland exploration and pastoral land acquisition
Surveys to open Australia's interior to European pastoralism

Blainey, G., *A Land Half Won*. Sydney: Pan Macmillan of Australia, 1995 (revised).

Lee, I., *Early Explorers in Australia: From the Logbooks and Journals*. London: Methuen, 1925.

Stephens, S.S., *A History of Australian Land Settlement*. Melbourne: Macmillan Australia, 1968.

Allan Cunningham's map of the Darling Downs, 1827

Cunningham, A., *A Few General Remarks on the Vegetation of Certain Coasts of Terra Australia, and More Especially of Its North-western Shore*. London: John Murray, 1827.

Cunningham, A., 'Brief View of the Progress of Interior Discovery in New South Wales', *Journal of the Royal Geographical Society*, vol. 2, 1832.

Hordern, M., *King of the Australian Coast: The Work of Philip Parker King in the* Mermaid *and* Bathurst, *1817–1822*. Melbourne: Melbourne University Press, 2002.

King, P.P., *Narrative of a Survey of the Intertropical and Western Coasts of Australia*. London: John Murray, 1826.

Hamilton Hume's map of Lake George to Port Phillip, 1825

Andrews, A.E.J., *Hume and Hovell, 1824*. Hobart: Blubber Head Press, 1981.

Boyes, R., *Overland to Port Phillip Bay: The Story of the Epic of Exploration by Hume and Hovell with Party. October–December 1824*. Moorabbin, Vic.: Interprint Services. 1975.

http://www.win.tue.nl/~engels/discovery/hume.html

Prest, J., *Hamilton Hume and William Hovell*. Melbourne: Oxford University Press, 1963.

Thomas Mitchell's map of the Nineteen Counties, 1834

Andrews, A.E.J., *Major Mitchell's Map, 1834: The Saga of the Survey of Nineteen Counties*. Hobart: Blubber Head Press, 1992.

Archives Authority of New South Wales, *Major Mitchell's Map of the Colony of New South Wales, 1834*. Sydney: Archives Authority of New South Wales, 1994.

Bradford, T., 'Major Mitchell's Map of the Colony of New South Wales 1834', *The Australian Antique Collector*, 60–63.

Eccleston, G.C., *Major Mitchell's 1836 'Australia Felix' Expedition: A Re-evaluation*. Clayton, Vic.: Monash University Department of Geography and Environmental Science, 1992.

Foster, W.C., *Sir Thomas Livingston Mitchell and His World 1792–1855: Surveyor General of New South Wales 1828–1855*. Sydney: The Institution of Surveyors NSW Inc., 1985.

http://www.personal.usyd.edu.au/nslaw/SuesPage/Mitchell.htm

John McDouall Stuart's central Australia expeditions, 1858–1862

Bailey, J., *Mr. Stuart's Track: The Forgotten Life of Australia's Greatest Explorer*. Sydney: Macmillan Australia, 2006.

Bonyhady, T., *Burke and Wills: From Melbourne to Myth*. Canberra: National Library of Australia, 2002.

Hardman, W. (ed.), *Explorations of Australia: The Journals of John McDouall Stuart, 1846* (facsimile). Perth: Hesperion Press, 1986.

http://www.cyburbia.net.au/Community/jmcdss/expedit.html

Mudie, I., *The Heroic Journey of John McDouall Stuart*. Sydney: Angus & Robertson, 1968.

Stokes, E., *Across the Centre*. Sydney: Allen & Unwin, 1996.

William Owen's atlas maps of the Australian colonies, 1869

http://www.nla.gov.au/ntwkpubs/gw/55/p11a01.html

Ernest William Pearson Chinnery (1887–1972)
Sketch maps created by Ernest Chinnery,
former Papua New Guinea patrol officer
Maps Collection

John Forrest's West Australian Exploring Expedition, 1874

Crowley, F.K., *Big John Forrest 1847–1918: A Founding Father of the Commonwealth of Australia*. Nedlands: University of Western Australia Press, 2000.

Forrest, J., *Explorations in Australia*. London, 1875 (reprinted Adelaide: Libraries Board of South Australia, 1969).

Forrest, J., *Journals of the Proceedings of the Western Australian Exploring Expedition through the Centre of Australia from Champion Bay, on the West Coast, to the Overland Telegraph Link between Adelaide and Port Darwin*. Perth: Richard Pether, Government Printer, 1875.

Forrest, J., *Report on the Kimberley District, North-western Australia*. Perth: Government Printer, 1883.

Forrest, J., *Notes on Western Australia*. Perth: Government Printer, 1884–1887.

http://absoluteastronomy.com/encyclopedia/j/jo/john_forrest_1st_baron_forrest_of_bunbury.htm

http://www.davidreilly.com/australian_explorers/forrest/john.htm

http://www.southwestlife.com.au/history1202.htm

http://www.uwapress.uwa.edu.au/titles/index/big_john_forrest

8 Mineral exploration and geological surveys
The importance of mineral discoveries

William Clarke's geological map of New South Wales, 1880

Clarke, W.B., *The Duty and Interest of Educating the Children of the Poor in the Principles of the National Religion*. London: J.G. and F. Rivington, 1833.

Clarke, W.B., *Researches in the Southern Goldfields of New South Wales*. Sydney: Reading & Wellbank, 1860.

Clarke, W.B., *Remarks on the Sedimentary Formations of New South Wales. Catalogue of the Natural and Industrial Products of New South Wales, Forwarded to the Paris Universal Exhibition*. Sydney: Government Printer, 1867.

Clarke, W.B., *Notes on the Geology of Parts of New South Wales and Queensland Made in 1842–43 by Ludwig Leichhardt*. Translated by Ulrich, G.H.F. Sydney: John L. Sherriff, 1867–1868.

Grainger, E., *The Remarkable Reverend Clarke: The Life and Times of the Father of Australian Geology*. Melbourne: Oxford University Press, 1982.

http://www.michaelorgan.org.au/clarke1/htm

Moyal, A., *A Bright and Savage Land: Scientists in Colonial Australia,* 2nd ed. Melbourne: Penguin Books, 1993.

Moyal, A., *The Web of Science: The Scientific Correspondence of the Rev. W.B. Clarke, Australia's Pioneer Geologist*. Melbourne: Australian Scholarly Publishing, 2004.

Peter Drummond's map of the Silver Mining Country, Barrier Ranges, 1884

Andrews, E.C., *The Geology of the Broken Hill District*. Sydney: A.J. Kent, Government Printer, 1923.

Blainey, G., *The Rise of Broken Hill*. Melbourne: Macmillan of Australia, 1968.

Blainey, G., *The Rush that Never Ended: A History of Australian Mining*. Carlton, Vic.: Melbourne University Press, 1993.

Grolier Society of Australia, *The Australian Encyclopaedia*, 4th edn. Sydney: Grolier Society of Australia, 1983.

Map of the Hannan Goldfield West Australia

Bennett, A.L., *The Glittering Years*. Perth: St George Books, 1981.

Casey, G. and Mayman, E., *The Mile that Midas Touched*. Adelaide, Rigby, 1968.

http://members.westnet.com.au/dunc/general/p2.html

http://walkabout.com.au/locations/WAKalgoorlie.shtml

http://www.clarelibrary.ie/eolas/coclare/people/paddyhannan.htm

Thomson, T., *Paddy Hannan: A Claim to Fame*. Kalgoorlie: Thomson Reward, 1992.

Turnbull, C., *Frontier: The Story of Paddy Hannan*. Melbourne: Hawthorne Press, 1949.

Turnbull, C., *Australian Lives: Charles Whitehead, James Stephens, Peter Lalor, George Francis Train, Francis Adams, Paddy Hannan*. Melbourne: Cheshire, 1965.

T.W. Edgeworth David's geological map of Australia, 1931

Branagan, D.F., *T.W. Edgeworth David: A Life—Geologist, Adventurer, Soldier and 'Knight in the Old Brown Hat'*. Canberra: National Library of Australia, 2005.

http://www.discontents.com.au/words/ocah_david.php

9 Land administration and management
Forms of land title

J.A.C. Willis' Binalong Police District map, 1864

http://grandpapencil.com/austral/intell24.htm

http://www.poemhunter.com/andrew-barton-paterson-%60banjo/poet-7296/

http://www.uq.edu.au/~mlwham/banjo/own_story/4_feb.html

Yass Courier, 1863–1864, various issues.

Thomas Kennedy's survey of Norfolk Island, 1860

Hoare, M., *Norfolk Island: A Revised and Enlarged History 1774–1998*, 5th edn. St Lucia: University of Queensland Press, 1999.

High country snow lease map, 1892

Andrews, A.E.J., *Earliest Monaro and Burragorang, 1790 to 1890: With Wilson, Bass, Barralier, Caley, Lhotsky,*

Jauncey, Lambie, Ryrie. Palmerston, ACT: Tabletop Press, 1998.

Hancock, W.K., *Discovering the Monaro: A Study of Man's Impact on His Environment.* London: Cambridge University Press, 1972.

Model of the Snowy Mountains Hydro-Electric Development, 1949

Wigmore, L., *Struggle for the Snowy: The Background of the Snowy Mountains Scheme.* London: Oxford University Press, 1968.

Charles Wilkes' charts of the Antarctic continent, 1844–1874

http://www.archiveshub.ac.uk/news/0308usee.html

Lambert, B.P. and Law, P.G., *A New Map of the Coastline of Oates Land and Eastern King George V Land.* 1959.

Mawer, G.A., *South by Northwest: The Magnetic Crusade and the Contest for Antarctica.* Kent Town: Wakefield Press, 2006.

Philbrick, N., *Sea of Glory: America's Voyage of Discovery: The US Exploring Expedition, 1838–1842.* New York: Viking, 2003.

Viola, H.J. and Margolis, C. (eds), *Magnificent Voyagers: The US Exploring Expedition, 1838–1842.* Georgia: Smithsonian Institution Press, 1985.

10 Urban planning

Town planning ideas

McCarty, J.W. and Schedvin, C.B. (eds), *Australian Capital Cities: Historical Essays.* Sydney: Sydney University Press, 1978.

McLoughlin, B. and Huxley, M. (eds), *Urban Planning in Australia: Critical Readings.* Melbourne: Longman Cheshire, 1986.

Proudfoot, H., 'Founding Cities in Nineteenth Century Australia', in Hamnett, S. and Freestone, R. (eds) *The Australian Metropolis: A Planning History.* London: E. & F.N. Spon, 2000.

Statham, P. (ed.), *The Origins of Australia's Capital Cities.* Cambridge: Cambridge University Press, 1998.

John Helder Wedge's map of Port Phillip, 1836

Billot, J.P., *John Batman: The Story of John Batman and the Founding of Melbourne.* Melbourne: Hyland House, 1979.

Bonwick, J., *Discovery and Settlement of Port Phillip: Being a History of the Country Now Called Victoria, Up to the Arrival of Mr. Superintendent Latrobe, in October 1839.* Melbourne: Goodall & Demaine, 1956. Reprinted Melbourne: Red Rooster Press, 1999.

Bonwick, J., *The Wild White Man and the Blacks of Victoria,* 2nd edn. Melbourne: Ferguson and Moore, 1963.

Campbell, A., *John Batman and the Aborigines.* Malmsbury: Kibble Books, 1987.

http://www.nla.gov.au/collect/newaq/200112.html

Harcourt. R., *Southern Invasion, Northern Conquest: Story of the Founding of Melbourne.* Blackburn South, Vic.: Golden Point Press, 2001.

Wedge, J.H., *The Diaries of John Helder Wedge, 1824–1835.* Hobart: Royal Society of Tasmania, 1962.

Wedge, J.H., *Narrative of an Excursion Amongst the Natives of Port Phillip on the South Coast of New Holland, 1835: Description of the Country around Port Phillip, 1835.* Archives Office of Tasmania, Reference NS 278.

William Light's survey of Adelaide, 1840

Dutton, G., *Founder of a City: The Life of Colonel William Light.* Carlton, Vic.: Melbourne University Press, 1991.

http://users.senet.com.au/~hitek/holdfast.datasa/HomeCL.htm

Philipp, J., *A Great View of Things: Edward Gibbon Wakefield.* Melbourne: Thomas Nelson Australia, 1971.

Whitelock, D., *Adelaide 1836–1876: A History of Difference.* St Lucia, Brisbane: Queensland University Press, 1977.

J. Roche Ardill's plan of Braidwood, 1859

Gurry, D., 'Dr. Thomas Braidwood Wilson, RN: Surgeon Explorer in

Australia', *Medical History of Australia,* vol. 5, 1991.

http://www.heritage.nsw.gov.au/07_subnav_02_2.cfm?itemid=5054706

http://www.walkabout.com.au/locations/NSWBraidwood.shtml

Maddrell, R.S., *Braidwood Goldfields 1850–1860: History of Goldfields, Braidwood District.* Braidwood: Tallaganda Times, 1978.

NSW real estate sales plans, 1860–1940

Daly, M.T., *Sydney Boom, Sydney Bust: The City and Its Property Market, 1850–1981.* Sydney: George Allen & Unwin, 1982.

Particulars, Plan and Conditions of Sale of a Grand Block of Property, Situate Fronting York Street & Clarence Street in the City of Sydney (… sold by public auction by Hardie and Gorman in conjunction with J.J. Roberts, esq, at their rooms No 133 Pitt Street, Sydney, on Wednesday, 23 April 1884 at 11.30 a.m. precisely). Sydney: [Hardie & Gorman, Auctioneers], 1884.

Pettit, J. and James, T., *'Excelsior': A History of the Excelsior Land Investment & Building Company & Bank, Limited Sydney, 1880–1928.* Sydney: John Pettit Pty Ltd, 2000.

Federal capital site map, 1909

Birtles, T., 'Finding a Site for Australia's Seat of Government', *National Library of Australia News,* December, 2006.

de Burgh, E.M., *Report on Water Supply for the Federal Capital: Yass–Canberra Area.* Sydney: NSW Legislative Assembly Papers, 1908.

Forrest, J., *Federal Capital, Proposed Sites (Minute by the Honorable Sir John Forrest on the localities in the Tumut and Southern Monaro districts of New South Wales, suggested as sites for the seat of Government of the Commonwealth).* Melbourne: Government Printer, 1904.

Oliver, A., *Report of the Commissioner on Sites for the Seat of Government of the Commonwealth.* Sydney: NSW Legislative Assembly, 1900.

Pegrum, R., *The Bush Capital: How Australia Chose Canberra as its Federal City.* Sydney: Hale & Iremonger, c.1983.

Scrivener, C.R., *Federal Capital Site: Papers and Plans.* Sydney: NSW Legislative Assembly Papers, 1909.

Watson, F., *A Brief History of Canberra: The Capital City of Australia.* Canberra: Federal Capital Press of Australia Ltd, 1927.

Wigmore, L., *The Long View: A History of Canberra, Australia's National Capital.* Melbourne: F.W. Cheshire, 1963.

J.T.H. Goodwin's manuscript map of Canberra, 1916

Birtles, T.G., *Planning Australia's Capital City: Differing Ideas for Canberra,* 4th edn. Belconnen: University of Canberra, 1997.

Federal Capital Advisory Committee, *Construction of Canberra: Final Report.* Melbourne: H.J. Green, Government Printer for the State of Victoria, 1926.

Freestone, R., *The Federal Capital of Australia: A Virtual Planning History.* Urban Research Program Working Paper No. 60. Canberra: Australian National University, 1997.

Headon, D., *The Symbolic Role of the National Capital.* Canberra: National Capital Authority, 2003.

O'Connor, M., 'Towards a Federal Capital: Some Early Maps and Concept Plans of Canberra and the Australian Capital Territory', *The World of Antiques & Art,* July–December 2001.

O'Malley, K., *Concerning Canberra: The Christening and Dedication of Australia's National Capital, 12 March 1913, and Its Dire Neglect.* Melbourne: K. O'Malley, 1936.

Read, P., *Canberra Following Griffin: A Design History of Australia's National Capital.* Canberra: National Archives of Australia, 2002.

Reps, J.W., *Canberra 1912: Plans and Planners of the Australian Capital Competition.* Melbourne: Melbourne University Press, 1997.

11 Military mapping
Naval hydrographic surveys and army field mapping

Australian Light Horse map of north of the Hunter River, 1907

Blackwell, F.M., *The Story of the 3rd Australian Light Horse Regiment.* Adelaide: Third Light Horse Regiment Club, 1950.

Hall, R.J.G., *The Australian Light Horse.* North Blackburn: The Dominion Press, n.d.

http://www.awm.gov.au/units/unit

http://www.imh.org/imh/bw/austock. html

http://lighthorse.org.au/military/ horsesin/htm

McKenna, T.P., *An Australian Icon: The Australian Light Horse, 1914–1918 War.* Henley Beach: Seaview Press, 2000.

Ritchie, E., *Crusaders of the Southern Cross: The Australian Light Horse in the Middle East from the Letters of Colonel Jack Davies.* Leichhardt: Roland Nigel Davies, 1998.

Starr, J., *From the Saddlebags at War.* Hamilton: South Cross PR and Press Services, 2000.

Plane-table surveys, 1910–1936

Cavill, J.A.L., *Survey Engineering: A Guide to First Principles.* South Perth: John Cavill, 1995.

Coulthard-Clark, C.D., *Australia's Military Map-makers: The Royal Australian Survey Corps 1915–96.* Melbourne: Oxford University Press, 2000.

Lines, J.D, *Australia on Paper: The Story of Australian Mapping.* Box Hill: Fortune Publications, 1992.

Raisbeck, J.J., 'A Short History of the Military Survey of Australia, 1907–1936', *The Australian Surveyor,* vol. 4, September 1937.

Australian aerial photographs, 1919–1994

Coulthard-Clark, C.D., *Australia's Military Map-makers: The Royal Australian Survey Corps 1915–96.*

Melbourne: Oxford University Press, 2000.

O'Connor, Maura, 'Aerial Photograph Collections in Australia', *The Australian Surveyor,* vol. 37, no. 4, December, 1992.

Tyson, B.T., *The Topographical Map Series of Australia.* Melbourne: University of Melbourne, 1965.

Automap and the development of Australian digital spatial data

Coulthard-Clark, C.D., *Australia's Military Map-makers: The Royal Australian Survey Corps 1915–96.* Melbourne: Oxford University Press, 2000.

Lovejoy, V., *Mapmakers of Fortuna: A History of the Army Survey Regiment.* Bendigo: Ex-Fortuna Survey Association Inc., 2003.

Royal Australian Survey Corps, *AUTOMAP: Automation Applied to the Mapping Process.* Canberra: Royal Australian Survey Corps, 1977.

12 Overland transport
Overcoming the tyranny of distance

Australian Heritage Commission, *Linking a Nation: Australia's Transport and Communications 1788–1970.* Canberra: Australian Heritage Commission, 2003.

Blainey, G., *The Tyranny of Distance: How Distance Shaped Australia's History.* Melbourne and London: Macmillan, 1975.

Murray–Darling river pilot charts

Bentley, K. and Bentley, L., *River of Islands: Charts of the River Murray Yarrawonga Weir to Hume Dam.* Adelaide: Kath & Leon Bentley, 1983.

http://www.rivermurraycharts.com. au/history.html

Roberts, J., Unpublished notes, 2004.

NSW railways and coach routes, 1905

Gunn, J., *Along Parallel Lines: A History of the Railways of New South Wales,*

1850–1986. Melbourne: Melbourne University Press, 1989.

http://www.abc.net.au/farwest/ stories/s1357882.htm

http://www.nswrtm.org/rail-history/ index.html

Lee, R., *The Greatest Public Work: The New South Wales Railways, 1848–1889.* Sydney: Hale and Iremonger, 1988.

Lee, R., *Colonial Engineer: John Whitton (1819–1898) and the Building of Australian Railways.* Sydney: University of New South Wales Press, 2000.

Paddison, L.I., *The Railways of New South Wales, 1855–1955.* Sydney: Halstead Press, 1955.

Charles Kingsford Smith's Pacific flight, 1928

Mackersey, I., *Smithy: The Life of Sir Charles Kingsford Smith.* London: Little Brown & Company, 1998.

Excursion map of Sydney and surrounds, 1887

Cannon, M., *Australia in the Victorian Age: Life in the Cities.* Ringwood, Vic.: Viking O'Neil, 1988 (reissued).

Sheila Scott (1927–1988)
Selection of maps used by Sheila Scott, aviatrix, in her flights across the Pacific and Atlantic Oceans
Maps Collection

Index

Titles of the maps are listed in a separate index, followed by the general index. Page numbers in *italics* refer to illustrations only.

General index

145

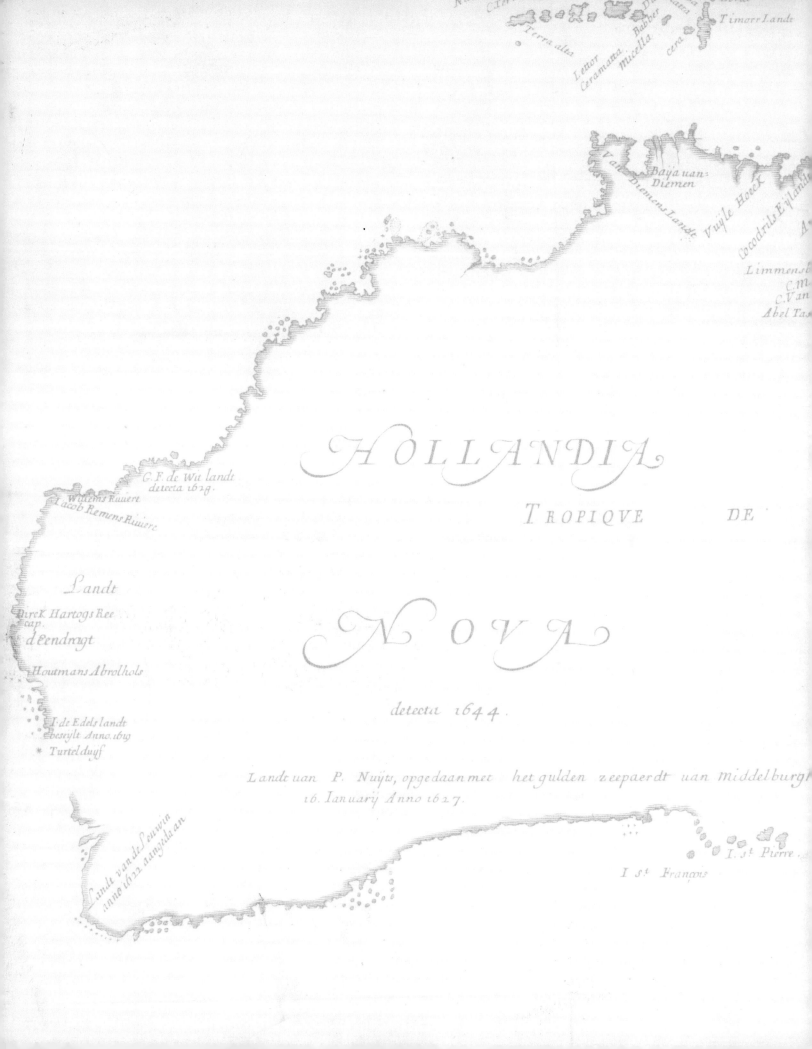

Nus
C.Ierta
Terra alta
Lettor
Ceramana
micetta
Babber
cera
Da matta
Loral
Timorr Lande

Timorr Lande

Van Diemens Lande

Baya uan Diemen

Vuyle Hoeck

Cocodrils Eijlandt

Limmensb
C. M
C. Van
Abel Tas

HOLLANDIA

TROPIQVE *DE*

G. F. de Wit landt
detecta 1628.

NOVA

Willems Ruuere
Iacob Remens Ruuere

Landt

Direck Hartogs Ree
cap.
d'Eendragt

detecta 1644.

Houtmans Abrolhols

Lande uan P. Nuijts, opgedaan met het gulden zeepaerdt uan Middelburgh
16. Ianuary Anno 1627.

I de Edels landt
beseylt Anno 1619

* Turtelduyf

Landt van de Leuwin
anno 1622 aanzida an

I. St Pierre

I St François